# Wake Up and Win,
# America

# Wake Up and Win, America

A Staunch Soccer Fan's Reflections
on the State of U.S. Men's Soccer

Patrick Carolus Melus

**Disclaimer**

This project is a creative non-fictional essay, previously published as *Wake Up and Win, America! Do It Now* by Patrick Carolus Melus. It is a work heavily based on a true story and events but conveyed in writing using anecdotes, comic blends and inspiring techniques. In some cases and sections, names of people, places and (or) photos have been either changed or obscured to honor privacy choices made. This implies that with the exception of all prominent celebrities, soccer players and important personalities that we are familiar with (most of whose first and last names are included); all other names, photos and places adopted are either fictitious or fictional. Any other resemblances to real people, living or dead, places or trademarks, are entirely coincidental. Opinions expressed here are based on the author's insights, investigations, informed and informal research. Some of the fitness and wellness suggestions made in this book are publicized for general informational purposes only. They are not intended as and should not be relied upon as medical advice.

ISBN 9780998027548

# Dedication

*I dedicate this title to the indomitable Marshall University 2020-21 Thundering Herd men's soccer team, their brilliantly dynamic coaches and smart technical advisers.*

# Contents

# Introduction

In the middle of 2021, the original version, *Wake Up and Win, America! Do It Now,* was replaced by a revised edition, titled *Wake Up and Win, America.* In this volume, aside from the change in the book and chapter titles, a few interior alterations, modifications and improvements were also made to facilitate and update reading. However, the number and nature of such changes were restricted by the desire to retain the substance and detailed framework of this popular volume. This creative writing and project began with my prolonged inner struggle and apparent disenchantment over the protracted inability of the US national men's soccer team to "win really big" in the previous World Cup soccer contests. The timing of this title, intended to promote soccer in the US could not have been better, especially at this time when the US women's national soccer team's (USWNT) performances appear quite attractive to the world. USWNT has continued to soar globally in popularity that more people and even previously "non-soccer lovers" in the US are beginning to put interest in this beautiful sport. The team's latest wins present yet another incredibly exciting moment with added significance to soccer in the US. Its victory continues to project an electrifying impression not only for the nation's boys and girls but for everyone. It is even more thrilling that the USWNT can now potentially be used as a benchmark with which to measure women's soccer performances in the world. Because of the team's steady performance, it is hoped that many will be reignited with interest in soccer. With the amazing performances of the USWNT, it is only natural that the American people's curiosity will grow over the men's national team with the burning desire to help it shine globally, too.

While much progress has been made and a few milestones marked in the US soccer program in recent years, fans and enthusiasts across the nation do not seem to be convinced that the problem in the United States men's national soccer team (USMNT) has been or will ever be fixed, at least, so soon. Soccer fans and supporters, have variously voiced their concerns, some articles have also been written by both soccer analysts and sports pundits. All these critical analyses and concerns point toward the urgent need to improve the US men's soccer for a better performance or attain a higher efficiency that is victory friendly.

Arguably, the nation's men's soccer system should, demonstrably and reliably, be able to represent it both in friendly matches and global soccer contests, at least, with appreciable successes and befitting victories. Public opinions and comments in this book suggest that while many soccer fans, sponsors and supporters are hopeful, they still lack confidence in the USMNT's ability to perform with flying colors in international soccer tournaments like its women's counterpart. Although basically similar in structure, the performance differences between both teams could not be clearer. However, with the hope-giving outings of some men's soccer teams across the nation and, particularly, the recent spectacular performance of the Huntington West Virginia's Marshall Thundering Herd men's soccer team by winning the first-ever Division 1 national championship in soccer, hope is high and the future bright in the USMNT. The Herd's team's style of play and coordination remain quite impressive and perhaps need to be replicated in the USMNT.

This new edition of *Wake Up and Win, America,* as piece of literature, retains its ridiculously simplified nature, a form of 'fictional realism' originally conceived as a simple but longstanding thought existing in the minds of staunch soccer lovers, and later fleshed out into a sizable volume. It is a wake-up call to all soccer-loving American fans, supporters, and advocates. I consider it a creative and tantalizing title, representing a clarion call to all American soccer fans, supporters and advocates. It is intended to promote and bolster the appreciation of soccer with its potentially huge future progress. It is a title that tells us that America's future in soccer is bright, despite all odds. It reveals that the world of people's thoughts, feelings, opinions, and ideas about soccer, as it is portrayed on paper, mirrors and closely resembles the ones that exist in the minds of so many American soccer fans and supporters as well as in the modern world of soccer that they inhabit. Title wittingly but fictionally captured American celebrities discussing soccer. Also, it contains important and teachable elements that can enable soccer leaders and managers to fashion out real solutions to the USMNT's soccer challenges based on people's comments and feedback that span over a decade.

There is no doubt that soccer, the most popular sport in the world, has grown in a couple of decades and continues to improve with relative ease across the US. A fair assessment of soccer in the nation would immediately present most of its outlook as promising. Arguably, the number of viewers for both local and international soccer tournaments in the US has increased dramatically, while the level and pace of its progress have left everyone hopeful for the future. With the increasing interest in soccer as a global sport, this book, like its original version, is certain to remain a "Johnny-Come-Timely" title, primarily intended to convey other people's, beliefs and convictions, including mine, on the progress, shape, and size of soccer as a viable and winning program in the US This volume also intends to shine a bright light on the value of soccer in the lives of ordinary people, soccer lovers, and supporters as part of a global sporting community. Nevertheless, the lingering question is this: "Why should a great nation like the US eternally maintain a mediocre status in major men's global soccer encounters despite her great population, strong diversity and richness in both human and sporting resources?" In this book, various suggestions have been subtly made by discussants and commenters on how to address those challenges that have for some decades now seemed insoluble. At least, the recommendations indicate that there are indeed several ways to approach those challenges and potential solutions to perceived hindrances.

Because the content of this project is partly fiction and partly real life events, it is intended to promote and bolster appreciation of soccer and its potential future progress. Also, because of its fictional underpinnings and exploratory nature, it is crucial to note that with the exception of the names of public figures and celebrities, other names were modified, abridged, or changed to suit the purposes that this title is intended to achieve. This book is a "must read" for all who aspire to make soccer as cherished a sport in the whole of the US as it is in other great soccer nations. The nature of this project is such that it might attract wide readership: married couples and those intending to get married, the old and the young, the great and the small, professionals, celebrities, philanthropists, soccer managers, coaches, and high school and college students who love soccer.

Although strongly anecdotal, with its appeal to emotions, passions, and feelings on the necessity to be a big winner, *Wake Up and Win, America* is a project that magically represents almost every person's opinion about the US soccer. It smartly touches upon almost every aspect of the American culture and life in general, while at the same time presents a fair evaluation of the situation of soccer in the US. While it recognizes Americans as exceptionally talented, and able to achieve whatever they set their minds on, this book aspires to be a fun, psychologically superb, and an inspirational project that calls for the widest readership possible. *Wake Up and Win, America* is a book you will desire to read or rue. It might change the way you think about soccer forever. Without doubt, its contents appear captivating, exciting, inviting, and irresistible. I am hopeful that this revised volume will still encourage readers to deeply reflect upon, recognize, and appreciate the importance of soccer, not only as a national event, but also as a global sport of great positive consequence. Thank you for reading!

*P.C.M*

# Chapter 1
## A Sweet Start

What a dramatic, sweet start!

Steve and Carol Bloom of Colorado Springs, vacationing in Atlanta in the summer of 1996 to attend the Olympics, caught sight of people driving to Sanford Stadium in the town of Athens for the soccer tournament. This couple and other avid soccer fans were excited because important things would soon be happening.

Flash forward a few days, to July 18, 1996. Remarking about the Olympic opening ceremony, which would usher in the great soccer event, Carol said to her husband, Steve:

"Atlanta has been making news these days, more than ever before. There's such a beautiful feeling in the air."

"It's understandable because of the upcoming international multi-sport events and, most importantly, because soccer is here with a sweet start," replied Steve.

"Yes, Olympic soccer is here and it's going to be great," concurred Carol.

The following day, this happy couple drove down to the stadium in Athens, where they witnessed athletes, fans, and supporters from various countries and continents discussing the upcoming tournament, which would begin on August 4. They anticipated the first shouts of "It's a goal ... goal ... gooooal!" in favor of their favorite teams.

Steve and Carol drove around Atlanta for some sightseeing before the opening ceremonies and events kicked off. From their newly-rented silver Cadillac Escalade, they saw malls overflowing with customers shopping for soccer T-shirts, hats, shoes, boots, sporting helmets, and jackets in an array of colors — blue, red, white, black, and yellow. Some fans had their faces painted in soccer colors. Signs advertised Nike, Adidas, Reebok, and Coca-Cola. Steve and Carol looked on in admiration.

Store managers were shouting at customers: "Welcome. Here is your great chance to create a soccer shopping list, as you sharpen your legs for the upcoming event. Shop like stars as you prepare to play like stars. We'll see you there soon, and we hope you come back to shop again."

"You're in the driver's seat this time," one of the visiting customers responded. "Just give us a good deal and we'll jump all over it."

The malls weren't focused on deep price discounts. Rather, they were bent on improving customer service, and expanded their personal shopper suites from two rooms to four. The soccer-item shoppers wanted to find merchandise in their price range without wasting unnecessary time or standing in line for hours. They wouldn't hesitate to buy "must have" items when those products were selling near or within their price ranges.

"Shopping for soccer and multi-sport events could be overwhelming and time consuming for players and fans," noted Carol, "as there are too many options to choose from."

"Of course, time is of the essence," replied Steve, "and it's far better to use one's time in a smart way. This isn't only true in shopping for soccer, but also true on the soccer field. Please, if there's something in your price range that you need, buy it when you see it, because there's no guarantee it's going to be on sale later in the season."

"Right." agreed Carol. "Even when I go to grocery stores, I have to decide what's absolutely essential for the kitchen and our kids. Same thing whenever I visit boutiques. I don't buy the things I want and love, but only the things I need. I've always heeded the voice: 'shop wisely.'"

"I do the same," Steve replied. "I mean I shop wisely whenever I go to Home Depot, to avoid walking around without a penny in my pocket. I want to save my wallet for the greater good."

Carol chuckled. "You're right, Steve. I never want to be plunged into abject poverty."

As they drove their way back to the Olympic Stadium, heavy traffic caused a rubbernecking delay. The traffic jam really tested Carol's patience, as she wanted to get back to the stadium at least a quarter hour before the opening soccer match.

"Don't worry; the soccer tournament won't start right away," declared Steve, "because they'll have the opening ceremonies first. The soccer tournament isn't going to take place here anyway. It's going to happen in a different stadium in Athens sometime in early August, probably before we go back to Colorado Springs."

"Do you think so?" Carol asked.

"I know so, as I heard that over the radio several times," replied Steve.

"Where and when will the match between Portugal and Tunisia take place?" Carol asked.

"That will take place tomorrow at 3 p.m. at RFK Stadium in Washington, D.C.," Steve revealed.

"Why on earth did they move it over to Washington?" Carol asked. "How are we going to watch the match?"

"That's how they normally arrange the Olympic soccer events," Steve replied. "We'll probably watch the match at the Olympic Stadium lounge here in Atlanta."

"Thanks, Steve, that's good to know," replied Carol.

Carol and Steve were hopeful that they'd get to the stadium on time and buoyed each other's optimism. Really, a sweet start. What a beautiful couple and expectant soccer fans! When they got to the stadium on time, they heaved sighs of relief. How good it was to be back to watching something they loved and enjoyed!

Carol and Steve loved soccer so much but they didn't skip the opening ceremonies at the Centennial Olympic Stadium in Atlanta.

The Olympic Stadium that Carol and Steve found on their arrival was an illustriously modern state-of-the-art structure. It had a complex design, holding 85,000 spectators. It had a traditional ballpark shape at the south end, and expanded northward to include a 400-meter track and additional seats.

From the VIP box, President Bill Clinton declared the Olympics open before the largest gathering of nations and athletes in the history of the event. Seated in the box was the 76-year-old president of the International Olympic Committee (IOC), Juan Antonio Samaranch, with his wife, Maria Theresa. Also present was the head of the Atlanta Olympic Committee, Billy Payne, and his wife Martha.

The crowd was roaring in the 30-second countdown to the opening ceremony, which featured fireworks in the final moments. According to Steve, the opening ceremony production cost about $15 million.

"I just overhead the commentator mention that amount," Steve whispered into Carol's ear. "Amazing, eh? Was that an approximation or what?"

"I think it's really expected to be that much," replied Carol.

The crowd waited to hear the thrilling "Call to the Nations." At the northeastern corner of the stadium were the Olympic spirits, who'd invite the tribes of the world to Atlanta. The spirits made trumpet-like calls through wind tunnels, with colored streamers waving above the spectators, who suddenly ignited with shouts of great joy and excitement. What an amazing spectacle for Carol and Steve!

The Olympic colors, represented and reflected on the wind tunnels, were linked to soul-stirring, rhythmic sounds of global music. Yes, musical wings and sounds of grand global beauty, wonderful to describe. The color Yellow stood for Asia, Blue for Europe, Green for Australia, Black for Africa, and Red for both North and South America. Responding to the calls from the Olympic spirits, each of the five groups of world tribes (numbering 100 each) organized themselves for the opening ceremony. They rolled out in a glitzy and glamorous fashion, mingling and interweaving with one another, and eventually forming the Olympic rings, as Carol and Steve watched with astounding admiration their costumes and skillful displays. What an elaborate protocol and beautiful event, which could be personified as a queen bedecked with jewels!

About 450 children, ages of 7 to 11 and dressed in white, glided to the center of the arena to form the big centennial number: one and two zeroes. Carol spotted a little boy dangling his feet while seated on the lap of his over-excited mom. This cute little boy was also nodding his head as he stared at the kids on the field weaving among themselves in choreographed calisthenics.

Carol grabbed Steve by the chin and pointed him toward the kid. Steve smiled lovingly.

Finally, the symbolic tribes, with the 450 children, formed the Olympic rings inside the stadium, coupled with the centennial year figure 100.

"Hey Steve, the figure 100 that you see right now at the center of the arena was boldly carved through the mingling of the kids dressed in white."

"Yes, Carol," Steve replied, "I saw the kids mingle and intertwine until they created the giant centenary figure 100. Look at that. What an amazing job they did!"

"Yes, the man sitting right beside me just mentioned that the Olympic rings were symbolic of the gathering of the entire global family in Atlanta, Georgia," whispered Carol. "What incredible and gorgeous costumes they displayed. It's simply glitzy and glamorous."

And it wasn't over yet. Carol and Steve now joined the mammoth crowd in watching Al Oerter, a legendary discus thrower and one of the greatest Olympic Gold Medalists; carry the Olympic torch into the stadium. Oerter set memorable records at the Olympics, representing the U.S. from 1956 through 1968.

A symbol of the Olympic Games, with its origins rooted in ancient Greek mythology, the Olympic torch commemorates the theft of fire by Prometheus from the Greek god Zeus. A fire was kept burning all through the ancient Olympics. That torch has been kept burning since the first Olympics, and has been part of every modern Olympics.

Carl Diem, at the controversial Berlin Olympics of 1936, introduced the torch relay of modern times, which transports the flame from Greece to the various designated sites of the games. Some ten thousand torchbearers had carried the torch thousands of miles from Athens to Atlanta. As Al Oerter carried the torch toward the stadium, a jubilant roar rose from the crowd. Carol jumped to her feet in excitement alongside Steve as Oerter handed off the torch to former Heavyweight Boxing Champion and Olympic Bronze Medalist Evander Holyfield, a favorite son of Atlanta, who received a standing ovation.

Holyfield carried the Olympic torch onto the huge elevated platform in the center of the stadium, having run through the center of a tunnel that took him underground to his destination. This dramatic display resulted in a joyously riotous show of excitement from the spectators. Who was next to take the torch from Holyfield?

As Carol and Steve looked on, Holyfield made his way through the athletes and a young-looking woman took it from him. It was Paraskevi Voula Patiloudou, who, at the 1992 Barcelona games, became the first Greek woman to take the Gold Medal in the 100 meter hurdles. With a gentle cheek-to-cheek kiss, Holyfield co-lifted the torch with her into the stadium, before handing it off to Janet Evans, a four-time Gold Medalist swimmer who was participating in her third and final Olympics. The spectators roared in admiration.

Making her way to the rear of the Olympic cauldron, raising one hand to greet spectators and supporters, she came to a stop at the center of the stadium. And who was next to take it?

The former Heavyweight Boxing Champion, Muhammad Ali. He was honored to light the cauldron. A giant figure and a boxing legend now trapped in the quagmire of Parkinson's disease, a progressively terrible illness. What a moment of mixed emotions, with great joy and tearful excitement written on the faces of the crowd. It was an emotion that Carol noticeably shared in, as she watched the shaking of Ali's left hand, caught in a tremor from the symptoms of Parkinson's syndrome. The entire crowd wildly cheered on as he struggled to light the gigantic Olympic cauldron.

"Look at President Clinton over there," Carol exclaimed, as she nearly shed tears. "He looks emotionally absorbed in this ongoing episode."

"Just like you, honey, I think he's also fighting to hold back his tears," remarked Steve. "What a kind-hearted man he's, indeed."

Carol cried in empathy for Ali, who got a huge response from the crowd. What a marvelous moment!

Finally, the giant Centennial Olympic Cauldron was lighted, raising waves of thunderous applause from the crowd. The torch that Ali ignited was self-propelled via a lengthy cable onto the waiting cauldron. The spectacularly glowing cauldron became a star attraction right away.

After the opening ceremonies, Carol and Steve drove back to their hotel room at the Hyatt Regency Hotel in Atlanta, where the staff welcomed them. The concierge was helpful, but Steve and Carol had to dodge an opportunistic panhandler who, faking politeness, offered them local sightseeing advice but then demanded money for an unsolicited service.

Their room was spacious and spotlessly clean. The couple loved the hotel because of its proximity to major attractions, like the Georgia Aquarium, Coca Cola World, museums, and shops. Unfortunately, it was also located in a noisy section of the city, with the windows not doing much to muffle the sounds of police and fire sirens, car alarms, and the shouts of drunkards and beggars in the early hours of the morning. Earplugs, however, proved an easy remedy.

The following day the couple went back to the Olympic Stadium. Hearing from someone in the audience that the soccer matches had started, Steve and Carol quickly hurried to the stadium lounge where a group of spectators watched, on a big flat-screen television, the battles between four formidable teams.

Steve and Carol enjoyed watching the match between Portugal and Tunisia, followed by the match between the U.S. and Argentina. For them, it was a red-letter day. But Carol and Steve were awfully disappointed when Argentina defeated the U.S. men's Olympic soccer team 3-1, with goals scored by G. Lopez, Crespo, and Simeone. Argentina would eventually become the Silver Medalist at the 1996 Olympics.

Nevertheless, Carol will remain ever thankful to Reyna, who saved Steve from heart failure by pulling off one goal in favor of the U.S. After the heartrending defeat by Argentina, Carol and Steve stayed at their hotel room and watched the next match between the U.S. and Tunisia. They were thrilled to see the U.S. trounce the Tunisian team 2-0, displaying an impregnable defense. Jovan Kirovski and Brian Maisonneuve, who scored those two goals, were their heroes.

The performance was so spectacular that Carol and Steve changed their minds and drove down to the Olympic Stadium to watch subsequent matches on television. What a joy it was for them to see the U.S. men's soccer team wake up and start winning.

"I think their coaches, Steve Samson and Bruce Arena, did a great job to put these guys together," suggested Carol. "What a wonderful selection! If they continue in this way, I think we're going to get to the finals at the Olympics, and maybe more."

"Likewise, honey," agreed Steve. "They still have the chance to get the Gold Medal."

"I hope so. Let's just keep our fingers crossed."

On July 24 they drove down to the Olympic Stadium, where they watched matches again on television. This time the U.S. team got a 1-1 draw with Portugal, in a match played at the RFK Stadium in Washington, D.C. Carol and Steve were still impressed, as the Portugal team was a pretty strong one. They weren't disappointed, even though they wished that America had won the match. They envisioned the U.S. team not only winning a Gold Medal in the future, but perhaps the World Cup as well.

Nevertheless, counting the team's points so far, they realized that the U.S. wouldn't make it to the finals. Yet they were resolved to watch the soccer matches until the last day, including the semi-finals and Gold Medal game, to be played at Sanford Stadium in Athens, Georgia. It was already dusk, time flies, when they left the stadium and headed back to the Hyatt Regency Hotel. They passed a cavalcade of buses conveying thousands of fans, who were exulting in victory or trying to ease the trauma of defeat.

Back at the hotel room, Carol called her sister, who was taking care of their kids in Colorado Springs. Steve immediately saw that she was relieved to hear the kids were doing well. They had a late dinner of lightly fried fresh salmon and fries with Italian sauce, and then downed two glasses of German malt beer. They topped off their meal with two slices of pizza and a piece of pie, and then finally sealed the evening with a few sips of *Cabernet*.

Steve recalled one of his Chilean soccer player friends telling him, shortly before they departed for Georgia, that Chile's Central Valley was among the few places in the world where nature has favored vineyards with soft ocean breezes and sunshine about 300 days a year. Not to mention the perfectly balanced soil components and clean Mountain Rivers which created an ideal microclimate for cultivating one of the noblest and most iconic of French vine stocks —*Cabernet Sauvignon.*

Turning toward Carol, Steve observed, "Honey, one of the intriguing things I've come to learn about the French is that aside from their penchant for and interest in soccer, they take their entertainments seriously and always inject them with an air of glamour, from decadent cuisine that you might find in a restaurant, to a thoughtful, sophisticated décor. I thought it might be nice to keep these images in mind, sweetie, as you plan a French-themed party for our soccer friends when we get back to Colorado Springs — but if and only if our men's soccer team eventually wins."

"Sounds good." Carol replied. "Trust me, darling, if our guys win, we'll break a record with a dinner party. First, with an invitation, we'll convey the promise of a super exciting evening they'll not want to miss. Secondly, we'll have a French cocktail, or an aperitif hour, to set the mood of the party, because there are two things that guests look for as they walk into a party: the mood and the drink. The party might also look a little bit like a Super Bowl feast, thereby bringing in a little bit of the American style, because variety is the spice of life. For those who like beef, we'll create a swanky smorgasbord fit for pro soccer linemen, including Kobe beef burgers, sliders, franks smothered in Kobe beef chili, and French fries fried in Kobe beef oil. Make no mistake about it, Kobe is one of the most expensive kinds of beef in the world, and Kobe cows are believed to get daily massages to make their meat tenderer. Overall, we'll create an alluringly indulgent spread. We'll start with a traditional pre-dinner cocktail that's been forever in vogue. It'll be nothing less than a refreshing cocktail that's both light and effervescent. This is the best way to start off a dinner at which heavier food and wine will be served. It'll be like a champagne cocktail that gets the guests in the mood for later festivities and encourages conversations, walk-arounds and look-arounds, while listening to some beautiful pieces of exhilarating classical music."

"Darling," Steve replied, "that's a pretty big lesson on both American and French cuisine. As you spoke, I experienced the refreshing chills people get when they hear their favorite music. It's the type of feeling you get when you win big in soccer."

"You got it!" Carol cried. "It'll be a golden entertainment. One more thing I've come to learn about the French is that they're masters in managing contrasting yet compatible images — sophisticated yet edgy, passionate yet cool, engaged but laidback, lively but never loud. Forget about low-key, casual parties with finger food and paper plates. Hey! Wait a minute, Steve. Hope we didn't take too much of that stuff tonight."

"What's that? Do you mean the wine? Give me a break. I've never been a heavy drinker."

"Yes, I hear you, honey." Carol replied while smiling brilliantly. "But remember that beer, wine, and pizza aren't the main focus of our trip down here in Atlanta."

This moment was overtaken by other interesting events. This cool, cloudless Atlanta night ended as they retired to their room for a sweet and wonderful night.

The next morning Carol woke up to victory, but it wasn't about soccer this time. It was rather about not drinking early in the morning. She didn't want to wonder if she and her husband had become drunks or alcoholics. They both recalled previous instances when a bad choice resulted in unpleasant consequences.

By 8 a.m. the weather looked a bit cool. Carol and Steve explored tourist centers and attractions in Atlanta. Their plan was to familiarize themselves with the major landmarks and attractions of the city in a short period of time. They headed to the CNN center, the new World of Coca-Cola, and stopping to inspect with admiration the Georgia Aquarium. On their arrival at the CNN Studio, they were given a walking tour and behind-the-scenes view of the studios, getting an exciting glimpse of live newsgathering and broadcasting. Their stay at the CNN center was brief but pretty exciting.

They then departed for the new World of Coca-Cola. Carol and Steve were taken through the spectacular glass tower into the lobby, and from there were conducted to the largest collection of collectibles and memorabilia in the history of the Coca-Coca industry, in all shapes and sizes and assembled from around the world. A thrilling experience for both Steve and Carol.

What caught most of their attention was a short movie featuring how Coca-Cola had become an icon in popular culture, and how celebrated artists and everyday people from across the globe expressed their creativity through Coca-Cola. This movie was introduced by a soccer advertisement, featuring a soccer tournament between the U.S. and Germany.

They then visited a station offering a wide selection of Coca Cola brands, a sea of choices that included Coca-Cola, Pepsi Cola, Diet Coke, Vanilla Coke, Coke Zero and Cherry Coke. Carol and Steve discovered that July was the busiest month for this giant company, with the main entrance, lobby, atrium, and passageways packed with visitors, patrons, and customer traffic. With their cameras and camcorders, Steve and Carol took pictures to share with their kids when they get back to their home in Colorado Springs.

The Georgia Aquarium happened to be close to the new World of Coca-Cola. The couple had secured a special-ticket package that enabled them to enjoy these two major attractions at a combination price. The aquarium offered the most spectacular aquatic experience. Carol and Steve saw whales and sharks. As they watched these beautiful creatures navigate their habitats, Steve told Carol how their water movements reminded him of how smart players brilliantly navigate their way across soccer fields toward their opponents' goals. Several "touch pools" provided Carol and Steve with an up-close encounter with sea creatures.

The tour provided them with a better and clearer understanding of some of the most misunderstood and stigmatized creatures on earth. They viewed a wide variety of animals found in African, Asian, and South American rivers and seas, including octopuses, alligators, small-clawed otters, sea turtles, lion fish, and more.

Among the creatures that Carol and Steve admired most were two small breeds of eight-year-old Sulcata turtles. Everybody at the aquarium knew them as red-eared sliders. Carol and Steve took time to examine those little creatures and fed them leafy fresh vegetables, which they reluctantly ate.

"This behavior will help us research them more to know what they need and how they feed better," Steve reasoned.

"Look at how cute they are." Carol remarked. "To me, they're like little kids. Our kids at home will love them. How I wish today was also Valentine's Day, so that these small creatures would be presented to me and my family as a Valentine's Day gift."

The aquarium director revealed that the turtles could live for another 70 years. Carol and Steve were astonished at this revelation. They had a large aquarium in Colorado Springs that could well accommodate those little creatures. Even though taking care of turtles would be a major commitment, they finally adopted those turtles (especially after hearing disgusting stories about people who bought turtles but didn't take good care of them). They ended up becoming not only soccer advocates, but advocates for the adoption and rescue of turtles.

"We've become a couple of crazy turtle lovers," joked Steve.

"Yes, I love that." replied Carol. "I wish they could play soccer like human beings."

"If we do only one thing here before heading back to the stadium on the final day of the soccer tournament, it should be to visit the Fuqua Orchid Center and the High Museum of Art," Steve suggested, voicing his heartfelt desire to Carol.

"Yes, of course, visiting those places will help us make the most and best of our vacation here," replied Carol.

They headed to the Fuqua Orchid Center to see the distinguished orchid collections. Its mission was to display and conserve orchids, and educate visitors about them. At this point orchids were the second most popular indoor flowering plant, after poinsettias. This year would hold indelible memories for Carol and Steve — their love for colorful events in soccer led them to the love of color and beauty in things of nature as well.

As they toured the Atlanta Botanical Garden, they saw its amazing new collection of montane orchids that grow at high elevations. They met other couples from New York, Florida, and California who shared their love for soccer and flowers. One of the couples tried to woo Carol and Steve into becoming members of the Botanical Garden, which they promised to seriously think about later.

Next, the couple headed to the High Museum of Art. They took a casual walk through the museum's permanent collection of more than 11,000 pieces, including 20th and 21st century American and decorative art, significant European pieces, modern and contemporary art, photography, African art, and folk art.

However, it wasn't long before two of their favorite soccer teams lured them back to the Olympic Stadium's lounge. This time they watched France defeat Spain 2-0.

On July 27 the couple was again on their way to the Olympic Stadium when they heard over the radio that an apparent terrorist bomb blast had killed a spectator named Alice Hawthorne and wounded 111 others, causing the death of Melih Uzunyol by heart attack.

It was a sad and heartbreaking day for the couple, who drove back to their hotel room with tears dripping down Carol's cheeks, while Steve was holding back his. The following day they drove to a local church for the 11:15 a.m. Sunday worship service. A visiting pastor was preaching fire and brimstone sermons, with the church more packed than ever before. Carol said she overheard two parishioners discussing the sermons. Interestingly, both agreed that the sermons were exhilarating, heartbreaking, but at the same time absolutely righteous.

During the sermon, Steve thought: It's been a long time since I'd let God guide me in all I do. Dad often liked to say in a booming voice, "The Lord is my rock and my fortress," and sometimes "The Lord is my shepherd; there's nothing I shall want."

He turned to Carol and confessed, "I was taught to depend on God for everything. But as I grew up, even during my college soccer years, I relied more and more on myself. But I give Him every thanks, now that I have you by my side, and for our love of soccer that brought us together in the first place."

They mourned and prayed together for the victims of the terrorist incident that nearly brought their summer soccer joys to a sudden end. They even considered returning earlier to Colorado Springs, but then decided to finish their vacation as planned. They saw this as an opportunity to exercise further resilience, as a time to wake up and move on.

Carol and Steve booked a hotel in Athens, Georgia, to watch both the semi-finals and finals set to take place from July 30 to August 3. It was a thrilling experience to watch players from countries other than their own. They saw Argentina defeat Portugal 2-0 in a semi-final match, and Nigeria overcome Brazil 4-3. On August 2 they returned to Sanford Stadium to watch the Bronze Medal game, where Brazil decimated Portugal 5-0. Carol had always been impressed by the Brazilian soccer team's style and methods. Given the chance, she'd try to remake the U.S. team in the Brazilian team's image.

On August 3, they saw Nigeria defeat Argentina 3-2. Nigerian soccer had made a strong impression on Carol and Steve, as it did on everyone at the stadium that day. It was quite magical how Nigeria defeated both Brazil and Argentina in the last few days. The couple mimicked the commentators, in a funny sounding, tongue-twisting verbal display, as they called out the names of the scorers: Kanu Nwankwo, Victor Ikpeba, Daniel Amokachi, and Emmanuel Amunike.

"Honey, aren't these Nigerian guys great?" Carol asked. "They lit up the world stage."

"They're really great." Steve agreed. "How I wish the U.S. team's strikers and forward liners were as great as those guys. With greater effort, I think they'll perform even better than these Nigerian guys. I strongly believe the U.S. has all it takes to get there."

"Why not?" added Carol.

The 1996 Olympics were now almost over, and the couple got ready to fly back to Colorado in about three days' time. For them, it was a never-to-be-forgotten vacation experience. It had been expensive, but well worth it.

On the day of their return flight, they packed their bags and headed for Atlanta Hartsfield International Airport. They made a brief stop at a McDonald's, where Carol ordered grilled chicken, French fries, and Coca-Cola.

They enjoyed these edibles as they drove on. Carol intermittently fed Steve, who was behind the wheel.

"It's getting more expensive to feed you these days than to feed two babies," Carol quipped.

Steve almost choked with laughter. It was another beautiful and exciting moment on their trip together.

They arrived at the airport, paid off the car rental, checked their baggage, and headed to their terminal gate. Carol called her sister Christine to let her know that they were about to board their flight and that everything was okay with them. They made it back to Colorado via a non-stop flight by about 8 p.m. that evening.

Carol and Steve were greeted by their two kids and Christine with immense joy and excitement. Christine promptly handed over driving to Carol, who drove the family half way to Colorado Springs, where Steve took over to finish the journey. During their drive, the soccer encounter between the U.S. and Argentina dominated most of the family's discussion, with the children noticeably excited to hear their parents' stories about the Olympics.

Fourteen years later, Carol raised the idea of vacationing in South Africa in 2010, to attend the World Cup soccer fiesta.

"I doubt that we'll go to South Africa," Steve responded. "It's really of no use because our country never wins big in men's soccer contests."

"When do you think our guys will begin to win big at the World Cup?" asked Carol.

"I have no idea," Steve replied. "It's really been disappointing and frustrating to watch the decline of our men's soccer team."

"Steve, you can never know what will happen. As far as I know, our guys have been doing their best. Is your frustration really enough to deter you from going to South Africa? Don't you know that more than 300,000 visitors are expected for the World Cup? And what's more exciting is the proposed introduction of the *Adidas Jabulani* as the world's first perfectly round soccer ball?"

"Ha. Do you mean to tell me that the previous World Cup balls weren't perfectly round?" Steve retorted. "If not, what were their shapes like? Were they like coconuts, watermelons, or doughnuts?"

"Very funny, honey." replied Carol, "I remember how the Brazilians complained in 2002 that the soccer ball was either too big or too light. As I talk to you, it's escaped my memory which country complained about the soccer ball in 2004, calling it a 'beach ball.' Was it France, Spain, or England?"

"If it escaped your memory, that's it," replied Steve, "because we rented a Cadillac Escalade and not Ford Escape."

"What do you mean?" queried Carol. "I only implied that it dodged my memory which country complained about the soccer ball."

"Ha-ha. If it just dodged your memory, honey," Steve teased, "sorry, but we're not driving a Dodge now."

"Haahaahaa. Oh, I see what you're doing. You're playing on words, even though you don't know how to play soccer that good. But it doesn't matter. I know that you're a happy-go-lucky guy who likes to make people laugh. Nevertheless, I'm just happy that soccer has brought us close together."

"I know, I know," Steve replied, "but I'd opt to stay away from South Africa this time, until I see some improvement in our men's national soccer team. I strongly believe that they can wake up and win big in soccer, as they have all that it takes. What a sleeping giant!"

Carol wouldn't give up on her dream.

"Oh Steve, how wonderful and joyful it would be to land in Johannesburg, not just for the soccer, but to feel my feet touch the continent I've loved and wanted to visit all my life. During my last two months in high school I learned a great deal about the African continent in general and South Africa in particular, and would love to be there in person. I've even learned their words, one of which is *ubuntu*. Steve, I know you're itching to know the meaning of *ubuntu*. The South African literal translation of the word is 'brotherhood,' but a better translation came from my friend Miriam, who said, 'Carol, the closest I can come to it's the expression I'm because of you.'"

Steve became slightly emotional and looked intently at Carol, experiencing feelings of uninvited guilt.

"Steve, I really am because of you," hinted Carol. She seemed to have accepted Steve's decision not to attend the World Cup, but said to him, mildly and politely, "As you please, honey. You're the big winner this time, but not in soccer."

# Chapter 2
## Soccer Again: South Africa

Far beyond the Soccer Olympics of 1996, 2000, 2004, and 2008, soccer events have gradually continued to grab the ears, eyes, and the entire being and attention of the American public, including Carol and Steve Bloom, even 14 years after the memorable story that was Atlanta '96.

To many it would sound like a dose of good news, as soccer was never expected to make that much of an impact on Americans. And that's because the U.S. has never been the world leader in playing or watching soccer. But this perception is beginning to look a lot like an age-old practice that is no longer in vogue. Now the U.S., along with the rest of the world, is getting massively involved in soccer, especially among the younger generation of ever-zealous fans.

"When it comes to developments in soccer," says Lady O., "it's beginning to look like a beautiful national experience, where providence has sent some special people to mend the 'cracks' in the walls of our sports."

Why is soccer beginning to get so much more attention now than ever before? Frankly speaking, previous attempts to portray soccer as exciting, no matter how often they were made, have failed in the US. It's not that Americans didn't think that soccer was important to them. But historically, **B**aseball, **F**ootball, and **B**asketball (BFB) have often come first in their minds, in their sporting interests, and in their personal agendas. BFB has achieved cultural dominance as the most popular sports in the nation.

"Having followed the current state of affairs in sports here in the U.S.," says Sydney P., "I prefer to leave people with this question and its implications. Isn't it fair enough to wonder why soccer, which has both international and global connections, occupies a less popular position in the minds of Americans than those three other 'parochial' sports? Of course, yes, it's fair enough to wonder. But, this time, instead of remaining glued to the games they'd always felt were more important to them, many Americans suddenly turned their attention a bit toward soccer, as a seemingly more important sport because of its major global connections. This gesture doesn't mean a total abandonment of the BFBs that remain popular 'loves of their lives', and beautifully tattooed in their psyches. They seem to have got the message without experiencing any imaginary tyranny from the majority. Strikingly, this better-than-nothing type of progress is a success in itself and, to some fanatical soccer fans, a non-vitriolic victory."

"It sounds like a slight change that soccer fans and supporters all over the U.S. will believe in," remarked Daryl, "following the coming of the new millennium, who could've imagined a better inaugural way to say welcome to the American soccer-loving fans?"

"It's really been a pretty long and arduous journey," agreed Paris, "for which everyone should be thankful. Soccer fans believe that it's one of the best and most beautiful things to happen in America. The more the nation invests resources in soccer, the more the attitude of Americans toward it will continue to get better."

Americans have started to quickly translate their soccer potential into a reality, but will they be able to match the feat in international soccer contests? American interest in soccer has grown slowly but surely. We have every good reason for hope — for more progress, yes, and hope for huge victories in future contests. No doubt, happy days and exciting years are coming.

"Soccer is here, again. Let's go for it and enjoy it, for it comes every four years, honey."

Expectedly, this declaration came from no other person than Carol Bloom who even though isn't a soccer fanatic yet loves soccer to pieces.

Steve replied: "If soccer were a type of religion and the World Cup a place of worship, then soccer fans, including my sweet wife, Carol, would take their seats, in large numbers, in the pews. Indeed, this trend shows a big sign of progress, as soccer grows in popularity now."

"Do you not think, Steve, that the FIFA 2010 World Cup may have broken the record for the number of soccer spectators in the history of the US?" asked Carol.

"You're not far from the truth, darling." Steve replied. "I recently read in a local magazine that about 19.4 million viewers watched the U.S. versus Ghana on ABC and Univision during the 2010 World Cup, compared to the same match that drew about 18.1 million viewers on the same networks. In a separate documentary, on television last night, it was revealed that the final of the Women's World Cup in 1999 between the U.S. and China drew about 18 million on ABC alone."

"Hmmmm," Carol murmured. "Why go there, Steve? Well, go ahead, I'm listening to you."

"I got your message, Carol. I went there to listen to the news and to watch only soccer, because I know that we both love soccer. What about it?"

"Haaa," Carol laughed. "I once read in a local newspaper where an admired clown said: 'Don't trust anyone over 50. They spend more, buy more gadgets, listen to the radio and watch the television more than anyone else.' Well, it might be a nice idea for people who once said 'I do' together to say it, at least one more time."

"What do you mean by that, baby?" Steve asked.

"No, never mind."

"But you just said something that's pregnant with meanings."

"Stop it!" Carol cried. "You're becoming a bit silly right now. I'm not pregnant."

"No, I didn't say that you're pregnant," Steve replied. "Do you no longer have pretty good ears, for which I've known you all these years we've been together? I said that you just said something that's pregnant with meaning. Could you explain further, honey?"

"Please, Steve, go ahead with your statistics. I just love soccer, and that really brought us together in the first place."

"Thanks to God Almighty, soccer did bring us together, darling!" Steve exclaimed. "But I know that marriage is no walk in the park. Except for waking up in the morning, every other thing gets easier with practice (laughter)."

"Shhhh," Carol urged. "Oh, you're laughing. There's really nothing funny about that."

Steve: "Do I have your permission to continue to talk, baby?"

Carol: "Yes, of course, go ahead."

"Are you sure, sweetie?" Steve asked. "Positive? Hope you're not learning how to grow jealous or suspicious?"

"Yes, I'm," replied Carol. "I just was worried about you and your implied hidden inclinations — and not about our women's or men's soccer teams winning."

"Shh ... hm," Steve replied. "Okay, thanks, honey. Another viewing record that I read in the New Jersey *Star Ledger* yesterday was that about 25 million people were believed to have watched the Spain versus Netherlands game on ABC and Univision. ABC was believed to have drawn 15.46 million viewers while Univision drew 8.820 million viewers. Have you any problem with this one, baby?"

"No, darling," Carol replied calmly. "I don't have any problem with that. Please go ahead with your statistics. It's all about our love for soccer and the desire to have a winning team in the U.S."

"Okay, thanks sweetie. Univision averaged 2.374 million viewers for the coverage of the 2010 FIFA World Cup, up 15% from 2006 and the highest average ever for the World Cup on the network."

"What an amazing job you just did, darling!" Carol extolled. "How did you come to memorize all those figures? You see, I've learned more from you than I ever learned from any local newspaper publishers. Tell me, how many gigabytes are at work in your head?"

"Haahaaahahaaa . . . You're sounding funny. It's my great love for soccer, honey," Steve explained, "and of course my love for you, too, which surpasses my great love for soccer put together."

"Okay, that's acceptable to me, honey," agreed Carol. "You're my hubby and I'm your wife and we'll continue to make positive things happen. Thanks a million times and please keep trying."

"You're welcome, honey, certainly," replied Steve. "You've always been the winner."

From this point on, Carol and Steve Bloom will gradually fade from the scene of the "wake-up-and-win" soccer journey, as other analysts, soccer veterans, players, celebrities, coaches, and supporters join our story. Relax and stay tuned, as it'll only be a temporary departure that welcomes the entrance of other contributors and discussants. This beautiful married couple has played the worthy role of heralds in this narrative, which has explored the progress in our men's soccer status and performances from a multiplicity of perspectives.

What a clear progress in the percentage and number of the U.S. soccer viewers in the memorable 2010 FIFA World Cup, as outlined above! It's a memorable event that will survive the test of time and go down in history as a thrilling, all-time event. Yes, it's pretty memorable when you recall the opening ceremonies, retrace the track and field events, and review in retrospect the almighty soccer fiestas of Atlanta 1996. The 19th FIFA World Cup event, taking place in South Africa from June 11 to July 11, 2010, is another international world soccer tournament that will make history.

"After watching the recent FIFA World Cup in South Africa on the television," revealed Steve, "a 14-year-old Texas boy, Keith O'Neil, who stands 5'2" and weighs 130 lbs., who never played soccer before except for line soccer, was said to have developed a profound interest in the game."

"I happened to know his mom Tina," Carol replied, "when I attended high school in Houston, Texas. She was not only my classmate, but also we're of the same age. Interestingly, she happens to be a WASP; haha…, as much as I'm, and we've both kept an unbroken and tight friendship until today."

"How beautiful!" Steve exclaimed. "What a friend indeed!"

"It might also excite you to know," Carol went on, "that Tina was one of my high school girlfriends who loves and appreciates soccer as much as I do. In fact, I spent about 30 minutes with her this morning on the phone. She brought to my attention that her son Keith recently expressed a strong desire and determination 'to play it now' after he moved to his new middle school. He considered himself mature enough in the speed and stamina expected of a good soccer player.

"According to Tina," continued Carol, "having been a good cross-country runner for about three years and pretty good at playing line soccer at the local gym, Keith's only concern was that he might graduate into the tenth grade without being sure whether or not he'd be able to make it to greater heights in soccer."

"Sorry, I don't mean to interrupt you, honey," Steve replied. "From what I read about him, Keith seems to be preoccupied with getting the necessary skills through further soccer drills and training. He's also thinking about the best positions he could play in any public soccer, with the rewarding feeling that people are beginning to recognize his good talents."

"What I learned from his mom so far," Carol replied, "is that he thinks that it's simply all about foot and legwork. He plans to try out attacking positions in his future drills and training, while hoping to get better at fundamental things, such as passing, crossing, and shooting. He's every expectation that he'll finally get there."

"That's pretty interesting for a young man of his age," Steve mused. "South Africa 2010 is believed to have left him with some transforming influence. I'm sure that he'll do well."

"Tina believes that South Africa 2010 was an event that Keith will seldom ever forget," Carol added. "He seemed to have found his heroes in the South Africa 2010 U.S. players, such as Landon Donovan, Clint

Dempsey, and Jozy Altidore. He deeply idolized them and, indeed, still idolizes them."

"Of course," Steve agreed. "That's what's normally expected of great soccer lovers of his age. As he played soccer with his peers in his parents' backyard, he'd call out the names of those heroes with excitement, as they dribbled along on their improvised field. Local soccer trainers, park goers, and other soccer enthusiasts have most likely spotted Keith playing soccer with his peers at community fields, playgrounds, and parks, with his friends thundering his name as they cheered him on."

"His was a humble but interesting start." Carol observed. "Moreover, Keith seems to have been inspired, blessed, and motivated by a Dad named Richard (Dick), who was said to have been a soccer player right from his high school days into his years in college. This revelation of family soccer ties is believed to have been profoundly illuminated in speech, as Keith once said: 'Dad was a great soccer player and a good guy. I'm sure he's going to help me a lot in soccer this summer.'"

Dick seemed to be pretty fascinated to learn that his son Keith might possibly become a later version of what he once was. He'd often share this impression with his wife Tina, who's been supporting Keith to become a soccer player, having realized that he was determined to follow in his dad's footsteps. For Richard, it would be a form of reincarnation, and it looked like another sweet start of great things to come for the family. Dick once remarked: "It's a fantastic feeling to learn that my son is developing great interest in soccer, and I'm filled with hope that he's going to do well. He's going to become a great kid."

Starting from the age of 5, Keith would watch his dad spend chunks of his precious time flipping through soccer magazines and newspapers, watching soccer on television, and discussing soccer events with his business associates and friends. Keith knew his dad wasn't kidding around with his friends when they all bought soccer materials for the World Cup and the 2010 Olympics, discussing with one another the possibility of traveling to South Africa.

Long retired from soccer playing, Richard continues to display great passion and exuberance for this beautiful game, and nearly made it to South Africa, along with his wife Tina, friends, and some of his high school soccer colleagues. But his tight business schedule prevented him from attending. As with the Bloom family, not attending the World Cup was for them a greatly missed opportunity.

About four weeks prior to the start of the 2010 World Cup tournament, soccer fans from Johannesburg were celebrating at Ghandi Square, because South Africa would be hosting international soccer's biggest contest of the century, with a kick off on June 11.

Hundreds of thousands of fans were flying to South Africa, with millions watching on television in anticipation of what was to be the biggest sport of the millennium. Despite the world's economy being in a deep recession, the demand for tickets was still exponentially high, making them difficult to come by. However, smart and well-heeled travelers and tourists worked with official tour operators to lock in their tickets, hotel rooms, and other travel arrangements to save themselves a last minute rush.

More than 100,000 Americans were said to be bound for the World Cup event. Indeed, the U.S. soccer fans, as widely expected, made up the bulk of ticket holders. Just as it normally happens in anticipation of every major sporting event, some concerns nearly got in the way. Indeed, there were some concerns that almost got in the way of people's great love for soccer.

Let's take a brief look at these concerns and questions, some of which might make people wince with surprise, especially those who know South Africa and its recent development. Could anyone have possibly imagined that these would be the concerns and questions from some would-be attendees? Perhaps, no. But in some cases, yes.

Notis: "Why would I go to a country with a less-than-stellar reputation and so distant from the US?"

Tricia: "Wouldn't it be brutally and oppressively hot over there, as many people have often thought?"

Thank goodness that South Africa gets chilly during this time of the year. It's actually the country's cold season, and this is especially true for Cape Town, which sits at the southern tip of the entire continent. Some soccer fans think this is the best time to visit South Africa, particularly to escape scorching, global warming heat waves. Judging from meteorology reports, the temperature during the World Cup could be as low as 45 degrees. Fans and other visitors were even advised to bring jackets or at least sweaters.

Most of the South African travelers and tourists believe that the World Cup coinciding with the country's winter season is favorable. They saw it as the summit of the safari season and held tight to the belief that low vegetation makes the environment, atmosphere, and climate better for both wildlife and soccer watching.

Owen: "Is South Africa ready to host such a huge event?"

These misplaced fears were eventually allayed when they learned that, among other things, some of the country's well-regarded and valued facilities, once threatened by ruin, had been restored and renovated. Moreover, each of the nine cities that were to host the soccer events had public transportation plans pretty well in place to accommodate the hordes of soccer fans. The nine cities were: Rustenburg, Polokwane, Nelspruit, Mangaung/ Bloemfontein, Nelson Mandela Bay/Port Elizabeth, Durban, Cape Town, Tshwane/Pretoria, and Johannesburg. These cities also have incredibly impressive natural and cultural sites.

Brooks: "Being a regular traveler to South Africa, I've come to discover that Cape Town, one of the host cities, with its distinctively European feel and good hotels abounding, is regarded in South Africa the way we regard Los Angeles in the US. And they hold Johannesburg in as high regard as we hold New York City. Suffice it to say that most of South Africa's gold comes from Johannesburg."

People may have gone to South Africa for soccer, but few would pass up the opportunity for sightseeing. Among the real charms would be a visit to the Apartheid Museum, the Safari Camp, the 30,000-acre Shambala Game Reserve, and the Arts Enclave in Cape Town. The apartheid museum in Johannesburg was running a special exhibition on Nelson Mandela. Usually crowded with visitors and tourists, this museum would encourage visitors to linger before venturing out to their respective soccer stadiums.

Another option might take visitors to the great city of Soweto, with its surprisingly cosmopolitan trove of the South African culture. They'd do well to explore this historically and culturally rich city, which occupies a vast expanse of land and is many people's favorite city in South Africa.

Some others might decide to take a shuttle down to the infamous Robben Island prison, which confined Mandela and other anti-apartheid activists for almost three decades. Depending on their interest, some would likely reward themselves with breathtaking views, and then cool themselves down with some classy wine procured from South Africa's world-class liquor stores.

Kruger National Park, illustrious for its safaris, is located a few miles away from Johannesburg. A visit to watch elephants, lions, Cape buffalo, rhinos, gorillas, and leopards would be gratifying. Guests and tourists have the choice to safari by car, elephant, or on foot. There's no doubt that this type of sightseeing might increase circulation in the legs, and alleviate pains in some strategic spots of a trip-maker's body.

Barry: "My visit to Kruger National Park during the soccer tournament was really rewarding. I saw many animals and other living creatures, including rare birds of prey. Among other birds of prey I spotted was a pair of bald and golden eagles that seemed to have started a new life. But surprisingly, the park director clearly explained to tourists and visitors that there hasn't been a courtship between these two birds, both of which were once critically endangered but were finally rescued for the park from Nairobi by the International Wildlife Service Corporation.

"I observed these birds through an outdoor show that allowed visitors to get up close and personal," continued Barry. I was excited to see their talons, which they use to catch their prey. I came to get an appreciation of the power and magnificence of the eagles, which are part of the Wildlife Conservation Society's outdoor birds of prey exhibit at the National Park. As the Park Director was conducting us around, I recalled that it was really rare to see an eagle in Minnesota when I was a kid playing soccer. But now I saw one, thanks to this trip to South Africa for the FIFA soccer fiesta."

Geraldine: "As a smart traveler to several global women's soccer outings, I must tell you that no one can ever completely know what benefits these sightseeing experiences can have on the human physical and physiological make-up. I'm just speaking from a positive perspective."

Aside from various park-and-ride and public bus plans, commuter trains were available to pick up passengers and soccer fans at various locations in the cities to transport them to the stadiums. What a shining privilege and honor for South Africa to be the primary host in the entire African continent for this international soccer contest! South Africa pulled off a major win, following an all-African bidding process that saw Morocco and Egypt as major contestants.

Tyra: "From my knowledge of civics and social studies, Morocco and Egypt are known as the two gems of North Africa. No doubt, these two countries, with their centuries-old royal hospitality, palatial hotels with sumptuous dining and cuisine, famous cities, excursions, monuments, and treasures, were believed by many to have had what it takes to host the FIFA World Cup soccer. But South Africa won the bid this time. That's okay. It's good for all of Africa and good for the entire world."

South Africa used her unique victory to celebrate the centenary of her membership into the Federation of the International Football Association (FIFA). They prepared well for this event and were ready to welcome people from other big nations. The South African government and businesses took great pains to make the entire nation tourist-friendly. Infrastructure in the host cities was renovated to accommodate the needs and tastes of visitors and tourists. South African ATM machines were modified to accept both Visa and Master cards, something that used to be rare in Africa. Credit and debit cards were rendered acceptable in places of business, with foreign currencies made easily accessible to pay for those services that wouldn't accept credit and debit cards. Several travel companies across the globe offered surprising packages and bargains, so that those who booked accommodations weren't disappointed. Pretty exciting.

Little wonder, then, that Carol Bloom expressed the profound wish and desire to spend another vacation in South Africa with Steve, and their other 10-year-old daughter Jessica and 8-year-old son Chris. It would've been an additional special event for this longstanding soccer-loving couple, who wanted to fly down to Johannesburg for the summer holidays to watch the games live. It would've been an opportunity for them to deepen the spirit of soccer that was already alive in their family.

Carol, Steve, and their two kids have been in the habit of playing soccer together every Sunday evening at the backyard of their house. They had sufficient open space to install two small goal posts. Playing the sport helped immensely in bringing the family together. It had been their desire and dream to pass on their love for soccer to their children, and grandchildren. They never felt that soccer could only be played on a field, as many families have thought, and so never left their home to play soccer.

This practice had attracted many soccer-loving families and friends to their house every Sunday evening before dinner, where they played the sport joyfully together. For those families and friends, joining the Blooms for soccer was a golden moment of golden togetherness, because for them such exercises afforded everyone a golden opportunity to catch up with whatever may have been happening in one another's lives. For them, it was also often a golden mini-soccer celebration. Together, they learned scoring skills and tactical dribbling.

Despite their inability to make it down to South Africa, the Bloom family still enjoyed the soccer games right in their home in Colorado

Springs, on their big family-sized-screen television. It was a special event for them, because they could watch the game with prize enjoyment and relaxation in the privacy of their home.

"Ever since I was a kid," recounted Carol, "I've lived for soccer in the summer. Sharing it with my parents, siblings, and now with my husband and two younger kids has often brought alive the bliss of summer."

The Bloom family watched the opening soccer match between South Africa and Mexico, which took place at Soccer City in Johannesburg on June 11 at 9.00 a.m. EDT. This match ended in a 1-1 draw. On the following day at around noon, Jessica reminded Steve and Carol that the scheduled match between England and the U.S. would begin at exactly 1:30 p.m. EDT at the Royal Bafokeng Stadium in Rustenburg.

This filial ingenuity earned Jessica the promise of a gift from her dad, Steve, who earlier thought he was cock-sure that the match would begin at 4:00 p.m. EDT. This costly presumption, had it not been challenged, would've been a heartbreaker for Carol, who was preparing with unsparing gusto to watch the U.S. versus England encounter. What an undesirable coincidence for this match to end in a 1-1 draw, the same as in the encounter between South Africa and Mexico the day before. The Bloom family seemed to have been satisfied with the performance of the U.S. team, but wished that America had defeated England to clear grounds for her possible advancement in the 2010 global soccer tournament.

They were hopeful that with upcoming matches — U.S. vs. Slovenia and U.S. vs. Algeria on June 18 and June 23 respectively — the U.S. had the chance to push forward and possibly reach the quarter-finals. This meant that the Bloom family never gave up. Being naturally non-discriminatory, they watched teams from other countries, with their children shouting, "Oh yeah, Mommy and Daddy, let's go Brazil!" or "Let's just go, Argentina." These exuberant shouts from the kids typified the shouts from many of the fans on the streets of Johannesburg before the summer Olympics.

"I understand, guys," Steve replied, "but while we wait for our guys, let's go watch Germany on Sunday and Netherlands on Monday. How's that?"

The kids stood listening. What Steve said really made sense to Carol, her sister Christine, and the kids. They watched the encounter between Germany and Australia and rooted for Germany because of their outstanding performance. Germany eventually took the match, 4-0.

On Monday, June 14, they watched the match between the Netherlands and Denmark, with the Netherlands winning 2-0. On June 15 they watched the match between Brazil and North Korea, with Brazil the victor by 2-1. At the end of the match the kids erupted with joy and sputtered with laughter, while shouting, "Let's go, Brazil!"

On June 17, the Bloom family watched Argentina defeat South Korea 4-1. Carol reminded everybody that the U.S. team would be playing against Slovenia the following day. She expressed the wish that the team would play as beautifully as either Germany or Argentina had in the past days.

The Bloom family watched the encounter between the U.S. team and Slovenia from their hotel room. The match took place at Ellis Park in Johannesburg and ended in a 2-2 draw.

"I never lost confidence," Carol enthused. "I know that the U.S. has a good team here. It's hard to take a draw game at this point."

The Bloom family never lost hope in the U.S. men's soccer team, even though they knew by this time that the team wasn't going to make it to the finals. They still looked forward to the match between the U.S. and Algeria on June 23. Meanwhile, they kept watching other nations' teams.

On Saturday, June 19, they watched Ghana and Australia, which ended in a 1-1 draw. The following day they watched Italy and New Zealand, while also deeply interested in knowing the result between Brazil and Côte d' Ivoire (Ivory Coast). They finally settled on Italy and New Zealand, which ended in a 1-1 draw, after which they switched over to watch Brazil and Côte d' Ivoire, with Brazil the victor by 3-1. The match between Portugal and North Korea ended in the scandalous score of 7-0 for Portugal. The lopsided defeat almost made the kids, in their innocence, shed tears of sympathy for the utter humiliation of the North Koreans.

On June 22 they watched the match between Nigeria and South Korea, which ended in a 2-2 draw. Carol was excited to watch the Nigerian team, yet was disappointed that they didn't perform as they did in 1996, when she first expressed great admiration for them.

"Compared to what I saw during the Atlanta '96 Olympics," she remarked, "I think that the Nigerian team isn't doing too well this time. What do you think, Steve?"

"I think you're right, Carol, but in my opinion they seem to be playing better than our guys, even though I may be wrong," replied Steve.

"Let's not draw any conclusions about our guys yet, until they finish up with Ghana," Carol added. "Never take our team at its face value, as they might spring surprises at any time."

"Ha ha. When is that going to happen, Carol," asked Steve, "as I'm no longer interested in watching them because they're not going to make it to the semi-finals, anyway?"

"Our guys aren't that bad, Steve. They're great guys. I like their way and style of soccer, but they need a little more brush up to enable them beat teams like Brazil, Argentina, Netherlands, Germany, and Spain."

"Ha ha ha, you're sounding funny, Carol. Beating Brazil? Are you even sure that they will be able to defeat Ghana in their next match? I don't see that happening."

"Those guys from Ghana are also great," replied Carol, "but I think that our guys might be able to defeat their team. Uh, I'm not so sure."

On June 26, the entire Bloom family watched the long-awaited match between the U.S. and Ghana. It was a tight match, but ended in a 2-1 score against the U.S. on a penalty kick.

Carol, Steve, and their children were saddened to see Ghana defeat the U.S., but decided that grumbling, yelling, or complaining about it wouldn't help. Rather, they handled the situation maturely with a laid-back approach.

"I told you so, Carol," affirmed Steve. "I'm not surprised at all. I've always said that our guys are good players, but they lack scoring power. Moreover, our defense is weak and porous in comparison with our guys in Atlanta '96. A lot of work really needs to be done."

"Their coach did a good job but more needs to be done," Carol pointed out. "If you add one more guy to Landon Donovan, Jozy Altidore, and Clint Dempsey, give the forward liners a little more drill, retain our goalkeeper Tim Howard, and establish the type of defense we had in 1996, believe me, we'll be able to hold our own in the World Cup or get to the finals. But this is simply my opinion, Steve."

"Indeed, all our players are good," he agreed, "but they need serious training and support. I believe that we can do so as a nation — winning the Olympic Gold Medal and lifting the global soccer trophy."

Chris and Jessica were really disheartened that the U.S. was defeated, even though it wasn't a humiliation as in the match between Portugal and North Korea. Nonetheless, they were demoralized, but managed to finish up the tournament by watching the subsequent matches.

Carol, Steve, and their children watched teams like Germany, Netherlands, Spain, and Argentina. The FIFA soccer fiesta finally ended on Sunday, July 11, 2010, with Spain pulling off a win against Netherlands by a narrow 1-0 margin.

"People love every FIFA World Cup soccer fiesta with much predilection, because it's unique in many ways," opined Carol. "It's unique because it's open to all the nations of the world. It's unique because every nation has an equal chance of qualifying for any of the contests or winning. Soccer unites people who belong to the same country, and people from different countries."

"You're right, Carol." Steve agreed. "I've got something to share with you. The movie *Invictus*, meaning 'unconquered,' which I recently watched, is an inspiring true story about Nelson Mandela, who, in his first term as president of South Africa, wanted to use soccer to unite his nation."

"Did it work for him?"

"Yes, of course." Steve exclaimed. "He eventually succeeded. Initially, though, some people, including politicians both white and black, expressed doubts about his ability to use soccer to bring unity to a country divided by 50 years of racial tension. But listen to how the whole thing worked. As Mandela attempted to tackle South Africa's largest problems, he attended a soccer match of the Springboks, the country's rugby union team. During the match, he noticed that non-whites in the stadium cheered against their home squad, because in their minds the Springboks stood for prejudice, apartheid, and white supremacy. He convinced members of the newly constituted sports committee, which was black-dominated, not to change the name or the color of the team, which was predominantly white. Mandela believed that if Springbok could gain the support of black South Africans in the 1995 Rugby World Cup the following year, the country would be inspired and perhaps end up being unified. When Mandela's theory eventually gained some prominence and traction, and acceptance by the blacks supporting Springbok, things began to change and positive momentum toward unity was created. Black men enthusiastically supported their national team alongside white men. Indeed, Springbok was seen as a game-changer, because it was the game of rugby that changed a nation's life forever."

"Thank you, Steve," Carol said, "for sharing with me that beautiful message about Mr. Mandela's accomplishment. It's touching. One of my friends recently shared with me a story about how one Wisconsin bachelor watched the entire 2010 World Cup on television."

Here is what the Wisconsin bachelor, Xerxes Grenada, observed:

"Watching from my room in Wisconsin on Channel 41, I beheld firsthand what it means to see soccer unite people from different countries."

Xerxes watched some of the opening ceremonies that kicked off the tournament in South Africa, which had also been watched by the Bloom family in Colorado Springs. For sure, he counted himself among many passionate soccer fans out there. But what could' have been more gratifying to him, at this time, than watching the live World Cup in South Africa? He enjoyed watching the matches on television to his utmost satisfaction, without fighting with anyone, real or imaginary, over the remote control, all in the privacy of his room in Wisconsin.

It's fine to remark at this time that the television is one of the home luxuries that the modern world offers, and very few people say no to it. Because of soccer, its value has been converted from something of a luxury to a necessity.

An American of Greek extraction, Xerxes Grenada migrated to the U.S. about 15 years ago. Interestingly, he didn't have an iota of trouble listening to the soccer commentary in English. That multiplied his pleasure, along with the amusing and attention-grabbing commentary of the soccer analyst, which delighted Xerxes.

"Soccer runs on many attention-grabbing events," Xerxes suggested, "and many people know that soccer is one of the most popular sports on the face of the earth."

Feedback in such big global events often comes from the numbers of spectators gracing each tournament. A sea of heads packed Soccer City Stadium for the opening ceremony and the first match between South Africa and Mexico, which ended in a 1-1 draw. Xerxes saw Brazilian citizens celebrating alongside people from Ghana shortly before the opening ceremonies that ushered in the opening match.

"What an excitement it was for me," he recalled, "to see them celebrating together, most of them draped in the jersey colors of their teams, beating the traditional African Zulu drums, dancing with special facial costumes, and rejoicing on both the broad and narrow streets of Johannesburg with a variety of interesting expressions, and other performances."

More touching was Xerxes' admiration for hundreds of African tribal dancers who paraded into the soccer stadium in colorful costumes, along with the South African trumpeter Hugh Musketeer and the American singer Ro Kelley. They entertained the huge throng of spectators, accompanied by a vibrantly fashionable fireworks display. It's time for Africa. Think for a moment about Shakira and her appealing musical companions, who entertained the spectators and visitors in a thrilling fashion with the piece, "*Waka Waka Eeh Eeh . . . Tamina amina Sangariwa . . .* It's time for Africa."

Among the dignitaries Xerxes saw on television were the Vice President of the United States, Joe Biden, and the South African anti-apartheid leader Archbishop Desmond Tutu, who at one point was almost dancing in his seat in sync and harmony with the ongoing music of the colorful moment. Who was conspicuously absent and why, although his spirit was present in the entire soccer city? Shortly after the opening ceremonies, supporters of the South Korean team and U.S. supporters were seen flying their flags together. For Xerxes, it was like beholding twin sisters or brothers playing and rejoicing together even before the games had started.

"A sense of pride for their individual nations shared together," he remarked, "was seen radiating on their faces, if not for any other reason but for qualifying for the 2010 World Cup. What an excitement for a people to realize that their nation is among the 32 nations to have qualified for the World Cup finals. For them, there was that sense of patriotism and support for their various nations."

Some people travel all the way to soccer hosting nations just to support and stand behind their national teams, staying in their team's camp all the way. Some express their support by wearing the team's jersey with the inscription of the team's name on it. What struck Xerxes most was the sight of hundreds of South African children and youth wearing World Cup jerseys with the inscription: "Go U.S.A.!"

For Xerxes, it seemed that they pretty much rooted for the U.S. players and perhaps hoped that they'd progress further than they did in 1996. For Xerxes, it wasn't about winning or lifting the Olympic trophy — rather, it was about the togetherness of the global soccer teams, from various nations and continents. There was no atmosphere of victor versus vanquished on the day before the start of the tournament. There was simply the anticipation of a brilliant soccer climate.

Just like Steve and Carol in the Atlanta, 1996, Xerxes watched as soccer fans across the continents counted down to the opening day of the 2010 FIFA World Cup. He was watching history being made again, as he wondered what type of month it would be, both for South Africa and the whole world. For some days, even an Alien Visitor from Mars would've noticed that soccer had arrived, as young people of African descent, dressed in beautiful and wonderful bright clothing, rallied along the streets to drum up support for the World Cup. It's true that nobody saw them swinging rally towels with flamboyance, as we would see in the U.S, but some of them carried placards in both English and local languages, portraying soccer as going hand-in-hand with world peace, unity, and mutual co-existence among peoples and nations.

The players and soccer fans took their turns on a broad range of instrumentation. This wide variety of instruments included the Zulu drums and, of special interest, the vuvuzelas or plastic horns that have a close tie to South African soccer tradition.

Aside from other soccer items and equipment, earplugs sold briskly during this month-long event, as some visitors, supporters, and even participants used them to protect their precious ears from the alleged and the presumed eardrum assaults of the vuvuzelas. The vuvuzelas, whose drone has gained notoriety for decades at soccer matches in South Africa, and especially during the 2010 soccer World Cup, are blown like there's no tomorrow by thousands of South African fans and supporters in favor of their favorite teams, to spur them onto great and meaningful action, or to simply urge them to Wake Up and Win. Although the vuvuzelas were inspiring and comforting to some, to others they were discomforting.

"As one of the soccer fans who was in South Africa for the tournament," recalled Frederick, "even though I didn't care for the earplugs, wearing them helped some of the foreign fans reduce the ear assaults from sounds that mimicked a loud zizz of angry bees headed on a combat mission. Some of those who wore earplugs confessed that without them, such earsplitting sounds could make the ears tingle without limits, but for the South African people and other genuine soccer fans, but it was all fun and enjoyable."

People heard the sounds of the vuvuzelas in Pretoria, Johannesburg, Gauteng, Tshwane, and in all the major cities in South Africa where the soccer contests took place. Some thought that the sounds mimicked those of a jet engine that was growing nasty. Some styled it the "vuvuzela drone," while the sound reminded others of a giant insect. Other visitors thought the sound was just fantabulous. What a truly vivid reality in the saying that "one man's meat is another man's poison."

One would be interested to ask the question: which of the preceding opinions would be held by soccer enthusiasts and even by the vuvuzela players themselves? Despite some expressions of dislike for the vuvuzelas, many fans still loved them to pieces, while some suggested that they should be used only for the soccer opening ceremonies in future events. They believe that it might create good feelings, just like the ecstatic feeling you get from a profoundly beautiful burst of ceremonial fireworks. There are many clear-cut ways of sharing in other people's cultures and traditions.

"It makes no sense using earplugs while watching soccer." says Jerry. "For me, it's better to get accustomed to that unique and beautiful culture. Using earplugs could also mean that someone has heard enough of everything in his surroundings. It sounds like the story of the old man who turned down his family's offer to provide him with a new hearing aid, insisting that he had heard enough. Soccer spectators and fans don't only watch, they also listen. Blowing the vuvuzela trumpet is all about boosting the morale of the players and fans. There are questions that linger in my mind: If you're a true soccer fan, could you possibly have heard enough? Have you really heard so much as to wear earplugs during beautiful and exciting soccer events? Amusing, eh?"

"I think you're right, Jerry." agreed Ivory. "It's about boosting the morale of well-meaning players and fans. In addition, I'd simply say, 'Good luck to all those who'd prefer to put on earplugs, but how would they communicate with each other so as to enjoy the matches together? How the players, supporters, and coaches would hear the sounds of the whistles and other important announcements, should they opt to use the earplugs as protective devices, would also be another good question to be answered."

People who couldn't stand the vuvuzela drones during the soccer games were said to have definitely become smart by literally allowing themselves to be subdued by what I'd prefer to call soccer *vuvuzexcitement*. Excited and smart visitors from other countries, including the US, discovered an easy strategy by which to escape from the alleged discomforting sound of the vuvuzelas.

What did they do? They simply joined the South African fans in the horn-blowing business. For them, joining in the exercise was absolutely fun and they wound up being joyfully excited in the long run. During the soccer contests, more than 50,000 vuvuzelas were believed to have been sold as a result of the participants' *vuvuzexcitment (and because they were pretty cheap)*.

Indeed, no soccer tournament promises to become a quiet occasion aware of the tastes of all involved. 'Noisemaking' and 'distractions' have a long history at major sporting events. Certain countries, continents and cultures, that are either communitarian or communalistic, have been known for beating drums and gongs, sprinting, chanting, singing, stomping, and making thunder-sticks.

What about shouting slogans and anthems, or yelling, cheering, or booing at someone during a match? It depends on the circumstances and the nature and demands of the event. Certain countries in South America, Africa, and Asia, such as Brazil, Argentina, Mexico, Ghana, Nigeria, Kenya, South Korea, and so forth, could be implicated in these types of field promo activities. But could all these emissions of alleged disquiet stop anyone from being a soccer lover or fan?

The best answer would be to ignore the sounds or noise coming from the vuvzelas (if you prefer to call it a noise). To some people it's a beautiful sound, whereas others have a different opinion. Perhaps one man's meat could be another man's fish.

"As a sports psychologist and soccer enthusiast," observed Allan, "I'm inclined to believe that it may be a part of the psychological strategies employed to intimidate the opponents, so as to gain the upper hand over them. It's also a way to raise the spirits of their darling team members, and to strengthen the solidarity and oneness of soccer fans in their support for their favorite team. All these are psychological supporting strategies that help a group of people gain advantage over others. They're all acceptable in soccer, so long as they don't disrupt the process of soccer playing itself."

"Of course, players should be able to distinguish between the earsplitting sound coming from the vuvzelas," added Lorenzo, "and the sounds of the whistle from the referee. The whistle sounds from the referees are unique to the ears of players, linesmen, and other field assistants. In summary, playing soccer requires the concentration and attention of the players, who should be able to ignore every other external noise or distraction."

"Great teams never complain about the sounds or noises from external sources," remarked Gregory. "Why? Because their players, coaches, and those on the reserve bench, along with their well-meaning fans, are never bothered by that stuff. External noises and sounds aren't important to them. What's important to them is to get the ball into the net. Only when that happens will you hear sounds and noises that are indescribable, a thousand times louder that the sound coming from the tiny vuvuzelas."

"From my long-standing experience in soccer playing," opined Jerry, "I've come to believe that external noises and sounds never distract or demoralize any well-intentioned and zealous players and fans. What's demoralizing is the inability of players to score goals. Nobody's ears are going to bleed from 'noises' that are in any way linked to good soccer playing."

"I was physically present in Johannesburg for most of the matches played," noted Derek. "I saw two dozen guys selling vuvuzelas outside in the parking lot. I also saw about six other guys across the street selling earplugs. What I found funny was that half the people around me in the stands wore earplugs. Fair enough, but what that meant to me was that I couldn't even talk about the game to the guy next to me. I didn't buy or wear any earplugs because I didn't feel I needed them, and because I'm a good soccer fan. I love soccer — that's why I had to travel from Chicago to South Africa for this event. Until this day, no one has complained that it has broken anyone's eardrum, including mine."

"I have a 15-year-old daughter who plays soccer in high school," noted Lucille, "we traveled down to South Africa on vacation and seized the opportunity to watch the soccer games. I believe that blowing the vuvuzelas is among the many off-the-field soccer activities fans use to help their favorite teams win. It was all about boosting the morale of their favorite soccer teams. They blew the vuvuzelas on some occasions in support of the U.S. team. I was sometimes a little bothered by the sound, but that didn't stop us from watching the beautiful soccer games."

"I'm studying sports psychology," announced Kevin. "Just invent whatever you need to help you win and be good at it. I don't care what it is. It's all about intimidation."

"Even though I'm a student of classics in Pennsylvania," responded Nancy, "I've loved soccer so much all my life and have watched soccer events on television, including the ones that took place in South Africa. Wouldn't someone be able to convert those vuvuzela sounds or 'noise' into a melodious musical experience to suit the overall soccer activities? I suspect that such a disputable concern could be simply moderated or resolved by giving huge awards for general comportment during the games, and seeing if the whole thing could be transformed into a beautiful musical activity devoid of discordant sounds, that otherwise would make the thing seem just 'noisy.'"

"Haaahaaaa. I love soccer," added Beverly, "and I loved the sounds of the vuvuzelas, too, when I heard them on live television. I later discovered that the vuvuzelas are South Africa's symbol to signify that soccer is here. It's a 'wake up and win' call to soccer fans, supporters, and team members. It's a call to rise up and shine."

A soccer tournament is a time to wake up and win and will continue to be. Players, fans, and supporters need some prompting; they need some motivation. Promptings and motivations don't always have to be sweet sounding to every ear for those spurs to do their job well. Soccer itself is larger than noise. From another perspective, the beautiful colors of the vuvuzelas, which represent all the major continents, can never be overemphasized. Its trumpet-like sounds can be likened to the calls from the soccer spirits in Atlanta '96 for the competing nations to wake up and win at all costs, but with mutual respect, love, and unity.

The colors and sounds of the vuvuzelas also give hope and inspiration to both the fans and other participants when their darling team members seem to be both down and dispirited on the field. They serve as a constant reminder that soccer is actually here.

And who was physically present as VIPs at the 2010 FIFA World Cup, and who was conspicuously absent at the opening ceremony? Guess who it was among the young and the old? Soccer makes the old feel and act young, while the young rejuvenate forever. What does it mean for the old to act young?

Recall that when South Africa won the bid to host the World Cup in May 2004, Nelson Mandela was among those who celebrated with vuvuzelas. Indeed, inside every old person there's a young person, as the saying goes. But what does that mean? For he who loves soccer, it simply means that soccer is here. Let's celebrate, even if it means counting one's chickens before they're hatched. Never forget that some people never lose their beauty, charm, handsomeness, graciousness, and sense of humor, no matter how old they are. Among the old people who attended the World Cup tournament in Johannesburg was the 91-year-old anti-apartheid icon and erstwhile South African president, Nelson Mandela. Though old, he looked relatively energetic and displayed dexterity with his joviality and a great sense of humor. He was always impeccably dressed and well spoken. Despite his age he keeps moving, just like an unstoppable soccer star.

Mandela had planned to attend the opening ceremony, to welcome the fans at the opening game on June 11, but he decided against it following the tragic loss of his great-granddaughter in a car accident as she was returning from the World Cup opening concert just two days after her 13th birthday.

The passing of Zenani Mandela, 13, was sudden, tragic, and a great loss for the former South African first family. Even though it's a big loss for him, as it would be for anyone of his caliber, his desire to see and welcome soccer fans, coupled with his love and predilection for soccer, remained undeterred. The 91-year-old briefly greeted the fans before the World Cup final at Soccer City, and then went home to watch the match between Spain and Netherlands on television. Mandela has always been loved, and adored, the world over for his resilience, never-quitting spirit, and philosophy of life. Despite the tragedy that befell him and his family, Mandela remained undefeated in the face of troubles and trials. He behaved like someone who had gained victory over difficulties and distress, appearing both victorious and undefeated.

# Chapter 3
## Victory and Defeat

Sports loving fans and soccer folks in the United States and across the globe needn't dive into the depths of sports psychology to learn about victory and defeat in soccer. Not necessary at all. Simple practical analyses from experienced players and other sports veterans will help explain the concept of victory and defeat in life's endeavors in general and soccer in particular.

Most of the time, success has been seen as leading to stability, whereas failure is seen as leading to possible upheavals. The old saying is that "success has a hundred parents, but failure is an orphan." Analyses of these concepts will enable us to understand the extent to which they can describe the outcomes of soccer encounters. They will help determine whether these concepts are changeable, debatable, or acceptable. This reflection and analysis will, of course, be of immense value to sports lovers, players, and students of sports psychology all over the U.S.

Just sit back, listen, and watch how the power of reflection and its application work in your life. A little bit of it helps.

"As a longtime soccer player," boasted Greg, "I've often asked myself, and others, these questions: What's wrong and not wrong with victory? What's wrong and not wrong with defeat? I appeared on the field prepared and expecting to win. I've at the same time seen the idea of 'playing not to lose' as a negative attitude in soccer. But with the positive spirit of playing to win, I've achieved great success in soccer."

"These questions that you ask yourself," replied Steve, "seem to pop up in many areas of human endeavor, underlying concerns about the failure or inability to achieve success, not just in soccer, but in other competitive encounters with opponents, rivals, contestants, counterparts, and even colleagues.

"Similar to what you've just said," Steve went on, "I once read a quote from Eric Davis: 'I think we've come to the park expecting to win, instead of playing not to lose.' This statement enables us to think more deeply about victory and defeat, about success and failure, but I desire to fight and win, and never fought to lose. Eric tells us that one shouldn't play not to lose, as that's not the spirit of sportsmanship."

"Yes Steve," Matt replied. "I believe that I've come across the same book that you read. I remember the clear portrayal of playing confidently to win, versus playing anxiously and desperately to avoid losing. This second approach could be dangerous for players."

"I understand what you're saying, guys," chimed Caroline. "I've played on a women's soccer team in Philadelphia for about five years now. From my experience, I believe that it's up to you as a person, soccer fan, player, team, manager, or coach to decide who and what takes a walk into your life. Also, it's up to you to decide whom and what you let stay in your life. The questions that remain are: Do you wish to keep someone in your life who desires victory, or someone who desires defeat? Would you like to keep someone in your life who desires success, or someone who desires failure? Do you wish to keep victory or defeat in your life? Would you like to keep success or failure? It's really up to you to decide whom or what you let walk away."

"I think that you're right Caroline." replied Alan. "But it's also up to you to determine who or what you'd refuse to let go; that's what you really need, indeed. Just give this advice a shot, and then send it as a soccer ball gift to your family, friends, or your acquaintances. When you've done this, then you may have learned to wake up and win, not only in soccer contests, but in life as well."

"Hi, guys," piped up Dorothy. "What all of you've been saying sounds like three different ways of saying the same thing. I think that it pretty much has to do with the attitude you have and the inspiration that comes to you at any time. Sometimes it's more difficult to try not to do something, than trying to do it. I'm looking at the issue from this point of view: we may be entertaining some fear when we're playing soccer only not to lose. No action ever succeeds if fear is the basis of that action."

"I see the point you're making, Doth," chimed in Yvonne, "because from my experience as a soccer player, when we play with fear, we're looking over our shoulders and wondering if we're doing enough to keep losing at bay. Moreover, any time we commit an error there's a tendency for us to begin to panic, because we have the feeling of getting a step closer to losing. At long last; when such feelings compound, the situation becomes pretty scary that it keeps us from winning. What's the use of such a winless attitude?"

The issue of victory and defeat remains an age-old issue. It possibly predates the origin of man as a social being. Every human being is subject to experiencing victory, success, defeat, or failure. It's natural for people to experience any of these in major life encounters and events.

"I wish to share my feelings as a former high school soccer player in Denver, Colorado," announced Kyle. "Whenever our team saw defeat, I often felt as if we'd allowed people to break into our home, eat our food and drink our wine, and then take our wives with them as they leave. That's the way defeat in soccer has always felt to me."

"Hahaha hahaha," laughed Tim. "I've often felt the same way, Kyle. Defeat is like people coming into your hard-earned house, kicking down the doors, polishing off the food, and sleeping in your well-dressed beds without caring to wipe their feet before doing so. To be honest with you, it would feel like some intentional disrespect. I wouldn't wish anything like that on anyone."

"Whatever points are being made here," concluded Alan, "I still think that all human beings experience either success or failure in life. They also experience victory or defeat at some point. However, experiencing constant failure is neither healthy nor conducive to anybody's total well-being and existence."

"How to raise your dreams and desires," advised Karen, "and how to get motivated remain key goals in every person's life. That which you want to create is of vital importance to you. But you need to look for the mentor within you to help push you forward to victory, if you so desire. Yes, the ultimate mentor is within you. The law of attraction to victory or defeat, failure or success, is within each individual."

"You're right, Karen," observed Arthur, "but you've got to create a big impression that you're out there making a powerful effort for the better in your life, in soccer, or in other professional commitments. If, for instance, you're spinning your wheels with time passing by, and victory isn't coming forth, you really need to pull back and start thinking: where do I want this to go and what do I need to do better?"

"People are often expected to learn that success and failure are just part of life's experiences," added Dave. "It's a fact sufficiently obvious to anyone who has accorded this issue more than a glance recognition. It's happening all over, in all sorts of sports, and not just in soccer alone."

"Have you ever taken the time," asked Steve, "to reflect on the sweetness of this message: 'When you win by scoring many goals, friends, fans, family, and well-wishers will go out of their way to praise and encourage you to make more of your talents. They know you've got a lot to offer.' What a thriller and morale booster! But, by the way, many people experience failure and defeat and fall away, while others come out stronger than before."

"I think that the problem most people have," argued Marti, "is falling down without the strong determination to rise again. It's possible to flee from the painful experience of defeat or failure to achieve victory or success, but we have to go back into the fight to achieve desired success. It's right to affirm that the one who achieves victory isn't the one who has always been victorious."

"Success and failure, like victory and defeat," noted Jamie, "can be like two sides of the same coin, depending on the situation. It's a lesson that I've learned and received from good friends, acquaintances, and relations, not to mention renowned present-day writers, philosophers, psychologists, anthropologists, and sociologists. And, I believe these statements are veritable and true. Honestly, I don't think this is an issue that should raise a single grain of doubt. I was recently having a chat with an acquaintance and soccer fan, who confessed that he struggled with the issues of success and didn't personally feel comfortable with victory or success. He mentioned that he felt uncertain about what he believed as regards victory and defeat."

"Jamie, I understand what you mean," replied Jennifer, "but no one actually knows why this acquaintance of yours would send out such a message. Some people believe that if you don't experience defeat or failure, it'll be hard to appreciate and cherish success or victory when it comes. Should failure and defeat be a necessity, then? Are failure and defeat in any way rewarding?"

"This is the way I look at it, Jen," jumped in Martha. "Because of his experience, having been raised in a soccer-loving family, his first few years in college, and where he played soccer, he may have brought on a chain of defeats and failures in all the soccer encounters he was involved in. These soccer events and experiences seemed to have pointed his thoughts and inclinations away from what I've always seen as the goal or objective of every person, which is victory and success."

"You're right, guys," agreed Jamie, "as we're all thinking the same thing. Believe me, when he said that, I really wasn't sure how to give a retort. I wasn't totally frustrated with my friend, but his message left me obviously flummoxed because he didn't sound like someone making any effort for a change or an improvement for the 'better' and the 'ideal.' He spoke about it as if his situation was incurable, and probably without any solution. But at the same time, he expressed no intention of remaining with the same mindset forever, and that's where I found my confusion."

"Hi, Jamie," responded Eric, "it sounds like persistence in awkward ideas and principles, but with a lot of questions left unanswered. He sounded like someone who either hates excellence or is at loggerheads with it, whichever way you view it. Do I sometimes have the same feelings as he does? I'm not quite sure … haaa haaa. But when it comes to experiences, I've, surely, seen victory and defeat, successes and failures, in various life encounters and involvements. However, I've come to the conclusion that the right thing to do at this point isn't to be frustrated with your acquaintance, who seems to be comfortable with failures and defeats, but to pray for, and sympathize with him and any person who doesn't feel comfortable with victory or success as really failure in human clothing, roaming about in turbans and singing the praises of defeat and failure in every one of his human endeavors."

"Haaa haa." chuckled Martha. "That suggestion doesn't really fly. Are you praying for someone who has chosen the way he wants to go, and basks in its imaginary bliss, that is, for me, the way of failure and defeat? That would be ridiculous. The one who delights in or feels comfortable with failure or defeat, has the seed of failure and defeat already planted in his or her bone marrow."

"Haaa haaa." laughed Jack. "But we could also look at the issue from another angle. The experience of defeat or failure may be positively viewed as a toolkit that helps us to better advance toward success and victory. Defeat or failure is simply a human experience, and shouldn't be seen as something that evokes disgust or despair. Rather, it should engender a strong desire for something better and more glorious — that's, the desire to wake up and win."

"That sounds good, but reasoning continues." chimed Keira. "I'm more of questioning that mindset of Jamie's acquaintance. If you really feel and believe as he does, then that's a big deal that really needs to be thoroughly reviewed and reconsidered. It's like taking great delight in being tossed and blown around by the wind."

"Wow!" exclaimed Jamie. "That was pretty bizarre. That sounds truly abnormal, requiring some form of psychological and, perhaps, spiritual counseling and intervention, if possible. I think that life has something much greater in store for us than feeling comfortable with failure and defeat."

"If someone is struggling with such a bizarre mindset," Richard pointed out, "that delights and glories in failure or takes joy in defeat, then don't sit back in mere observation and end up missing out something important. Just call 911."

"Haaaahaaaa." laughed Dennis. "That's right. A normal human being isn't supposed to be comfortable with defeats and failures. If we delight in defeats and failures, then we lack the capability and desire to either encourage others or to be encouraged ourselves. If that's something someone believes in, then it's outlandish, unorthodox, and below general acceptance. I think it's an open wound that needs to heal —indeed, a knife in the heart!"

"I must let you know," affirmed Jamie, "that I came away from this discussion absolutely confused and scandalized. Since then, I've been thinking . . ."

"Haaa haaa," chuckled Ben. "I'd like to be without defeats or failures all my life, but I know that sometimes I'm going to experience them and, indeed, do experience them. But that doesn't mean we should desire failure or defeat as something as delicious as our favorite dinner, or as something good and noble. They may be natural, but that doesn't mean that they're desirable, good, and noble."

"We've come into the world to become successes and not failures," interrupted Angelina. "That has always been my strong belief. The desire for failure or defeat in any known human culture would be considered a crime or an abomination. We can't accept that mindset at all, because it really stinks. We should try our best to get away from such a crippling mindset, and start to think absolutely about waking up and winning in every human endeavor. Our commitments should tilt toward excellence and nothing less."

"The call to success and excellence," noted Steve, "is a call we get every day of our lives. To desire or work toward anything less would be a clear sign of abject imbecility."

Carol joined in: "Failure or defeat is a pothole in that flat land that belongs to victory and success alone, while the desire for failure or defeat will constitute, in itself, a big black hole in that presumably inaccessible universal space field. No one desires to have a career that's low in wins."

"It's one thing to profess one's feelings," observed Sandra, "and another to assimilate, accommodate, and uphold them complacently. It's one thing to think of something or an idea like success or victory, and another to put it into practice. This is one of the good decisions I've made in eight years of engagement in competitive sporting events, like women's basketball contests."

"It's been my discovery," revealed Meryl, "that when defeat is an unusual experience, it becomes a lot more painful to handle. No one actually knows what the impact of defeat would be both for the victor and the vanquished. Whatever turns out to be the situation in an encounter or tournament, it helps someone ascertain the level of difference between the victor and the vanquished. Most of the time, it helps both the victor and the vanquished size up each other's strength. Does that mean that one wouldn't be able to possibly match the other's success? Not quite."

"Some people worry about being defeated to such an extent," reasoned Eli, "that it robs them of an increasingly rare opportunity for growth, through exposure to events and people with different knowledge, culture, gifts, skills, and talents. Your behavior in any situation; (of either defeat or victory), depends on how you picture, value, and present yourself as an individual or as a group. Again, it depends on how you assess, estimate, and evaluate yourself, and how you put those measures and impressions into practice. If a team has a low concept of its ability, the team's expectations will remain low. If a team enjoys a high social status, esteem, and support, the expectation for that team's performance during the tournaments will be high."

"People's reactions following victory or defeat," Eli went on, "also depend on how they value victory and success, and the meaning they accord to failure and defeat. The majority of people in the American culture see winning as something good, while they consider losing as something bad. For them it's a good thing to win. Indeed, every human being wants to rise. People feel elated whenever they win and embarrassed when they lose."

"A crystal clear realization," Jacob noted, "that most of the frustrations and sorrows in our lives are due to our perception of events and hence our responses to them. Knowing this can be of immense value in finding solutions to certain problems. I'd think that it takes forgiving oneself, abandoning negative mindsets, and having an absolute resolve to persist in the face of adversity. Forgiving oneself and one's team are crucial steps in avoiding giving attention to negative ideas, not to mention reducing stress."

"Our willingness and readiness to concede that there are many ways of looking at things, including victories, successes, defeats, and failures, can easily transform our lives forever," argued Paul. "It calls for endless watch over our various perspectives about the events and changes in life. Bracing ourselves to face various problems and challenges in life is eternally indispensable."

"Withering in despair," suggested Jenna, "is never a solution to any problem, but weighing various options can lead us to possible solutions rather than to ultimate failure. It's rewarding to combine this insight with a lucid appreciation of our real potential. Does this piece not sound true to you? Most people have at one time or another been tempted to avoid the problems and challenges of daily living because they fear failure or defeat. By so doing, we seldom accomplish anything more than make a bad situation worse."

"People are encouraged to come to grips with their everyday challenges," observed Ruth, "so that it'll be easier for them to tackle the big ones if and when they come. It's not good to give up easily just because of the fear of failure. It's better to think of your problems, challenges, and defeats in life and to talk them over with others. You may get a novel slant on the situations that will make them clearer, brighter, and easier to solve the next time you encounter the same situation. Defeat or failure doesn't matter. Even though you may not have achieved your objective in a successful manner the first time, you can still do what you've set out to do, if you know and learn to do it in a better way."

Bryan added: "I just want to mention that the Tibetan Dalai Lama once said that if the rope is broken nine times, we must bind it together ten times. From my perspective, this implies that even though you might have fallen over and over again, you've got to get up and keep on trying again and again. We slip, we fall, we tumble, we fail, but what's most important is that you continue to move on by pushing yourself to your limits."

"Just as you've mentioned," recalled Stephen, "I think there are no obstacles to success and triumph as such, only challenges in our various journeys through life. All we have to do is to simply figure out how to get around those challenges. Allow me to quote Larry Pedrie, former head coach of the Flames at the University of Illinois: 'Although striving to win is important, how you end up winning is far more important.' That 'how' begins somewhere, and I'd totally suggest self-confidence. But we know that it takes a lot to build self-confidence."

"You seem to have hit the nail on the head, Stephen." agreed Dolores. "Self-confidence, and all it implies, is also thought to be the first requisite to great undertakings. I believe that if we have self-confidence and the expectation of winning, we'll enter our soccer contests from the position of strength. What's important are positive expectations that can give us the strength we need to achieve our goals and objectives."

"What do you think about learning to live for ourselves in whatever we do?" asked Ann Marie. "Our goals, our objectives, and our ideals are indispensable in the real-life contests of the world today, soccer events included. It's advisable to do things for our glory, and good results will come from them. These results include both victory and success. It's understandable that defeat can sometimes set in because of circumstances beyond one's control. But what happens next?"

"Really, what happens next is, in fact, what matters," quipped Dorothy. "Imagine an athlete who's in the throes of a major contest. The joy in the heart of this athlete is immeasurable and unimaginable, especially for someone who's in the first place in an athletic contest, whereas previously he was in the last position. A great sign of improvement, indeed, and his heart is beginning to sing: 'Let's celebrate right away, as I can't wait to get home to enjoy my triumph with friends and family.' Think of those involved in car races, or in horse races like the *Kentucky Derby*. Imagine yourself as one of them. What happens when you or your horse begins to lose strength when you're about to reach the finish line, and you see another competitor closing in on you, who's about to take your hard-earned first position?"

"That's a striking example," agreed Eleanor, "but I strongly believe that it's a question of how you feel at that point, and of course thinking affects how you feel. It's natural to feel that the heavens are coming down on you, while inner struggles of frustration set in too. Of course, you're not yet disappointed until anticipated victory is completely taken away from you. Unless you try to reframe the defeat or failure, a deep-sized disappointment or possible depression logically intrudes, especially when you remember how much talent and skill you put into training for that contest."

"Hmmmm." mused Jeff. "I give you an A plus for the content of your message, Eleanor. This isn't far from what we see in real-life sports, going by the expectations of fans and players in today's soccer arenas. Isn't it true that life is all about what you choose for yourself? I've been in favor of the idea that good thinking, good plans, superb preparations, smart strategies, and good organization are crucial before any games begin."

"Speaking from previous experience," observed Christine, "I do surmise that the World Cup carries so much glory that every team wants to win and each player desires to score! What's wrong with a defeat is that it makes you look weak and inferior in that area of life. That's why no one likes to accept defeat. I think the same applies to soccer."

"Of course," agreed Laurie. "No one wants to be defeated in his backyard or be told that he's destined to be a good loser. Not so soon, never ever. 'Show me a good loser and I'll show you a loser,' boasted George Steinbrenner, who was the head of the New York Yankees from 1973 until his death on Tuesday, July 13, 2008 at the age of 80. In real life, there are victories and defeats, but the most pressing question is: 'Which direction do you aspire toward?'"

"I guess that everybody knows that success, in the form of victory, doesn't come to anyone easily," opined Gabriel. "No one is born to be a winner or a loser. That speaks for itself. Every person experiences many victories and defeats during his or her lifetime. I believe that no one person is born to be either a steady winner or loser. Hopefully, no one aims for failure, in the same way that no one aims for success every day and achieves it."

"There are people who don't accept any defeat," opined Marcel. "There's a saying: 'Whether you finally succeed or not depends on how you handle life's defeating circumstances.' It takes experience and maturity to accept things the way they're and to accept things that we can't change. Some people complain and blame others for their defeats in life. Some go as far as antagonizing people, families, and even communities."

"The revelation that I've experienced over and over again," observed Nestor, "is that no one is successful all the time. You can win today and lose tomorrow. Isn't failure really success in disguise? Your failure today may be a sign of tomorrow's success that's hidden from you. Be energized and never say die. I guess what's important is learning to keep your head cool and calm, and doing your best, regardless of the outcome."

"You hit me where it feels good, Nestor!" enthused Kathy. "I recall that our classics and Latin teacher in the late 1980s would once in a while interject a question as follows: *Quid est optimum tuum*, which means "what's your best?" The question that lingers, even as you listen, is "what's your best?" This sounds like a pretty good question. Does your *best* imply the expectation of the *worst*, even as you keep working to achieve success? Everyone really wants to win. It's believed that you're never defeated until you think you are."

"Wonderfully put, Kathy!" Lorraine interjected, "Wisdom is power. The desire to learn something new makes your ideas pretty fascinating. There are many things and ideas running through the minds of people. Life is a join-the-dots-journey that begins with thinking and then is followed by working things out. We're what we think. Our thoughts are like seeds that are sown in a soil that produces plants. But the nature and type of plants that grow depend on the nature and type of the seed sown. Your journey begins with your thinking, and it's in thinking that the foundations of either success or failure are laid. The same is applicable to success in all its ramifications, and soccer isn't an exception."

"Your idea now led me right back to my home, thinking about dad." revealed Rose. "Dad, who had been a good soccer player and a renowned psychologist, taught me that you never succeed in doing anything unless you think you can do it. Yes, the human mind is a home or factory where success or failure is originally manufactured. The seed of either of the two opposites, success or failure, is sown from there. For everything you can think of in life, the fruit will often be the same as the seed that was sown."

"It's believed that the absence of happiness and joy in our lives is the offshoot of the absence of balance in our thinking," remarked Jerome. "It's easy to blame others for every problem that we encounter, but that won't yield any benefit unless we first think about addressing our problems and challenges. I think that it would be a fulfilling and rewarding experience for someone who never thought about lifting the World Cup mega trophy to begin to think of the possibility of winning the World Cup in a major soccer tournament."

"When it comes to the analysis of success or failure," observed Herbert, "we often miss out that success and failure often end the way they began. Let me take you down memory lane with a question: What's in a cliché? Employing the simple cliché "Yes I (we) can" and other clichés you consider meaningful might help. It's motivational and encouraging to realize that you can do anything you want to do. This mindset is endemic in the American culture. All that someone needs to do is to think in one's mind that he or she can do it."

"Similarly," added Sylvia, "we also need to remember that once you achieve success it can't be changed, and the same is applicable to failure. Don't give up; stick with me, as I have this new idea in me to share with you: victory represents for the victor and his associates an important morale booster. It can help people establish a sense of national unity and patriotism."

"Even though the discussion is about soccer," replied Ken, "I'm a basketball player. But I love soccer so much that I once considered resigning from basketball to get into soccer. One thing I want to put forward now is that when people gain victory, they often tend to see it as a reward for the efforts and hard work they put into their day-by-day living. They consider themselves as having made a good run. It's like an outward sign of latent, inward greatness — a spirit within the team that observers don't ordinarily see. I'm going to leave you with that."

"I'd say that's great idea from you, Ken!" exclaimed Ray. "I thought about it, with the determination that hard work and teamwork will always get any team to the highest point of achievement. *Waking up and winning* entails battling successfully every force and resistance that pulls you back from achieving your desired goal. The message is: 'No matter the situation and circumstance, win anyway, even if it's your only achievement.'"

"My musing," said Karla, "is with people's reactions after victory or defeat. I'd say that reactions after victory or defeat can be quite spontaneous and emotional, sometimes irrational and wild. On the one hand, reactions after victory are often characterized by feelings of elation, happiness, satisfaction, and excitement, while on the other hand, reactions after defeat or failure are associated with feelings of anger, disappointment, frustration, and, to some extent, hopelessness and depression. How can the listener understand my points and agree or disagree?"

"There's no point in disagreement," remarked Lisa. "I absolutely agree with you, Karla. But I think that people can experience more positive and sensible reactions to defeats and failures with the benefits of a good sleep, quiet thinking, reflection, and relaxation. I believe it's all in the feelings and thinking. It's important for people to take some time out and be by themselves."

"After a defeat," noted Frances, "people have been awash in booze, stumbling back home late at night in an effort to forget defeat. My boyfriend Dick, Who's a strong soccer fan, told me that he drank to excess with his friends following Ghana's 2-0 defeat of the U.S. Moreover, I overheard some people say that they wouldn't follow soccer anymore out of frustration and disappointment."

"I had a different experience when the U.S. was successful against Algeria," observed Janet. "I now recall how thousands of U.S. fans celebrated wildly on June 23, 2010, as the U.S. team scored in extra time against Algeria at the 2010 World Cup tournament. Think of the soccer fans' reactions. They were literally dancing, both at the stadium and inside bars across the U.S., where they all huddled together watching the match."

"I saw exactly what you saw, Janet!" cried Eve. "For the players, the coaches, and the fans, the victory of the U.S. team over Algeria was beyond mere congratulatory responses, because for many American fans such a gutsy performance from the U.S. team was for them one of the best games of the World Cup soccer tournament. Very moving and touching, indeed."

"I can imagine what you mean." responded Keri. "A similar reaction was seen in the streets of London when England suffered one of their worst World Cup defeats at the hands of Germany. It was a sad day to be an English soccer team supporter. But what disgusted me was the sight of one of the British fans trying to burn the German flag. For me, this was an eyesore."

"I understand what you mean, Keri." chimed Sarah. "I'd like you to think deeply about the U.S. and Slovenia soccer encounter. One thing you should keep in mind is that someone who's defeated could feel that he's been either destroyed or devastated. But all I know is that despair after defeat gets no one anywhere. It's rather an ill wind that blows nobody any good. There's a saying that 'when you win, confidence rises high.' Just keep winning."

"That's a good reflection on the effects of defeat and failure," noted Mary. "What a wonderful job we've done, guys. I wish to add that, depending on the circumstances, defeat or success can bring about negative relationships among people, unless external causal contributing factors accounting for the poor performance of the individuals or group in question are otherwise implicated."

"Great point, Mary!" exclaimed Stuart. "This is a real intellectual exercise and that's where my knowledge of philosophy seems to be helpful.

I think that the implications of those external causal and contributing factors would help members of any team discount negative feedback. On the other hand, if those external causal factors could've helped to promote and facilitate a better performance, then the coach, fans, team members, and others would have a genuine reason to either apportion blame or accommodate any negative feedback. The same applies to possible self-serving factors and excuses."

"Philosophy and intellectual exercises apart," argued Allison, "all I know and am convinced about is that trust and confidence in a soccer team can either grow or diminish, depending on the team's performance. Showing visible signs of trust in a team can serve as a strong motivation for that team and their supporters. This attitude can serve to bring out the best in people. The question remains: how do we build trust and confidence in a team?"

"It's true that trust and confidence take time to build," replied Jay. "One of the things I discovered by working for the U.S. Soccer Federation in the past two decades is that a lot of great players found greatness because they began to believe that they could make a difference in each one of their soccer encounters. Generally, one must be confident in oneself to be successful in life. You're not going to be successful if you don't think you're going to do well. So, maybe confidence really takes primary place in our journey to victory and success in all of life's endeavors."

"Confidence for me is the ability to throw off fears and insecurities in all endeavors," enthused Terrence, "including soccer and doing what feel right for you and for the team. Then you've got to keep doing it for the rest of your life. Some people might say: 'Enough! We don't want to win a battle and lose teammates to injuries, 'for life doesn't keep office hours.' To that assertion I'll answer: 'Sorry, no one who aspires to win in a soccer contest settles for the choices of a coward.'"

"I do seriously think that players need to believe in themselves," preached Michael, "believe that they're good players. Confidence goes with the power of positive thinking and is definitely an attitude. Brimming with confidence is an attitude that everyone needs to cultivate — an attitude that propels me to believe that I'm really going to win in future soccer engagements. Now, hear what you may be missing. Confidence is like feeling good, which starts in the mirror. It's often said that when you look good, you feel good and play good. How you see yourself helps a lot."

"I'm in the same boat with you, Mike." agreed Jay. "When you think that you're confident in soccer, you tend to play confidently as a result.

But when you're lacking in confidence, chances are that you're not doing the right thing. However, this shouldn't come into conflict with acts of humility. There's no humility in soccer. Humility is only a virtue."

"I must compliment you," affirmed Janet, "and agree with your discussion so far. One other thing you should know is that no matter how the performance goes, positive feedback is preferable. When someone expresses 'negative' feedback, let it be handed down in the form of constructive criticisms that will help to build rather than destroy."

"You're not alone, Janet, in that thoughtful journey." declared Megan. "I think that it also serves to boost the morale of players, which leads to maximizing their potential for a better performance. While negative feedback weakens the spirit, positive feedback reinforces effort and zeal, leading to better achievement. It's enthusiasm that helps bring about success. It's the visible offshoot of what we call human motivation. Hope this helps."

"May I ask a question that I consider thought provoking," requested June, "and I'll provide you with an answer if you please. It'll differ from what we've said so far, but it'll also provide some continuity in the same direction. From whom do reactions come after any soccer tournament? Reactions normally come from the coaches, players, fans, and the mainstream media, and obviously from the whole nation."

"As a soccer coach for almost a decade in the state of Georgia," recalled Jeremy, "it struck me when you mentioned coaches first and you're right. Let me talk about coaches a little bit. The coach is seen as an important figure in the scheme of things. Of course, cameras are often focused on the coach, to monitor his or her reactions during soccer. People want to see how you react, look, cheer, direct, or whatever else you do during a game. I think that the media has glorified the coaches."

"My thoughts and guesses are as good as yours, Jeremy," noted Frances. "I've been a coach myself in Baton Rouge, Louisiana for almost 12 years now. It's the belief of most coaches, including myself, that all eyes are on them to produce winning teams. Such perceptions make you feel like you're the most influential person in the world and in the players' soccer lives. Know that your relationship with the players can have a huge psychological impact on them, positive or negative."

"With our discussion moving in this direction," added Camille, "someone would be interested to know what happens after someone or a team has been unsuccessful or defeated following a soccer tournament. The question remains: What's next for the defeated? Many fans are believed to carry the trauma of defeat for months, years, and decades, depending on the nature of the game and its scope. Could they not have seen it as a game, or recognized victory in the face of defeat?"

"This sounds like a good suggestion, Camille," countered Jay, "but it doesn't work for fanatical fans and die-hard soccer aficionados. Some of the fans see the games as not only part of their lives, but also as part of themselves. Little wonder that we hear the joke: 'It poisons testosterone and flattens progesterone.' It's possible that the impact of soccer contest can increase or decrease stress hormones, depending on what's happening in each person, as soccer fans shout, raise their hands, and even spring out of their seats either in celebrating victory or mourning defeat."

"What happens in the event of defeat is a pretty good question." argued Melissa. "What should be crystal clear to everyone is that on every index of human endeavor, someone who's defeated isn't necessarily destroyed. There should be a rational and forward-looking thought. Defeat is never the end of a man's life. The person who failed or the one who's defeated isn't ruined, and neither has he (she) been undone. He (She) has only lost a contest, and can always wake up again and win."

"You've come right back to it, Melissa." admitted Rebecca. "I think that it's all about waking up and winning. Various nations have experienced defeats at the hands of their competitors, opponents, and rivals. I believe that the U.S. is quite virile in the field of soccer and not impotent. What I'm convinced is needed at this time is resilience, which is the philosophy of the strong ones never quitting when the going gets tough. Resilience will make you feel stronger, more courageous, and more powerful in resuming the fight to achieve a whole new level of greatness that you never thought possible."

"As I was listening to you, Becky," observed Lauren, "it came to mind that it might be time to adopt Richard Fenton's five secrets to help you turn failures into successes. It'll serve as a blueprint toward a better way of thinking and living. The first secret is changing one's mental models of 'success' and 'failure.' What does success and failure mean for the players, coaches, and soccer fans? Does failure mean total destruction for you, or is it in fact a necessity for someone who'll someday become great or achieve greatness?"

"To achieve significant success in today's world," argued Elaine, "one should be ready for and be open to failure, which along with success should be construed as the opposite sides of the same coin. Does success mean remaining in the middle at all times, because that's what it means to be virtuous in the field of soccer? Virtue stands in the middle. Is that what guides us in our soccer engagements? Go ahead, Laurie."

"Okay, thanks, Elaine." responded Lauren. "The second secret paradoxically suggests an intentional increase in one's failure rate, which means to 'just go ahead and try it.' This is based on what Fenton referred to as a counter intuitive, reverse thinking philosophy. It means don't be afraid of failure as there's no harm in trying, especially when there are both inner and external voices discouraging you with a big 'No.' This leads us to the third secret, which recommends that you don't listen to any 'no' discouragement, but rather set success goals and keep on moving with all the 'yeses' in life to make the sky your limit."

"Lauren, I think that it's about learning to keep people in the game, whether it's soccer or any sport," suggested Andrew. "But that's, especially, the essence and spirit of every soccer commitment."

"What I found unique, amazing, and apparently controversial," rejoined Lauren "is Fenton's fourth secret, which has to do with learning to celebrate your failures and successes. How many people and soccer fans will agree with this? As far as I know, few people celebrate their failures."

"Wait a minute," Margaret wondered, "celebrate failure? We naturally get excited by successes but grow sullen in spirit with failures. It would be hard to remember the last time anyone rewarded herself for failing or losing. Maybe someone might decide to give it a shot. Lauren, you seem to believe that it's worth trying, as that might lift someone's spirit up, but that depends on what people consider a failure or defeat. If, for instance, your failure means that you're one step closer to success, then you should have the courage to celebrate instead of mentally punishing yourself for not succeeding or winning.

"Of course, punishing yourself means abusing yourself again after a failure," she continued. "The result of this will be the absence of peace, joy, and happiness; a knife in the heart! By mistreating oneself after defeat, this self-inflicted anger is bound to manifest in various ways and might snowball into a depression."

"You've got to love this discussion on success and failure," advised Heather. "Let this be an eye-opener that will enable you, in a timely manner, to achieve success and victory. I think buying your colleagues cups of coffee, ice cream cones, or ice cream cups can do this job. The idea isn't to let failure have a negative grasp on your thoughts and emotions, as that will definitely affect your performance."

"Certainly, the truth is that negativity can ruin a person's or a group's hopes and dreams," suggested Lauren, "not discounting its attendant heartaches and depression. It's far better to see courage as a muscle, which is the fifth secret of Richard Fenton's writings. With this secret, you're no longer seeing failure as something negative but rather as a vehicle that can eventually transport you to success, with courage serving as the fuel. Courage is like any muscle — you must develop and strengthen it with lots of exercise. At this stage you're looking fear in the eye and taking action anyway. As you take action, the courage muscle gets stronger. The long and short of the whole message is changing your mindset about success and failure."

"Well spoken, Lauren!" interjected Elizabeth. "My gut tells me that the idea you've just advanced is guaranteed to work, not only in the field of soccer, but also in the personal and professional lives of everyone. One thing I'd like to throw in at this point is that when Ghana defeated the U.S., when time finally ran out on the Americans on what I prefer to call that "unfaithful Saturday," some of our players dropped to the ground as the backups who had watched from the bench trudged out to console them. Looking at what was happening made me feel really bad, when I considered how our players, who had really done their best on the field, reacted to such an undeserving defeat."

"I felt really bad, too," noted Juliet, "as much as you did, Lizzie, when I saw the reactions of some of our players. But I felt more relaxed and was ready to get over it when I saw Jay, one of our soccer team's defenders and who I thought had a hand in surrendering the first goal, stride toward the stand, where thousands of American fans had spent the night cheering and applauding the team. 'There's always disappointment when a great tournament like this comes to an end,' he explained later. 'But I think it's a really special time for the U.S. soccer. There's a reason why the U.S. sold more tickets than any other country: these people care about soccer.' To show our appreciation for the players, win or lose, is the important thing. And even when letdown or regret is at its highest, it's perhaps the time to show the most recognition."

"Jay's message might mean that he was taking the defeat maturely." observed Robert. "His message might sound comforting to some people, but on the other hand it might have seemed weird to the listening ears of many soccer fans who were there to see the Americans win and win big. It's like his message was simply thus: 'Enjoy the moment, whatever the outcome of our soccer tournament. Enjoy it, anyway.' People from nations that happen to be defeated in soccer don't normally feel good about it because they're competing to win. Permit me to mention, in this last part of our discussion, that when it comes to global soccer, every country's national soccer team remains a 'beggar' because they're all begging to win, or, at least, to be allowed by other nations' teams to win. All of them, therefore, are beggars who wish to ride on victory horses, if given the slightest chance."

# Chapter 4
## The Defeat of the
## United States

Beggars riding on victory horses: an age-old English proverb has it that "if wishes were horses, then beggars would ride." Wishes don't often come true the way they'd appear in the minds and hearts of many. People's thoughts live comfortably with issues related to victory and success, whereas failure and defeat, for various reasons, are always unwanted.

"Tears nearly ran down many cheeks of those who rooted for the US," observed Karen, "following their undesirable and chilling defeat by Ghana in the 2010 World Cup soccer tournament. Those who couldn't fight the tears that rushed into their eyes clearly cried like babies, if you have the courage to rewind it on television."

"Under normal circumstances," observed Billy, "it would've sounded ridiculous ever to suggest that a country of about 25 million people would make any headway toward defeating, in whatever form, a country of about 310 million people. It would've been ironic to imagine that a country of only 10 regions would have enough power to outscore a country that's made up of 50 states."

"How has the mighty temporarily fallen?" lamented Mike. "But it's temporary. I hope so. It's like the defeat of a giant by a lightweight, but this giant will rise again in the field of international soccer, all things being equal. It'll be like the rising of a Mighty Star ushering in a great day."

Even though this encounter resulted in a minor defeat, a type that's never deserved or desired by the US, her true friends and admirers, at the same time it's also a defeat that wasn't absolutely unexpected. But we can, for now, comfortably hang on to the consolation that it's only a minor "defeat." Simply relax now and don't recoil from any embarrassment. Relax! It's only a defeat, not a shellacking or humiliation, because even though the U.S. was unable to salvage a tie, she was able to pull off a score on a penalty-kick award, courtesy of the great midfielder Landon

Donovan. Half bread is believed to be better than a piece of cookie; is it not so? Could it have been worse? Of course, yes. However, it's good to look on the bright side of life no matter how undesirable and embarrassing the circumstances might have been.

"When it comes to soccer and other sports," commented Walter, "there's been that feeling, and desire, deeply engraved in the minds of fans by nature herself, that sporting folks should never attempt to concoct means, or a habit of moving about exciting people, especially supporters, any time they see themselves as either half-ready or virtually unprepared. An all-time impression and conventional message that "nearly doesn't kill a bird" keeps people unsettled, since people are, by nature, pretty prone to looking for meaningful results, especially the ones that don't leave them unsettled. The same applies to any situation where they're left with a hope that ends up not being fulfilled or realized. The simple suggestion is: 'Never attempt to do so, as that will possibly frustrate, as much as irritate, friends, family, and fans, or perhaps leave them with some false hope.'"

"For me this preceding lengthy message from Walter sounds like the story of a robot that was made by a smart guy," mused Holly. "This robot does nothing but keeps touching and punching people, and every other imaginable passer-by, instead of moving the furniture out of the way. "Hahahahahahaha. Anyway, the U.S. soccer team members didn't punch or scratch anybody but seemed to have taken the undeserved defeat gracefully without much whining. The U.S. men's soccer team never, ever tantalizes its fans. The team was well-prepared and was impressive all through the contests, but only ran out of luck this time. That's really what I think happened. But they accepted defeat graciously."

"Yes," agreed Tiffany, "in the most recent World Cup soccer tournament, America has shown what I'd describe as the flip side of her super-competitive nature by remaining gracious in defeat, having shown a willingness and readiness to take some good-natured ribbing whenever the opportunity called for it, whether it's about not performing as expected, or for not being able to score big and to win big. Surprisingly, they looked upbeat and shinning again afterwards."

"I understand your argument, Tiffany," responded Gina, "but if they actually did, why were people fighting apparent tears, as clearly seen on television? Maybe because our guys didn't deserve it, having really played hard during the game, but for me that was pretty embarrassing."

"I'd wish that you change this topic and discussion, please!" exclaimed Priscilla. "That's not worth discussing now. I mean, how nice it's for them to win something. Anything, once again, is better than nothing at all. Some nations out there could've missed that rare chance and opportunity of scoring, even with such a big privilege and comforting award as a penalty kick."

"Haahaaahaaaa." laughed Kelly. "As far as I know, the U.S. has always been humble in accepting defeat in such an unpopular sport, like soccer. I remember so well that during one of the World Cup contests in the 1980s, in 1986 or thereabouts, one of the past presidents of a country well-known for soccer was believed to have spewed out, as announced by a prominent international soccer commentator, that if France defeated his country, 'All the citizens of his country would commit suicide.' What an awful statement!"

"That's unbelievable!" cried Mira in disbelief. "Did he really say that? How the hell could a president of a civilized nation make such a gravely unguarded statement? But it could've been worse, as someone suggested. But at least no action was taken, even as they ended up as defeated anyway, thank goodness. However, let's drop this right here for many reasons, as I'm no longer feeling comfortable discussing that right now."

It might sound right to recall that when the U.S. secured a beautiful victory against Algeria in June 2010, shouts of joy towered and soared into the skies as happy fans yelled and cheered: "Yuh . . . Es... Eeh... (USA.)" Those fans weren't merely cheerleaders, but were positively impacted by the performance of the U.S. men's soccer team. Ironically, before the end of their final match with Ghana, elated and zealous soccer fans, in support of Ghana, were dancing and sprinting, beating drums in jubilation, while tears were almost running down the cheeks of the earlier-excited and cheering soccer fans who were supporting the U.S. team. What a shift in development; indeed, a stark contrast to what had previously taken place.

"I saw the great stars and stripes coldly folded around the brow of a sad looking and apparently horror-stricken American fan, with the word *America* boldly written on his face," recalled Emily. "With sadness on the face of the always-cheerful and gleeful Bill Clinton who was so nice to attend this tournament in one of his beloved countries, South Africa. People clearly saw how much he loves this great nation and Africa in general."

"Yes, Emily," agreed Tricia, "I did see the reaction of the former President when the U.S. was barely defeated. His reaction, of course, is usual with every ex-president of the U.S. He wanted his country to win. Clinton watched closely in person from his seat at the stadium, having observed for himself how far the encounter had come and how far it had yet to go. I saw everything."

"What left me stunned," chimed Brooke, "was that our military men and women in Iraq and Afghanistan, who not only cheered with standing ovations from distant lands and were elated to see the general performances of our guys in South Africa, were brought to a sudden silence by the traumatic defeat. What I observed as I watched was that they might've surely come to know that World Cup contests are not the same as military combats, that soccer is far from a tech contest, nor is it an air-defense maneuver or a space engineering contest."

"I understand what you mean, Brooke!" echoed Mania. "But inasmuch as we shouldn't see soccer contest as a military combat, we'd also take soccer seriously too because of the hugeness and criticality of what it represents, especially since the world is going global now and will continue to go global."

The World Cup soccer fiesta somehow presents nations in some unimaginable perspective to contestants across the globe. There's a fine line existing between the battlefield and the soccer field, but we need to cross over it and make our high marks also in soccer. Isn't that right? In summary, activities in the battlefield, though sometimes necessary, aren't conventionally pretty and their pleasures, if there are any, aren't immediately clear, but soccer is always pretty, with its pleasures abundantly clear.

"What immediately came to my mind," noted David, "when the U.S. lost to Ghana, was a paraphrased anticlimactic excerpt from Marc Anthony's speech in the drama *Julius Caesar*: 'How has the mighty fallen!' I mean, when it's applied to this soccer encounter. For me, it was like the defeat of a giant by a lightweight, but that giant will rise again in the international soccer. Oh yeah! But again, I asked myself these questions: Has the U.S. been a giant in soccer before? Could it now be reduced to a lightweight in the name of soccer? However, it's not about stature, since being a lightweight or a giant doesn't make any difference in the mind of the Creator."

The difference that we observe in human stature simply lies in the distracting deception that comes from our finite human perception. It's certainly not about Goliath and David. By the way, who's Goliath and who's David in this soccer encounter? Everyone's got a funny story to tell in every life situation. Tell people yours, and when they listen to it or watch it acted or demonstrated on television, people will keep laughing and, of course, laughing all the way to the college campus, to the bank, mall, boxing and wrestling rings, soccer fields, and perhaps get well suddenly from being sick in bed or at any hospital. That's how life really goes.

As a follow-up to the preceding interesting discourse, a drama Moderator Extraordinaire has a pretty interesting message in store for us. Please welcome him.

Moderator Extraordinaire: "Good Morning. We'll now recall the story of a lightweight who's on an elevator, pushing the button to go up. Just before the door shut, behold a hand coming through and opening the door. A huge man, presumably of a typically tropical extraction, was seen entering the elevator. The lightweight stared at him and says, 'You're the biggest man I've ever met or seen.' The man smiled and nodding his head, replies: 'I'm 6-7, weigh 265 lbs., and I have 14 inches… I'm Abariye Akadoba.'

"The lightweight briefly passed out. After returning to consciousness, the lightweight asked the man to repeat himself. So, he did as follows: 'I just said I'm 6-7, 265 lbs., with 14 inches shhhhh…es, and my name is Abariye Akadoba.' The lightweight heaved a sigh of relief and, looking somewhat happy, broke out in a big laugh and asked, 'Do you mean your soccer shoes?' And they had the following conversation:

Giant: "Yes, of course, I love to perform on the soccer field, as that's my favorite place to be."

Lightweight: "The inches you mentioned would be too long for your shoes. For a second, there, I thought you said your name is Abracadabra."

Giant: "Sorry, it's a name that has no English equivalent."

Lightweight: "And what do I need to do so as to be (appear) like you and to do better in soccer, as you claimed that you do? I mean, appear like you, generally?"

Giant: "Haaahaaa. Appear like me? We've got to get together as soon as possible so I can teach you the secrets and the rest of the great soccer stuff, now that I know that you also play women's soccer for your country. But please, promise me that you're not going to teach the soccer stuff to any other person because it's a secret — it's only between you and me."

Stepping further away, the lightweight, who also has a great sense of humor, wondered: "Why is your English this good? Anyway... You don't even look to me like a soccer player; you appear more to me like a wrestler or a body-builder, hmmm ... mmm . . . Will you be able to go for the ball and run around the field?"

Giant: "Hahahaha. Of course, yes, I do that every day."

Lightweight: "I'm just beginning to think, but God forbid you needed to get out of your apartment real fast and the elevators weren't working. Maybe you ought to get yourself a pretty good parachute, but that will work only if your windows are well-functional and big enough to let you out."

Giant: "A parachute? For what? I could possibly parachute into the Chicago soccer stadium for a soccer kick off, but not from my apartment. I'd rather do it from the sky, perhaps from an airplane or helicopter. But I'm not interested in skydiving and don't want to skydive, either."

Lightweight: "Haaahaaa. Will you be able to make your way downstairs through the stairway?"

Giant: "Of course. I'll vanish through the stairway and leave all the doors of my apartment wide open to history."

Lightweight: "Haaaa haaa. Are you serious? That's pretty funny and ridiculous."

Giant: "Ridi . . . what? Well, don't worry about that now. Don't worry about me, either — worry only about yourself. You never saw an elephant running faster than a rat?"

Lightweight: "Haaa haa. You may be right. But that rat you're pointing at right now can deflate an inflated elephant and gnaw a big bag of tricks open from the inside out. You don't want to mess with or be on the wrong side of that rat. It's almost worse than crossing the picket line. Those who picket will know what I mean . . ."

Giant: "Haaahaaaaheeeheeeehoooo hooo. We're not fighting, my lady gal . . . friend, simply exchanging pleasantries. I'm not that big bag, and you're not the rat. Just kidding, only kidding."

Lightweight: "All right . . . that's not a problem. It's about the ability to play soccer and play it well."

Moderator Extraordinaire: "All jokes, folks, and a true humor, but all in soccer uniforms. Hope you invite me again for this little joke and drama. Goodbye."

What an irony! What a real paradox! Fair enough, a country like Ghana has never been that giant in the soccer field, but neither can we describe her as a lightweight in soccer. In the same vein, the U.S. has been a great nation but was never a giant in soccer; neither can we describe her as a lightweight in soccer. Fair enough, but the million dollar question remains: to which of the two sides and statures, dramatized earlier, is she leaning toward? Perhaps her stature in soccer lies in the middle. Virtue lies in the middle?

Indeed, the U.S. has never been that soccer giant, but it'll rise and win big in future global soccer fiestas. But she's to confront head on the challenges facing her, with soccer already labelled in some quarters as either boring or more suited for women.

Is soccer only for women? Did Brazil begin their soccer with women? Did Argentina, Germany, Italy, France, Spain, and even Britain begin their soccer with women? What of the rest of the world?

That might have been true in some cases, but did they all begin their national soccer teams with women's teams? It would be a lame excuse to hide under such a slight and dispiriting hint, but even if they actually did begin with their women's teams; our U.S. women's team has several times proven that they're the best in the world. Say bravo to every one of them for doing our country proud and lifting us high several times. They are the giants. It's true that much of history has it that organized soccer was exclusively for men, but we've seen that It isn't absolutely so in the modern and current history of soccer.

Soccer was believed to be a recreational and intramural sport in some women's colleges and high schools, and was further powered with changes in educational amendments in the 1970s in the U.S., when it was no longer seen as a threat to men's soccer. Village and local soccer contests were sometimes informally staged in scattered areas in much of Europe and America, for fun between married and unmarried women. Funny enough, in some developing countries soccer was and is sometimes organized between married men and women, with women sometimes bragging that they can play better than men.

As time rolled by, organized women and ladies' soccer teams were formed in various European countries, including the US. This trend seemed to have started from about the end of the 19th century and running into the early 20th century, despite conflicting religious beliefs and some nations' idiosyncratic socio-cultural and psycho-cultural belief systems.

A brief evaluation of our women's soccer performance: our women's soccer team has reached the desired pinnacle of success. They showed how far the U.S. has gone in soccer, with the signs of a global superpower coming to the limelight despite formidable opponents in the top women's teams across the globe, such as Germany, Russia, Canada, China, Norway, and Denmark.

"Some people would like to argue that in soccer, the biggest doesn't mean the best," observed Darcy. "That seems correct, because even though countries like China and India may be the highest or second to highest in the world's population, they're not doing so well in soccer. Both teams were eliminated from the 2011 Asian Cup in the first round. Even among the world's military superpowers, with the exception of the Unites States, Russia isn't finding it easy when it comes to soccer. So apparently the U.S. seems to be doing better than all of them and that's my humble opinion."

"Of course," agreed Gabrielle, "there's something unique with the US. We don't expect the U.S. to become either China or India in the field of soccer or Russia. I believe that we're more sophisticated than that comparison.

Americans have always had a different way of thinking. The same applies to their mobility and operational pattern when it comes to sports in general. In fact, there's something uniquely and awesomely exceptional about the U.S. One or two of the nations mentioned above was once believed to have a history of leaking goals in their defense, lacking invention and creativity in their attack systems. I'm not sure if the U.S. has those types of awfully exceptional gifts in soccer. We have all the resources we need to out-compete other nations in all the major sports. The way we've always performed in BFBs, and the shinning performance of our women's soccer team, will testify to what I mean."

"One exciting point that I'd like to strike on the head, Gabby," noted Xochilt, "is that the U.S. women's team plays a close game, even if they're not invincible. They've really won big on several occasions, coming back with Gold Medals and never disappointing the U.S. They're looked up to as the world's best. They passed the real tests in tough and tougher contests, and have produced top-flight players that are primed to keep moving on, except when due for retirement."

"Of course, for our women's teams, I believe that many more successes, victories, and triumphs will surely come," agreed Jonathan. "It's interesting to recall the build-up of fans and supporters whenever our women's national soccer team is engaged in soccer contests. Even though our women's team, which has attracted much attention and support from fans, has filled a major gap in soccer, our men's team cries for a better attention than what it's been getting now. For the time being, attention is focused on our men's soccer team players, as they need to wake up and win to do us proud. What does this mean? It means that the scoring power of our men's soccer team has to rise much higher than their current performance for them to get better attention from the U.S. public and fans."

"Certainly, their scoring power and prowess have to rise almost as high as in our home-grown sports, like **B**asketball, **F**ootball and **B**aseball (BFB)," noted Luis, "all of which are adored by many fans within the US. It's pretty common for fans to get frustrated and sometimes bored watching two teams play for almost two hours without either side coming out as a winner. What do you think? The question remains whether those 'weak minded' fans will remain patient for far too long. Will their patience stick until the end of the game, or will it suddenly fizzle out in between their waiting toes? What happens when they see the referee keep making genuine or wrong calls for off-side play? What happens when they see him give yellow cards, and, in some cases, red cards, to a player or players that they admire and love to pieces in the field of soccer?"

"Hi, Luis." said Craig. "Thanks for the points you're making. I thank the other guys, too. I'd like to make some comments on what the previous speakers said. It's simply to remind them that the FIFA World Cup had been generally as interesting as it's dramatic. It really gave us some mind-blowing surprises. Among the beautiful surprises was that Africa got the unique privilege of hosting the highest global soccer tournament for the first time. Let's not forget that about 204 teams in the world played the qualifying series, and the U.S. men's team happened to be among the only 32 that eventually made it to the World Cup. When it comes to performances, let's remember that great teams and big names like Brazil, Italy, France, Argentina, Portugal, and the rest of them were also disgraced and took the exit door. Even Nigeria, which used to be a young rising power in soccer globally, was practically unable to beat any team. But the U.S. team was able to beat at least one team during the World Cup. Please, give me a break."

"Thank you, Craig." replied Sylvester. "Permit me to mention one more thing that keeps my spirit down. I get sick to my stomach when I hear people put our guys down just because they happened to have lost a match where the opposing team won by what I consider a questionable penalty kick award. Listen, I've been watching their performances and I can't find a better team in the whole world. These guys are nothing less than superstars going by their performances. I promise you, guys, that our men's soccer team will crush any team they will face in the future, be it Brazil, Argentina, France, Germany, or the rest of them. Believe me."

The last speaker and contributor to this composition and project is a good soccer fan, and soccer lovers are simply fans and not fanatics. Please take it kindly with them and cherish their positive opinions and optimism. They're useful and quite effective.

It's true that real soccer fans might sometimes find it boring or dizzying watching a depressing scenario in soccer, previously hinted, or hearing a few discouraging comments from people. They might begin to think and ask themselves: "What's the gain in a game that leaves us winless? Why should we waste our time there?"

In all honesty, teams and fans may sometimes experience such intense emotions that they might even wish that the game ends quickly, no matter the outcome. Nonetheless, the U.S. can't but strengthen its momentum in soccer and move on to future global soccer contests, but the only way to do it's by waking up and simply winning big in future World Cup soccer. Wake up and win! This is the way and the only way the U.S. men's soccer team can get itself together and win the world's respect once again. It's another way to become doubly enamored, endeared to the rest of the world, and become the attraction of all eyes in the global soccer village. The time has come for us to have a Brave New Soccer-Playing America.

At this juncture, let's have a brief but thoughtful review of the previous global soccer encounters of the U.S. men's team.

Reporter: "The overview of the U.S. soccer matches in the FIFA World Cup of 2010. The match between the U.S. and England at the World Cup in South Africa, which many millions of us tuned into and watched, looked like the much expected soccer of this historical tournament. Words couldn't describe the height of euphoria that swept across states and cities in the U.S. after the tie game with England in the 2010 FIFA World Cup tournament. For many American fans, it was more than amazing. Although not everyone was pleased with the draw game, the 1-1 tie seemed to have been a great and stunning outcome for American fans, because popular and cheerleading fans more heavily favored England. The encounter enjoyed much coverage, as the trio of our wonderful goalkeeper

Tim Howard, and the star players Landon Donovan and Clint Dempsey, proved themselves soccer-field dynamos. They featured prominently in such a manner that we'll remain proud of them as long as our memory of the 2010 FIFA World Cup lasts. Recall that President Obama, in a uniquely friendly gesture, called the British Prime Minister David Cameron, and bet a beer on a foreseen American victory. It would be difficult to speculate now on what actually did happen after the tie. Of course, it wouldn't be inappropriate for brews to be exchanged, with at least one bottle from each side to signify the tie. It would simply have been a mutual exchange, as the score justified.

"The match featured several desperate attempts by the Americans to break the hard-nosed British defense," the reporter continued. "Our men were pretty aggressive. It may have been that the U.S. men's team adopted an age-old soccer style of soaking up the pressure from the other side while playing off the counter. One might also suggest that the U.S. team didn't play so well in this encounter, as they seemed to have lacked creativity in the attack, thereby finding it grueling to contain the English players who were on the offensive. Thanks to goalkeeper Tim Howard, the British scoring came about only through sheer luck. Why not play to win when the opportunities are there, to prove that we have a better team than the English? Some fans saw the American goal by Clint Dempsey as a gift from the English goalkeeper. But whichever way you look at it, England seemed to have had a better technical advantage over us."

Josh had the following comment: "However, the U.S. did withstand the onslaught and challenges posed by England. They threw more shots at the U.S. in the second half. But to celebrate in jubilation because we secured the draw by simply not losing could lead to mediocre and uninspired performances in future matches. Why should it have taken a major goalkeeper error by our opponent to enable us to salvage a draw with the English team? I believe and think we could've done better than that."

"I don't care." countered Paige. "No matter how the score came about, it remains a big win and will forever remain a big win, period. It's wonderful and we have to celebrate, because even though we're expected to lose, we tied, right?"

"In the 40th minute into the match," announced the reporter, "Clint Dempsey sent a shot into the hands of Robert Green, the English goalkeeper, who got both hands on the ball but somehow allowed it to slip off his hands into the net. What a catastrophe for England and what huge luck for the U.S. Clint Dempsey got a pretty loud ovation as the hero who saved America from what would've been a terrible embarrassment. This outcome was both antithetical and ironic because, for American soccer fans, the tie was a great result, but for the British it was a clear loss."

"Of course, in soccer," observed Kevin, "one man's treasure could easily become another man's thrash, depending on what happened. It wasn't about a big brother/little brother relationship or a quarrel about the British Petroleum's gulf oil spill. It was a global soccer contest."

"But that could be used as an analogy, Kevin." retorted Judith. "The 1-1 draw may have signified that neither nation was guilty of the winning spill. Who knows? The U.S. was, however, satisfied to take a point from the encounter, while the British were disappointed for not taking three points. They couldn't succeed in beating Tim Howard, our renowned goalkeeper, despite several chances."

"It would be too laughable to claim that we earned the tie," advised Annie. "It was only by sheer luck that we managed to squeeze a point out of this powerful and historical soccer rival."

"While I appreciate your remarks and concerns," noted Cathy, "I believe that such a win put us in good stead, to qualify for the next round to face countries like Germany, Ghana, and Serbia. It's a big victory for the U.S., who was hitherto expected to lose by some spectators. A little bit of luck does wonders, both for the underdog and for the hopeless, right?"

"But who's the underdog or the hopeless in this encounter?" asked Solomon. "Is it America? What I found friendly and lovely in the relationship between allies was that five hours before the long-awaited World Cup match Saturday between the U.S. and England ended in a tie, the English and American fans mixed and mingled. They blew vuvuzelas at one another, and ate steaks and sausages together."

"During the military commanders' confirmation hearing in June 2010, aired on C-SPAN," announced the reporter, "Republican Senator Lindsey Graham of South Carolina kiddingly mentioned that the World Cup was going on in South Africa and that he was a supporter of the U.S., but he had no idea what they were doing when it comes to soccer. Senator Graham may have been quite right, since the U.S. seemed to have, for so long, remained in her 'small' world when it comes to soccer but until now."

The match between the U.S. and Slovenia took place on June 18, 2010 at 9:00 a.m.

Reporter: "Some people who watched the match ended up describing it as schizophrenic, but what would that mean for a good U.S. soccer fan? However, we can count ourselves fortunate in this match, as our men didn't miss their few chances to score in the second half, when at last those chances miraculously came. Whoever saw Michael Bradley in his celebratory mood, with a pile of his jubilant teammates, after scoring the draw goal against Slovenia during their Group C match in Johannesburg, would know right away that the U.S. team did a great job even though it came out as a draw game. It was a great score, because for about 45 minutes into the game, the U.S. team appeared to have been helplessly subdued by the Slovenian team with a 2-0 lead, until the jinx was eventually broken, thanks to Bob Bradley, who surprised people by sending forth his most aggressive forward lineup on an offensive mission to rescue the most powerful and wealthiest nation on earth from an apparent embarrassment in soccer."

"I was watching the game," observed Carl, "as Bob Bradley made those changes, and I figured he hoped to open up the floodgates of goal scoring against Slovenia, and to temper their attack system. I saw this effort as having affirmed the strength of our men's national soccer team, leaving it with chances to move on and on again."

Reporter: "For a country as small as Slovenia, there's always the saying that there are more Americans in American prisons and jails than there are Slovenians in the entire nation of Slovenia. Think about it — a comparison of human population would place the inhabitants of Brooklyn as probably more in number than those in the entire Slovenian nation. In this soccer contest from the American side, players like Landon Donovan, Michael Bradley, Clint Dempsey, and Jozy Altidore undoubtedly remained shining stars. On the other side, the Slovenians were skillful in countering many of the chances that the U.S. team had to score and in dominating a major portion of the field in the first half. They adopted slow-but-steady attack tactics against the U.S. team, with some of their passes unchallenged by our men. Some of the attempts made by our men to catch up with their strikers were painfully slow, to the point that someone would ask these questions: America, Where's our tactical soccer-rival killer instinct within 18 yards of the goal? Where's the never-say-die spirit and mentality of our veteran and founding soccer players? Where are our lightning-quick interception and soccer-zipping, opponent-stoppage tactics? Where are our opportunistic ball utilization skills and relentless soccer expertise? Where are our pretty smart low push-pass soccer styles? Where are our subtle and clever latches onto deflected-ball crossing skills?

"If we Americans have never had traditional soccer powers, styles, and mindsets," the reporter continued, "indeed, the time has come. It has really come. Indeed, these afore-listed necessities should be part of our soccer play styles, among other desirable styles and tactics. The U.S. needed a win, if for no other reason than to build up confidence and trust among her beloved and expectant fans. The ending was as extraordinary as it was dramatic. Even though it ended in a tie, it could open a gripping page in the history of the U.S. men's soccer team. But, anyway, there was one more step ahead that might put the U.S. team atop its group for the first time in the modern era of soccer contests. It was an opportunity that might usher them into the knockout stage. The long and short of the message about this match was that if the U.S. team didn't seem to have impressed thousands of red, white, and blue clad fans in the first half, than it really did in the second half."

The match between the U.S. and Algeria took place on June 23, 2010 at 9:00 a.m., with a 1-0 win against Algeria.

Reporter: "It was believed to be a picture perfect day in Pretoria, with the sun brilliant and the breezes gentle. To some people the whole match was so entirely boring that it was advisable to check your pulse. To other people, it was riddled with excitement, an amazing match, even if you don't appreciate soccer for what it is. Some saw it as a U.S.-Algeria throw down, a U.S. miracle win, which resulted in many soccer converts. Even though the U.S. World Cup campaign came to what some emotional fans saw as an intolerable end, it simply proved the uniqueness of the American way of feeling and doing things.

"This match," the reporter continued, "was a great win for the U.S., for all those who keep track of soccer history. Why? Because, Algeria, like Nigeria, Tunisia, Ghana, and Egypt, has proven itself to be among the strongest soccer teams in Africa. She was one of Africa's last hopes in the World Cup soccer fiesta. What did this game mean to the U.S.? It was a game that sent the U.S. to the knockout round stage with her dramatic winning goal. A draw with Algeria would've sent the U.S. home after three consecutive and unwelcome ties. This is the highlight. It couldn't have been more dramatic and heart wrenching than the previous encounters, with their misses and lost scoring chances, which were agonizing to some fans and spectators. However, by comparison, Algeria shouldn't have presented too many problems for the U.S., if the U.S. team had done its job well enough on the field."

"From my observation," remarked Mike, "the U.S. seemed to have dominated the match in the first half, and as long as the minutes dragged on they appeared more aggressive than the Algerians in the attacking side of the game. But we saw a litany of squandered opportunities, and what would've appeared to an impatient coach as unforgivable misses, which at one point almost got ridiculous. But thank goodness we had a patient but dynamic coach in Bob Bradley, although he may have been wondering what had been going on in the game if you looked closely at his countenance."

"We know that Algeria had a few chances that they snuffed out at the beginning," added Francis, "but we know that when you're rooting for one team, you're really not worried about their opponents because you want your own to win. It's simply a major world contest. It's about waking up and winning big in soccer for America. We're only talking about the U.S. men's team performance in their various 2010 FIFA World Cup soccer encounters."

"What do you think of those fruitless struggles near the goal posts and those cross bar hits?" asked Randy. "What do you say about . . . whhh ... h? What about a few over-the-bar blasts? These are important questions, but whatever may have transpired, the efforts of the players, the coach's passion and master strategies, were what eventually paid off. The U.S. finally showed that it could play."

Reporter: "A goal by Clint Dempsey at the 20-minute mark of the first half was disallowed because of apparently mangled and controversial offside calls against him by the referee. Some spectators and fans believed the calls were gravely inaccurate, while others believed they were accurate, but that's one of those 'some believe this, others believe that' messages. It looked like an offside, but it was confusing and a close call. Whatever one's belief or conjecture, soccer rules can be confusing, too. Sometimes it takes forever for novices to figure things out. That's why every player has got to be careful and somewhat meticulous on the field of play. During what became depressing minutes for soccer lovers, as the match lingered without a score, Bob Bradley attempted another strategic surprise package as he did during the U.S. and Slovenia match, to give the game a liftoff in favor of the U.S. and perhaps chalk up a win against Algeria.

"Now," the reporter continued, "the question is: could this package of strategic surprises do the trick? Bob assembled quite a strike force in players like Buddle and DaMarcus Beasley and urged his team forward. It's a tactical change for him. But the game became a bit more complex as desperation set in. The team wasn't able to launch a cohesive and coordinated dismantle of the opponent's defensive lineup. In the 92nd minute of the game, Landon Donovan scored a clean, clear, and spectacular goal as the result of properly coordinated teamwork. It was an incredible feat and thrilling moment for every U.S. soccer fan worldwide."

"As a longtime soccer player," Peter added, "I've developed the conviction that scoring requires perseverance, hard work, combined efforts, and proper coordination. From my view, this score and the way it was coordinated, gave this soccer journey a conspicuously positive spin that sent the U.S. on to the elimination stage of the World Cup and spared it an undesirable setback for a long period of years. I hope our guys will endeavor to keep it up."

The U.S. versus Ghana took place on Saturday June 26, 2010 at 9:00 a.m.

Reporter/Commentator: "With its 1-0 victory over Algeria on Wednesday and atop Group C, the indefatigable U.S. men's team was poised to seek a place in the quarterfinals with its scheduled meeting against Ghana. Meanwhile, Ghana was the only surviving African national team in the second round, the round of 16 survivors in the World Cup.

"Five minutes into the match, Ghana scored a goal. During this match, Landon Donovan had proven himself a strong anchor for the U.S. team and had been consistently reliable all match long. An opportunity arrived for a penalty kick in favor of the U.S., an opportunity he used brilliantly and with amazing composure, snatching an equalizer for the U.S. team to make it a 1-1 tie. Draws are almost always unacceptable at the knockout stage, as opposed to a win by at least a goal, either way.

"In the third minute of overtime," the reporter went on, "Ghana got a chance to score, which was successful, with the U.S. team having already run out of chances to secure another equalizer. Ghana succeeded in eliminating the U.S. team by a 2-1 score to advance to the quarterfinals of the World Cup, and they did it with a penalty kick award."

Let's listen to some instant analysis.

"I think that with his performance," noted Alice, "Landon Donovan has proven his excellence in the field of soccer. The U.S. hasn't looked so great, but she (the U.S.) looked simply great. The U.S. team could be considered lucky because Ghana seemed to have been the best team that they'd be able to contain and manage in the round of 16, or, as the saying goes: 'Choose your fight.'"

"Even though some people believed that the Ghanaians were running up and down the soccer arena for almost five hours after their first score," recalled Robert, "they still managed to knock out the U.S. team with a penalty kick, anyway. For me a win is always a win, no matter how it came about, as long as it was genuine."

"Ghana may have been considered weak by some other great soccer nations," observed Kate, "but they sent us home with their strong determination and doggedness. We shouldn't forget that the same Ghana defeated the U.S. in 2006 by 2-1. This 2010 global soccer contest would've been a golden opportunity for the U.S. to erase the memory of that controversial defeat that was decided by a penalty kick, and achieve a successful rematch with such talented players."

"You're right, Kate." agreed Lisa. "It would've been a chance to redeem ourselves by avenging our loss to Ghana in the 2006 World Cup that eliminated the U.S. from the tournament. One thing I discovered was that many people were either jubilant or joyfully ecstatic when Ghana won, and not because they hated the U.S., no, not at all. It's because they believed Ghana was pretty passionate and cared more about soccer than the U.S., and should be encouraged to advance further."

"It really shouldn't have happened," complained Sharifa, "had the U.S. used all the chances they got. For me, as an American, it's a match during which the disappointment and negligence of the U.S. ended up becoming Ghana's great joy, because Ghana happened to be the lone African nation that advanced to the second round."

Reporter: "Ghana's soccer fans were believed to have arrived at the soccer stadium in Rustenburg aboard a motor coach inscribed with the phrase: The Hope of Africa. These fans got off their bus and danced at a breakneck speed, almost through the duration of the game. 'We fought for the African continent and fought for Ghana,' bragged a Ghanaian midfielder. 'I pray that our continent is proud, and that we've made a lot of Ghanaians happy.'"

What follows are some honest evaluations and comments:

"People who watched the 2010 soccer tournament in South Africa, which involved the US," opined Robert, "would always give it a beautiful description, even though the U.S. team ended their first two games in unwanted draws. We seem to have acquired a culture that tends to describe things that would otherwise become depressing in a pretty nice way, thereby giving it a pretty good outlook. How about that? Some errors were made during multiple opportunities to get the go-ahead score, with each shot sailing over the bar or narrowly missing, plus other technical challenges."

"On the positive side," added Chris, "I believe that they played well. In her group stage, during the last match and with about three minutes remaining, the U.S. finished a draw with Algeria. Overall, the players did well, courtesy of Landon Donovan, Clint Dempsey, Jozy Altidore, the rest of the players and the goalkeeper Tim Howard. On the flipside: Were there missed chances during the tournament? Yes. Were there shouts of 'it was nearly a goal'? Of course, yes, as always. But we all know that 'nearly' doesn't and will never kill any perching bird."

"When all is said and done," added Matt, "it's important to remark that soccer requires patience, but it also needs perseverance, hard work, strong efforts, and proper coordination. It may have felt trying, this time, not to be angry or frustrated at the U.S. team, but I'll say: wait a minute. Kindly hold off negative criticisms, anger, and bitterness. Let's drop the issue about the defeat of the US, and focus on what they did well this time. Let's put away all the 'should've, could've and would've' stuffs for now. Let's find a better way to move forward." Some others maintained that their achievement was remarkable.

"The U.S. team deserves big congrats and bravo," remarked Drew, "because making it to the second round of the global soccer contest isn't a small achievement. It's pretty significant. They qualified for the second round, even when soccer giants like France, Italy, and even Nigeria didn't make it to that point."

Others noted their graciousness, overall composure and comportment.

"I think that our guys are pretty passionate," declared Carla, "as they know their soccer pretty well, but they were also gracious during the whole encounter. Even though it wasn't a perfect performance, it remains a thrilling tournament, overall, with an excitingly huge U.S. involvement. The legacy that they'll leave for future generations would be their uniquely clear and exciting games, which have, of recent, got many Americans attracted to, and involved in, matters related to soccer. With these beautiful remarks, among others, their 2010 appearance could simply be seen as a clear success."

"It's true that our men's soccer team has suffered defeats against top soccer nations' teams," conceded Cedar, "but they've also been on the winning end, too, with some good results. I recall that the team had been amazing defensively, looking at their performance during the 1994, 1996 and in the 2002 World Cup soccer."

"The world loves the U.S.," opined Cheryl, "and would always wish to see her get more involved in soccer as a global sport. In essence, what some people see as a disappointment in this past U.S. global soccer contest might surprisingly turn out to spell increased attendance and interest in soccer from now on." Finally, there were several comments about the team's spotless resilience.

"An encouraging saying goes that, 'when the going gets tough, the tough stay on and get going,'" observed Noelle. "The U.S. soccer team's players went into the game well and kept fighting to the end amid difficult circumstances that were strategic — that's what I think makes them *giants*. Moreover, this fighting spirit was almost physically present."

"The U.S. has been known for its staunch spirit of resilience all through history," remarked Russell. "In brief, our men's team defied all odds in the face of adversity during their various soccer encounters. They didn't put themselves in a hole in any match. Mark this — not too many teams across the globe would've continued to survive, let alone held on to their caliber of determination, after their two goals were canceled in the first round of their encounter with Slovenia."

"You're absolutely right, Russell." agreed Abby. "They didn't crumble, but rather went ahead to become great winners in their group, even above their most dreaded competitor and arch soccer rival, England. The odds were against them in their final encounter with Ghana, even as they struggled and gave their all, in the latter part of the contest, to secure an equalizer against a team that was formidable."

"Our U.S. men's national team players, though not that old in global soccer, remain potential soccer giants that are yet to rise," concluded Annie. "They will rise higher than ever."

# Chapter 5
## The Giant Will Rise

*Rise, and let the sky be your limit!*

This message, which stands out in the imperative, is neither a snarky one, nor is it a scornful appeal for us to do well in future soccer engagements. It isn't an attempt to spoil or soil an ardent soccer player's soccer journey. It's rather an attempt to boost the morale of any soccer player and all soccer teams in the U.S., both great and small.

Great fans and lovers of soccer incontestably deserve the highest encouragement they can get from their environment, regardless of how challenging and competitive the sporting environment might be. It's a statement that can boost the hope of our national men's soccer team, and all those local, league, and club players who are aspiring to reach great heights. It sounds like a wakeup call that we really need today, to stand snug and secure so as to digest the urgent message of the need for the U.S. to brace up to the challenge of reversing the tide of "never winning big" in our men's soccer outings. This message highlights the suggestion for the U.S. to become an arsenal of soccer victories in the world. Our superpower status must be matched by our strength and stature in soccer, and, especially, in our national men's soccer machinery.

A spectrum of enlightened discussion from varied personalities would serve as an appropriate introduction, leading us right into the message that this section is set to provide.

"Some people have always believed that if any sport exists at all in 'heaven' above," observed Roman, "then it would be soccer, because of what it does for people and nations. It brings people together, among other things."

"You seem to be making great sense," agreed Arthur, "but as a follow-up to such an exalting and positive soccer promo statement, a question like this would naturally arise: is 'heaven' not a place of ultimate happiness and joy for the giants of virtue?"

"Permit me to say, yes it is, Arthur." rejoined Roman. "But let's not wait until we rise from the sleep of death and get into 'heaven' to find out if soccer really exists there or not."

"I think that I do understand where Roman's going!" exclaimed William. "Just as it'll take a resurrection to make it to heaven, it'll likewise take "rising and waking up" to make it to great heights in soccer. Let's begin to figure out how to get there, since making it to heaven is also about strong determination, grace, ultimate victory, and success; victory and success. The long and short of this message is that hard work always pays off, even in soccer, too."

"Wait a minute." Harris jumped in. "Hope you're not planning to transform our U.S. playgrounds, stadiums, parks, and recreational spots into shrines, temples, mosques, synagogues, and churches under the guise of religion? Are we talking about 'heaven', or are we talking about soccer? Why the detour at this point? Sorry, I'm not a religious person and I'm too busy to bother with that stuff right now. But that doesn't imply that I'm an axe-grinding and freewheeling atheist. Nevertheless, the detour is a non-starter."

"Even if you're an atheist of whatever description," suggested Patricia, "hopefully, that status shouldn't, in any way, be equated with ignorance or arrogance. There's always a lot more to learn in life, especially when it comes to figuring out whether or not there's a God and more to life than what we have here. However, this effort will be fruitful so long as the *learner* doesn't choose to remain a thought-dropping secularist and keeps massaging the issue of religion as a myth. Now, let's get a cook to make you a good dinner and let's see if you'll not believe in her."

"Haahaaa, I couldn't agree with you more, Patty." declared Daniel. "You gave the issue a thorough pat down. I've been a good soccer player in the state of Iowa for over 12 years. I used to be a nominal atheist, but I'm no longer one. I'm now a believer, thank God. Let me mention that my recent encounter with faithful believers revealed that despite their longtime belonging to the fold, they're still on a dogged search for a more spiritual and theological knowledge and those they confessed, as having been helpful to them."

"Thanks, Dannie," said William. "Your message is as clear as the day. I've reason to believe that the same discovery you made, which led to your conversion would also be applicable to soccer playing and growth in soccer performance, in general. In soccer there's always something more and new to learn — a revelation I've come to experience, over and over again, as a retired soccer player in the state of Arkansas."

"Please permit me to ramble a little further," appealed Susan, "as I have to do it right away; in fact, I have no choice but to do it, without betraying any slightest sign of diverted attention away from soccer, as that would be implied in the message that I plan to pass along. People who understand themselves, their daily lives and life careers, should often think of these issues deeply. Questions such as: when their career, be it soccer, coaching, or whatever, is over, then what next? These questions should come up once in a while, if not on a daily basis."

"That's right, Susan." agreed Robert. "But I also think that at some point in our pilgrimage in this life, we have to stop and think of what happens next when life finishes here; that's what makes us "religious." These questions and similar ones help you become religious, in need and in deed. So, I think that everyone is directly or indirectly religious, whether you admit or not."

"I understand that thoughtful diversion," remarked Paul, "but we'll do well to reconnect to soccer eventually, as quickly as possible. After all, it's a necessary shift because religion teaches us how to believe, and we need to believe in something to be faithful to it. Likewise, we need to believe in soccer to do well in soccer; there are no two ways about it. The practice of religion can even give us some insight into how to do well in soccer, believe it or not. In some countries where soccer is prominent, the fans sing to a being they refer to as "The God of Soccer.""

"Now, I'm beginning to experience and understand," noted Isaac, "the frustration and sadness that people go through when someone drifts from one discussion to another seems irrelevant. It's clear to me, once again, how fans feel when they see their team not playing to win, but inadvertently doing something else in the field of play. It's the same pain and frustration that you're going through now. But when they begin to play well, rising and shining brightly on the field of soccer, the fans are once again happy. However, the sense of religion will help us believe that this giant will rise, and I strongly believe that the fans will be happy again when this giant rises and shines. This discussion will still lead us to where we're going as ardent players and fans."

"I have no problem with the drift," agreed Chris, "Each of us can recall at least a moment in sports when people dropped to their knees, crossed themselves or bowed their heads and prayed, as the cameras zoomed in and millions watched. For me, it's always a beautiful and touching moment! People like that become heroes not just because of their victory, but because they shared their humanity and belief with us."

"Yes, even though we're here to have some discussions about soccer," interjected Frank, "I think there's great knowledge and deep insight into everything popping up here, guys. It doesn't even matter to me if anybody decides to take us far into religion. After all, I read recently that soccer has been worshipped and taken as a religion in most parts of the world, because people's love of the sport has conquered not only their minds but also their souls. Think of countries like Brazil, Argentina, Germany, and Indonesia, among others, where people have loved soccer so much that a winning spirit is enkindled in them. At this point, wouldn't it be nice for us to build three booths here — one for soccer, one for religion, and the other for well-meaning atheists?"

"You're right, Frank, haaaa haaa." laughed Richard. "To me this discussion will be enjoyable, even to players who once in a while need some time to relax and have fun among themselves without quarrelling or fighting. Anybody listening to us might be thinking that we've foolishly moved away from soccer, or that we're moving away from our main discussion, but we assure them that we know what we're doing. This little 'dance,' I assure you, will take us right into a deeper discussion on soccer. Just stay tuned! People who think that they shouldn't be bothered with religion haven't realized that religion is as necessary an activity as eating, sleeping, walking, working, and playing soccer on a field. Please wait — don't argue now."

"If their inclination is to ask who, why, when, and how," argued Joan, "then at least they will begin to ask the question about who's ultimately responsible for my being alive, eating, working, moving, playing, and roaming about in this beautiful life of ours, where we also play and enjoy soccer. That's when they discover that a Being is at the center of every existence — that's religion. No wonder players from various nations, including our guys, often get together to pray and give thanks before and after every soccer encounter, and, more so, after each victory, no matter how small. Now I see where you and others are going, Richie. Do you now imply who's responsible for scoring the goals to help us win? I see where you're gradually going, guys. Good job."

"I'd ask your forgiveness beforehand, guys," pleaded Lawrence, "and from all those who might be listening to me, because I don't mean to take you too far away into religion, but permit me to mention that I did read in a local newspaper recently that in the midst of the Civil War, Abraham Lincoln, while acknowledging the nation's sufferings, took note of America's vast abundance as the gracious gift of God, who, though angry with us for our sins, also remains merciful.'"

"Thank you, Lawrence, for your deep sense of history," said Victoria. "It's history that exposes the gift that we received from God, which has to do with unity, diversity, and resilience despite difficult circumstances in life. It's a sense of history that reveals that we Americans don't succumb to defeat of any kind. We've been naturally made a giant and will always rise and become victorious. This has been one of the major reasons Thanksgiving to a Supreme Being was declared a national observation here in the U.S. Shall we not do the same any time we win globally in soccer contests?"

"Indeed, that's our aspiration." agreed Jack. "The whole of American people, both those who are at sea and those sojourning in foreign lands, unite every year in one heart and one voice to acknowledge this reality, to give thanks to whatever 'God' in whom they believe. Why do they have to do so? They have to do so because, despite its travails and differences, the U.S is still exceedingly blessed. What a remarkably successful and special experience and demonstration of religious pluralism in a nation. Despite our travails and differences, we can always unite together as a nation to do wonders and magic together in various areas of human endeavor, and great soccer triumphs aren't excluded."

"I'm getting excited, by the way, our discussion has gone," enthused Julia. "Good job, guys. With our spirit of resilience, unity, and togetherness, and our sense of religion, this great nation and sleeping soccer giant will rise and march toward greater heights in our men's soccer program. This great giant will rise again."

"Here we go again," sighed Robert. "This great giant will rise again in the field of world soccer *fiestas*. For now, it's about sports, and, most especially, about soccer and a sleeping giant rising and winning big in international soccer. We're now talking about soccer because the joy that's in soccer takes you out of this world for good, especially when you're a big winner. Remain a big winner. Who among you knows the joy you feel when you win big in soccer, and even when you score to help a team win?

Please don't forget that Paul, in the scripture, tells us, as mentioned above, that all the runners at the stadium are all running to win, every one of them."

"You're now beginning to sound again like a good churchgoer," remarked Thomas, "but let's think of how to fix soccer in the U.S. so that we can win big, too, just like the runners in the stadium. Of course, church going has helped me through my career in life, because I couldn't do much without God. He helped me during my career in soccer in the state of North Dakota, and finally in my business and family life too. Ask the Brazilian Pele who, to me, was the greatest and most celebrated soccer player that ever lived, if he wasn't and isn't a good churchgoer. But that's by the way, anyway."

"Yes, Paul in the scripture," noted Anthony, "spoke of runners at the stadium and, of course, running is also involved in good soccer playing. It also takes a good runner to score a goal, too. That's fine. I've always believed that it takes a giant and a super-giant to rise. It also takes a giant stride to rise to stardom, or superstardom, in soccer. I have reason to believe that we'll be quite able to do so. Imagine what it would feel like watching the U.S. in any World Cup finals winning, and winning big. It would be fascinating."

"I agree with you, Tony." chimed Stacy. "A giant doesn't get boxed up in a cage. He's got to stand outside the box to think well, act well, fight well and play well. Giants, even though they may have been sleeping, seldom lie low. Our gifts and the blessings of utilizing resources, pluralism, diversity, and, above all, unity, can have everyone eating out of our hands and plates in the international soccer arena."

"I'm inclined to think that since it has been freshly overtaken by other superstar soccer nations," observed Joseph, "the U.S. would now seem to be standing at the threshold of a new but rising movement, perhaps leading the way for countries to follow in its wake, sooner or later, to greatness in soccer. In a world where contest is increasingly apparent, the U.S. men's senior soccer team can still reveal what it means to outgrow growth. It's not difficult to find solutions to our soccer problems."

"Your brilliant ideas and suggestions," remarked Richard, "have the potential to make a major impact and even lift us as a nation in soccer all the way to the top. Does it really take a giant to fix a problem? Not necessarily. Fixing the problem of soccer in the U.S.? It's never too late. With their increasing growth, the population, resources, and diversity in the U.S. have shown that this country still has its head and shoulders high up. She's a big, affluent, and sports loving nation, and shouldn't be contented with anything mediocre or small. The same should be applicable to its journey in the world of international soccer."

"It's been my contention," added Mildred, "that the U.S. future in soccer shouldn't be shrouded in feelings of unwarranted fear and uneasiness. We should save soccer for our future in the world and for a rapid globalization in this 21st century, since the world is also going flat with soccer, and not only with computers and the internet. What I'm saying is that we'll not rest on our oars until the tummy of the world becomes flat, too. That's when soccer, as a beautiful game, becomes a great success in the US."

"Soccer can serve as a unifying force in the world," suggested Carmela, "and the U.S. should take the lead as well — a winning lead, too. I predict that the U.S. will soon be known as a flourishing soccer nation after many years of apparent soccer slumber. No matter what happened in the past, I've always believed that when one door closes, another opens. I believe that a big wide door is opening for us to win big in future soccer contests. I mean, get the Gold Medal home in our men's national team. Bravo!"

"The great future of soccer in the U.S. shouldn't be in doubt, in any way, at all!" exclaimed James. "Now, soccer momentum in the U.S. is building at a breakneck speed. The time is fast coming when we'll make our strategic soccer presence felt around the world. The good news is that any time we attempt to recount our blessings and strength in our great resources, plurality, and diversity, we also spur our potential to come out on top in any future global soccer encounters. That's the way I see it."

"Preparing for FIFA World Cup soccer is to me like writing a perfect speech for the president of the U.S.," opined Craig. "I've always thought that it's all about the soccer director coming up with an acceptable championship plan as his primary focus, in agreement with his colleagues. But he must open to new ways of going about it. Openness to new ideas and modern soccer stuff can attract all sorts of interesting people, different ideas and experiences."

"The good news," replied Michael, "is that what Americans have been waiting for is due to arrive and when it arrives, this could be a cause for celebration. Any better attempt to harness our resources, and use the strength of diversity in our men's soccer team, will be of immense value. A strong men's soccer team will become our stimulus in global soccer progress. By helping our men's soccer team rebuild and by integrating foreign players with our existing great soccer players, we'll do great. It'll go a long way toward making us a great pillar of strength in the world of soccer."

"Some people believe that we can regain our confidence fully," noted Nancy, "if we could recruit future players from the younger generation of soccer players in the U.S. About two years ago, I watched a television documentary where soccer experts and analysts suggested the possibility of recruiting a new breed of youngsters in their late teens and early 20s, who might be trained to launder the inferior image of soccer in our nation. Yes, I think that's a good idea."

"Yes, I think that's a good idea too," agreed Bertram, "because at those age brackets, their energy and stamina levels are probably racing at the highest peak, so there's not much they can't achieve at that stage. My recent visit to Freeport in Long Island, New York, gives me the impression that soccer will grow more in the U.S. if better promoted."

"It sounds like a coincidence," noted Christopher, "as I was also in Freeport from July 1 to September 30, 2010. On August 23 or thereabouts, a good and reliable friend whom I met in Church was telling me how Mayor Andrew Hardwick had congratulated and welcomed Coach Mario Espinoza and members of the Freeport PAL Red Storm Boys Soccer Team to the Village Hall, in recognition of their winning streak in the Long Island Junior Soccer League. It's a visit that saw the Mayor place a Gold Medal and the town of Freeport pin on each member of the team, after which he took a photograph with them and wished them continued success."

"The report of your visit is quite informative," beamed Olga. "What an encouraging gesture of support from the Mayor! What an inspiration and motivation for the coach and the youngsters to see a familiar face boost their morale! What does that tell you? For me, I'd love to believe that for us to rise in global soccer outings; we'd start now to work toward it. Moreover, we need to open our doors to everyone and have soccer everywhere, if possible. From what I've learned about The PAL Red Storm Boys Soccer team, it's said to comprise boys under the age of 14, all of who have been involved since they were under the age of 10. It looks like a radical move to reclaim our lives in soccer, starting from scratch."

We then shared thoughts and observations of the 2010 High School Boys' Soccer Recap.

"My discovery after watching the 2010 High School Boys' Soccer Recap in the tristate area of New York, New Jersey, and Connecticut," recalled Jared, "showed me that hard work pays off. There's always an exciting feeling in the air whenever we learn that high school boys' soccer teams in the U.S. are improving, continue to improve a great deal, and seldom lose sight of the goal they're seriously working to accomplish, regardless of the obstacles that seem to be placed in their way. They had phenomenal seasons with regard to the tournaments. I saw these soccer seasons as big opportunities for the boys to develop basic skills, tactics, and strategies, teamwork and the spirit of sportsmanship that will help them learn to win — or lose — with honor. This exposure will also enable them to easily adjust to the demands of their future college soccer engagements and beyond. One of the striking things about high school soccer is that if you love soccer this year, you're going to love watching college soccer for the next four years."

"The boys were really good." agreed Kevin. "Their outings have been awesome and laudable in many ways and for many reasons. For those of us who watched those seasonal matches, it's like reliving the biggest moments, best games, and top individual players in boys' high school soccer in the US. In the tristate area, especially in New York, New Jersey, Long Island, Connecticut, the Hudson Valley, and Westchester, we find great and solid players and terrific soccer teams, like Scarsdale, Fordham Prep, Staples, and Wreckers. For me, Scarsdale was a physically tough team with tough players, such as Gregg Shaheem (19 goals) and Hiroki Kobiyashi (10 goals). They have a great style that everyone would admire as they sit back and watch. For me, it's always been a great pleasure watching the great midfielders from Scarsdale, whose next stop, I believe, will be in college soccer."

"The boys played excellent soccer," concurred Keith, "exhibiting their talents and great love for the sport in the field. Great teams among them advanced to the regional finals. I think that Hiroki Kobiyashi (10 goals), Andres Torres (23 goals), Neilon Lambert (23 goals), and Donovan Fraser stood out as the top players and forward liners. I place these great young and dynamic players on top of their teams' performances during this past season."

"In addition to Long Island, where the boys had a hugely exciting season, as we saw among the Chaminades and Brentwoods," noted Damian, "we also have a lot of other champions among the Staples, St, Benedict Prep, Pingry, and Chatham. They are among my top soccer teams here in the tristate area. Their performances were nothing less than spectacular. Aside from the players in the field, I wish to remark that we saw a great goalkeeper in the person of Mike Nadal, who did a great job with his two hands that he wound up helping Glennrock advance to the semi-finals in the Group 2 tournament. Coming to Connecticut, I discovered that soccer is a terrific program with great soccer performances beginning and ending with the Staples. I also think that they got a great goalkeeper in Sebastian Tomayo, who had great saves of striking varieties in the defense area. I was asked to pinpoint who my great soccer player was, and I answered that my great player of the year was Brendan Lesch (13 goals), who belonged to the Staples. He scored terrific goals. I'd say without qualification that his performance was my top moment of the season."

"The season saw great performances," agreed Pat, "with Pete McNamara as my great player of the year. What I did observe among the boys was that there's much passion and precision in their soccer styles. Most of the great players among the boys were two-footed and skillful. They can play on the right or the left and through the middle. They're composed finishers and adept in beating opposing players. In their overall performance there were no stupid shots, as you'd often observe in some teams, no dumb fouls, and above all their scoring methods were balanced."

"It's been an exciting season for the teams from Long Island, New York." observed Carl. "I must mention that the performances of the boys, for me, were a glorious spectacle. The Brentwood boys' soccer team is a class organization with a classy operation. By this I mean that they adopt great styles and win big. What I love about the Brentwood boys' soccer team is how they're adored by the community that comes out in large numbers to watch their matches. When you go to the Brentwood soccer games, note that after the team wins a match, the players go out to greet the spectators with handshakes. What a beautiful and terrific atmosphere."

"What I'm going to tell you now, isn't a rumor." declared Kevin. "It's about a great defense. On Long Island, the Chaminade boys' soccer team played so well on defense that in 22 games they had 19 shutouts. I can't tell you what a unique and amazing combination it's to have a strong offense and impenetrable defense. Their defense did as good a job as their forward liners. I saw no difficulties in corner kicks."

"In New Jersey," replied Lou B., "we also think of top teams, like St. Benedict's Prep, Pingry, and Chatham high schools. These teams made it all the way to both state and national championships with talent-packed rosters. When we take a look at the 2010 Boys' Soccer Recap Special Show and the performances of our high school boys in the tristate area of New York, New Jersey, and Connecticut, we see that our future is bright. They're pleasant to watch, with a wonderful combination of size and speed. In these boys we saw absolute magicians, judging by the style of their ball kicks. They adapt those amazing styles and go ahead to win."

"What impressed me and gave me hope for the future." affirmed Jared D., "is the performance of those young players. Here are their names and the number of goals scored during the year: Matt Slotnick (29 goals), Neilon Lambert (23 goals), Juan Colorado (18 goals), Donovan Frazer (17 goals), and Nihad Musovic (7 goals). Other players who had a nice combination of size and speed were Andres Torres, Fernando Ascalona, Mike McNamara, and Jonathan Abasela."

"I also wish to add," noted Penn, "that it's always a joy to spotlight star players in other parts of the country, like Brian McBride, who though a retired American soccer legend, was reported to have scored the 80th goal to crown his stellar career in Major League Soccer with the Chicago Fire, beating Chivas USA, 4-1. Some of these young players reminded me of him. Let's also extend our appreciation to a place like Indiana, where the leading goal scorers Brad Horn and Andrew Rosenberg are averaging over two goals a game."

And now, some comments from our Special Reporter:

"Let's take a general look at the states of Texas, Georgia, Florida, North Carolina, and Oklahoma. In youth soccer, when we look at the championship summaries, the under-14 boys' soccer produced Lonestar (96 goals) Red (South Texas) as the highest scoring team, with Andrew Lopez (52 goals) as the highest scorer. In the under-15 boys, Concorde Fire Elite in Georgia was found to be the highest scoring team, with Cameron Moseley (54 goals) as the highest scorer of the year. In the under-16 boys, RSL Florida (93 goals) was the highest scoring team, defeating Concorde Fire Elite by 2-1. Adrian Alabi of Concorde happened to be the highest scorer (68 goals), followed by Lakota Thomas (42 goals) from RSL Florida.

"In the under-17," the reporter continued, "Alpharetta Ambush Elite Red in Georgia defeated GSA (93 goals) Phoenix Red in Georgia by 4-1, with the highest goal scorers as Ambush-Algagi Toure (76 and 117 goals), Karl Chester (95 goals), Jaime Sanclemente (120 goals), and Lain Smith (90 goals) from GSA. In the under-18 boys' soccer, TUSA Gold of North

Carolina (91 goals) beat Edmond OFC in Oklahoma (92 goals) by 4-1. The highest scorers are Sebastian Garner (45 goals) of TUSA, Robert Lovejoy, III (53 goals and 78 goals), Zabarle Kollie (84 goals), and Andrew Hall (63 goals). In the under — 19 boys, Andromeda (91 goals) Navy of North Texas beat Black Rebels (91 goals) by 1-0. The highest scorer was Alexei Reyes (36 goals). I'm excited, and my advice is that we should encourage continuity, which means letting those young guys who played together, stay together as we keep matching on."

"Of course, when we see such performances," confirmed Gerard, "we heave and give out some sighs of relief, knowing that unique opportunities are quickly heading our way for future big wins in international soccer. Moreover, when you prefer to think of pedigree in high school soccer championships, it might be a good idea if you could go to Dowling College, where the speed of and feelings for soccer playing are so much harder and quicker than you would find in high school soccer."

"I'm familiar with the Dowling College's great soccer performance!" exclaimed Lloyd. "This college men's team has former Comsewogue High School players who were part of the state championship teams. As of the end of 2010, they're headed for the NCAA Division II Final Four for the fifth time in their soccer history. Dowling was said to have won the national title in 2006."

"Hi Lloyd," announced Stanley, "you spoke of a high school I know so well. You're quite right. It might interest you to know that the Comsewogue soccer program had been structured in such a way that it's potentially a winning type. Also, the team's players know how to win, for that has been hugely important to them. They feel good whenever they win the state's championship. They have great players, like their sophomore back, Anthony Forlini, midfielder Sean Dougherty, and Aidan Pagano, Who's also a midfielder and who played on the 2008 state championship team, whereas freshmen forwards Gerassimos Magoulas and Keith Vigorito played for the 2009 championship team."

"Sure, Stanley." agreed Lloyd. "May I add that these young players know that winning is what matters in soccer encounters. Specifically, Dougherty was said to have initially taken a different path by heading to NYIT as a freshman, but later changed his mind and transferred to Dowling to meet his fellow high school players. When I heard that, I thought that it must have been quite awesome — getting the opportunity to play with his friends again. To him, of course, it would look like high school again."

"One of the ideas I came away with as a former high school soccer player in Tennessee," recalled Mark, "is that there's always a need for continuity with teammates and co-players, as that has always created great advantages in future soccer wins. From what I learned, Dougherty led the team with nine goals. He made a big difference as soon as he arrived on the squad by getting several game-winning scores or helping them get tying goals. He took advantage of his soaring popularity and ended up making it."

"The coach and the team," remarked Rodney, "were said to have been thrilled to have Dougherty transferred to them, because they knew he was bringing something unique and outstanding. A pleasant surprise. His fellow players have always thought that he's the great commodity of speed, and are all delighted to have him not just for scoring goals but for playing exceptionally well. I think that every team would need him and players like him."

"I'd like to mention," added Stanley, "that their coach, John DiRico, has guided the team to 13 postseason appearances and has secured straight academic awards from the National Soccer Coaches Association of America. DiRico has always respected his team for one thing — their passion for winning and their absolute hatred for losing."

"This short moment of listening to your discussion," observed Meryl, "has been for me an uplifting moment of revelation, which can help a lot of people begin to see soccer from a different light and come away with the feeling that we can overcome any obstacles in soccer. Of course, we can always begin somewhere, the earlier the better, but there must be some continuity for real progress to be sustained."

"I'm impressed by these discussions," noted Josh. "But my great joy is that, finally, soccer is gradually made available to kids who aren't able to pay in order to play. We shouldn't forget that about 97% of great players in the world today came from poor backgrounds; the same is applicable to the American basketball and football. This championship team, shortly discussed above, is part of the Long Island Junior Soccer League, one of the largest youth soccer leagues in the US."

Another program featured discussants who were suggesting recruiting and buying up players from other countries as one of the ways to fix our men's national soccer.

"It's good to know that there's no international event," remarked David, "that inspires as many player exchanges among different nations for the World Cup. As a nation of immigrants, it's often wrongly thought that the U.S. has a national men's team that consists of many foreign-born players. Not quite, because we're a nation that basks in our pluralism and diversity, where our major strength lies. We can achieve quite a lot with our blessings of diversity."

"Indeed, diversity has always been our strength," concurred Malcolm. "Sports have for some decades now become increasingly diverse. Diversity has been our strength in many ways, that we've become a successful people. Diversity influences our superb decision making, whether in education, politics, business, arts, government, or sports. I think that this diversity should be extended to soccer, at all costs. Diversity influences our group performances and activities positively, and can lead us to the greatest heights in soccer performance."

"What you've said is excellent!" exclaimed Gayle. "Diversity can lead to the highest victory in any sports, including soccer, but the players have to stay together for quite a long time for them to know themselves well and to overcome possible challenges of negative group dynamics. Once that's done, then the sky is the limit of our performance in soccer. That's where integration comes in, and there's no big deal about that."

"We can always reap the benefits that diversity can offer in all fields of our endeavors," suggested Carl. "I don't think that we'll have any problem increasing the benefits of diversity in our men's national soccer team, since the identity of a team is easily shared among players and that elevates group performance. I'm talking from my experience as a former soccer player in the state of Michigan. Our team was virtually stacked with people of diverse origins, but all Americans. I can tell you that in our 12 soccer encounters, we narrowly lost only three. Indeed, we were rarely defeated, and I believe it was because of the power of diversity that blessed our soccer team."

"Carl, I think your message is clear, but what would you say about recruiting foreign players?" asked Sampson. "In my opinion I'd say yes, as they could be usefully drafted into the squad that we already have, but they need some time to familiarize themselves with other players and get fully acclimatized to our existent system."

"Buying up players from other countries?" mused Carl. "Yes and no. Of course, a fresh influx of properly controlled and well-regulated smart players from other countries will provide fresh impetus, contest, and confidence to our unstable men's soccer team. But we can do that, too, if it comes to the point of looking for external support. Again, the problem we may be having could be seen in possible miscommunications and misunderstandings, which are more likely to arise. This might cause frustrations and resentments, and perhaps damage team performance. Such a scenario can weaken morale, coordination, and commitment to the soccer team. But we can invest more in ourselves and in our nation, as human resources and wherewithal abound in this country."

"Look," gestured Gwyneth, "the U.S. isn't a small country and we're not okay with anything small. All I know and am convinced about is that it's time to say goodbye to mediocrity. We have everything it takes to be great in our men's national soccer team. That this giant of a nation will rise in soccer remains the cliché of this debate and our preceding discussions."

"Wake up, America." exclaimed Joyce, "and let our young soccer guys log on to the internet and watch great American soccer players, like Cobi Jones, Landon Donovan, and their companions, or click to watch women players like Abby Wambach, Mia Hamm, Michelle Akers, Kristine Lilly, Julie Foudy, Hope Solo and the legendary goalkeeper Briana Scurry on YouTube. What of Carla Werden Overbeck? Great! Please wake up all and win big, so as to become more successful on the global soccer stage."

"Of course, when the U.S. awakes," agreed Lynn, "the world of soccer will tremble, as it nearly trembled in 1996, and somewhat again in 2010, as Carol and Steve Bloom of Colorado Springs did once observe. Bravo to the coaches and all the players. I don't care what people might be thinking or saying now. Yes, this sleeping soccer giant will pretty soon be awakened with a comeback in this important sport."

"All you need to do," advised Ashley, "is give out the names of some of the world's greatest soccer players ever, and let our young ones in both high schools and colleges log on to websites and chose their heroes and superstar model players. All I have to do is name them all in alphabetical order. Here you go: Adriano, Pablo Aimar, Roberto Baggio, Michael Ballack, Gabriel Batistuta, Franz Beckenbauer, David Beckham, Dennis Bergkamp, Jared Borgetti, Omar Bravo, Gianluigi Buffon, Eric Cantona, Fabio Cannavaro, Roberton Carlos, Nery Castilo, Petr Cech (goalkeeper), Bobby Charlton, Hernan Crespo, Johan Cruyff, Kenny Dalglish, Deco, Didier Deschamps, Landon Donovan, Didier Drogba, Freddy Edu, Michael Essien, Samuel Eto, Luis Figo, Gennaro Gattuso, Steven Gerrard, Gheorghe Hagi, Thierry Henry, Cobi Jones, Oliver Kahn (goalkeeper), Austin Okocha, Ricardo Kaka, Roy Keane, Kevin Keegan, Jurgen Klinsmann, Miroslav Klose, Philipp Lahm, Frank Lampard, Jens Lehman, Gary Lineker, Diego Maradona, Lionel Messi, Roger Miller, Pavel Nedved, Kanu Nwankwo, Alessandro Nesta, Micahel Owen, Pele, Michel Platini, Juan Riquelme, Rivaldo, Robinho, Romario, Ronaldinho, Ronaldo, Christiano Ronaldo, Wayne Rooney, Hugo Sanchez, Peter Schmeichel, Alan Shearer, Carlos Tevez, Marco Van Basten, Rudd Van Nistelrooy, Patrick Vieira, and Zinedine Zidane."

"Thanks, Ashley," responded Jill, "for this exciting list of famous and great players on the world stage. Our young ones will, no doubt, find it helpful. Indeed, the need for this giant to rise in soccer is what the national and mainstream media should help promote ceaselessly. I'd recommend that it be best put this way — that the U.S. should no longer be overtaken, eliminated, humiliated, or knocked down from the top-spot global soccer position, toward which she can't wait any longer to aspire."

"The prospect of this giant rising in the field of global soccer," noted Leonard "isn't as remote as some people have always considered it to be. Think of the Soccer Under-Appreciation Syndrome (SUAS). Many Americans once thought that soccer couldn't be truly American because they bore supreme loyalty to football, baseball, and basketball. But with our women's soccer team, which has done us proud, their opinions and attitudes about soccer suddenly took a positive turn. Let's not cling to stereotypes or wallow in basic misconceptions when it comes to our status in soccer."

Shawn pitched in: "Even though, internally, the U.S. seems to have inherited and become trapped in, a deep and near-agonizing economic downturn and sky-high joblessness, as many other countries are suffering now; the U.S. is not awkwardly bent. A game that's able to boost the image of a nation externally could also enhance her popularity. It can also help the economy grow anew, create employment, make individuals, groups, and families happy, and raise our national hope. Soccer is a game that ought to be looked into closely for some possible overhaul and necessary reorganization."

"I'm absolutely sympathetic to your opinion, Shawn!" cried Charlotte. "Surely this recommendation doesn't smack of poor performance on the part of the managers or the coach, but we want to do better. We're not going to say: 'This is good, keep it going.' We want to say: 'This is good, but we can do better and want something truly outstanding. We want to be the best.' It makes no sense to leave the system in abject mediocrity or let it gradually die."

"Thank goodness," replied Carmela, "the U.S. hasn't acquired any ill-deserving notoriety as a difficult place where the soccer industry has come to die. Our job is only to restructure, as soon as possible, the already-existing soccer machinery in the nation. To change the direction of any game, including soccer, you need what it takes to get the job done right. Needless to say, this country could easily be transformed into a soccer-industry colossus."

"You're right, Carmela." enthused Allan. "But what exactly it would take to let this apparently sleeping giant rise in soccer remains an urgent and vexatious question. Listeners shouldn't be at a loss as to the best way to tackle this problem. It takes an irrevocable commitment to the desired goal of waking up and winning. We needn't have a widespread protest before something better is done ahead of the next World Cup in 2014, when our men's soccer team shouldn't be allowed further excuses for not clinching the World Cup. This must be done out of a deep conviction that the U.S. needs to claim and acquire a pride of place in the comity of nations, both within the continent and across the globe in the field of soccer."

"I think that this great feat could be achieved," noted Bonnie, "by forging a common front to produce a pretty formidable men's team, which will rejuvenate and energize our entire sports entertainment industry and social system. What of rebuilding the obviously declining public interest in soccer contests? It reasonably calls for some re-strategizing in the U.S. Soccer Federation leadership and organization. One may wonder if we don't, at this time, need some form of hyper-transformative leadership in soccer, with sharpened focus, undeniable energy, skill, and charisma based on seasoned experience, honed on a necessary interface between economy and nation-building."

"I've always been of the opinion," observed Perry, "that the leadership of the U.S. Soccer Federation hasn't been tested enough and, so, needs to be more tested so as to be more trusted by Americans. It's high time we asked ourselves some serious questions about what we want to accomplish in soccer, and then, having answered those questions, rejoin the entire world of soccer to make it happen. What seemed so difficult yesterday and in past decades could seem laughably easy today."

"International soccer may not have changed one bit," added Tipper, "but our attitude toward it can change and that's what could make the difference. The U.S. stands the best chance, more than ever before in the past decades, of fixing her feeble men's soccer system, with the current President Obama as a former basketball player and soccer enthusiast. With his charm and perspicacity, I'm sure that he'll not stand idly by to see the image and face of soccer in the U.S. completely tarnished."

"I read recently," said Ashton, "that in late May 2010, Obama and former President Clinton, the honorary Chairman of the World Cup bid Committee, were said to have hosted the team at the White House, after which the team was bused to prepare for a tune-up match against Turkey in Philadelphia. Good enough. These are signs of progress, but how did our men's soccer team members perform when they played with Turkey?"

"The only thing I heard," recalled Macaulay, "was that they did their best, but we definitely want to see a true atmosphere of change in the way our national men's team performs in the next World Cup come 2014. My request is this: 'Why not bring the soccer World Cup home in 2014 or 2018 or stop trying?' We have an ample opportunity now to begin to prepare, and recruit the best talents in the country."

"If the U.S. can win the global soccer contest once or twice," reasoned Ellen, "then the whole of the U.S. will, undoubtedly, begin to develop serious interest in soccer, because soccer, more than any other field of play, holds great promise in the sleepless journey of our beloved nation toward globalization. What does it take to do this job? What does it take to bring some change and reform into our soccer system?"

"It doesn't necessarily take too much," suggested Ronald. "Just a committee of about 12 people, both men and women, who'll give the U.S. soccer a good restructure and a radical overhaul, can get the ball rolling in the first place. What does it also take to win the World Cup soccer tournament? Apart from creating better training programs for the players, assessing and evaluating the quality and effectiveness of those programs, the committee should be able to lay out a blueprint for restructuring the entire soccer system, open to suggestions from the citizens and popular soccer veterans in the country."

"I think that you're making an important point, Ron." noted Portia. "With good ideas from the members of the committee and intelligent contributions from the citizenry, a lot of progress will be made to save us future embarrassments in the field of soccer. We can begin to organize, in an impressively superior fashion, soccer juggling and dribbling contests, 'score for a reward' and skill-challenge contests, in both high schools and colleges across the country."

"These strategies you just mentioned, if properly implemented," responded Sandra, "will help the youngsters appreciate the special talents and skills that they can employ for the good of any soccer team in which they're involved. Without special talents and skills, the entire team can easily lose. However, whether the plan of the committee will strengthen or weaken the system we already have will depend on how the committee fleshes out the details of their plans and ideals."

"You're in the right track, Sandra." interjected Cleopatra. "But I think we need to get some men below the age of 40 to do the hustling job. It isn't expected that the process will involve much rigor to get the ideas to work. One best player from each of the 50 U.S. states will do the trick. The implementation of this initiative in the player-recruitment strategy will in fact quadruple the 11 men that are needed for one good soccer team. Who knows what will happen if we get up to three or more wonderful players from each state?"

"If I properly understand the point you're making," replied Guy, "your message implies that to be prepared for each soccer tournament, the U.S. must produce at least one prodigious soccer player for each wing to get us what we've been longing for. It's doable. But for this proposal to be achieved, the committee in question will have to conduct a search around the globe, beginning in the U.S., for a soccer coach who has attained wizardry level in the field of soccer. The search needn't diminish the importance and precious contributions of both the present and previous soccer coaches."

"You've got a nice idea, Guy." agreed Harvey. "Of course, these steps aren't difficult to take if the U.S. government prioritizes soccer among her other major sports, because its scope is critically and undeniably global. It isn't just parochial, like our other traditional sports, such as baseball, basketball, football, hockey, and so forth soccer is also massively global. It'll be interesting to know how the government helps to promote soccer as a global sport in the U.S."

"Sure, it'll be," added Julian, "but it's hard for me to tell if the current national system of soccer in the U.S. encourages the sport in both primary and high schools across the nation. If it does encourage soccer in primary and high schools, how exactly it does so remains a trillion dollar question. The system will be progressive if it inspires governments to give credits, rewards, and incentives to schools that do well in soccer and the ones that improve their performances. It may introduce new elements of strategic importance, which might include giving scholarships, up to the university level, to great soccer strikers and defenders who have proved themselves indomitable, unstoppable, and impenetrable on the fields."

"These initiatives sound sensible and significant enough," noted Jason, "as long as the performances that'll be rewarded and the incentives are worthwhile in achieving our great goal — the rise of a lame giant in soccer. This plan might even help improve academics, as no right thinking leadership would wish its school system to be popular only in soccer, while relegating its academic life to the background. It'll help to move the entire school system ever more forward, if such attempts are properly integrated. How about giving players a befitting welcome, a red carpet reception, when they do us proud? How about that?"

"Good question, Jason." replied Nellie. "It may sound naïve to some people, but I think that will be one of the most public honors an American soccer player can receive — to be given a huge financial reward as if he won a big lottery. That's, when they succeed in winning the World Cup. It'll have a huge psychological impact on those who are striving to do well in international soccer."

"What of offering free-housing benefits," Kanye chipped in, "or brand new, top-notch cars to the best performing players when they make it to the semi-finals? Thinking of players who served us well in past soccer contests, with special reference to the 2010 World Cup, players without whose presence and involvement we would've gone back home much earlier. Such players should be treated as heroes and popular lightning rods for soccer enterprise, expertise and zest in the US."

"These are great ideas," responded Courtney. "Moreover, the gestures will show to all the value of the achievement and the nation's excitement, even if such gestures make the feat appear bigger than it's worth. Also, the nature of the rewards will depend on the nature and degree of the accomplishment. For instance, a striker who gave us a winning goal should, of course, get more rewards than a midfielder who did the engineering, but didn't succeed in scoring."

"I think that your suggestions make sense." reasoned Kim. "Why? Because not only is there something especially fitting about rewards and incentives, but also because not every soccer contest is necessarily about tactics, strategies, and mid-field engineering, although these are absolutely necessary. It'll help the players become interested, as well as desire to rise and shine. We all know that the game is all about performing, but ultimately it's about winning by scoring. Getting the job done means getting us goals, and as many goals as possible. Fans often jokingly ask players: 'How many goals did you get us when you had the chances to do so, buddy?'"

"The idea, culture, and practice of receiving players," suggested Trent, "and appreciating their soccer feats, can never be faulted by any generation of Americans. Players who achieved excellent results in soccer deserve to be rewarded. In my opinion, the coaches should also not be left out of the dollar and reward gains."

"That's a pretty good idea." agreed Robert. "In some countries when the national soccer team wins, the President will welcome them in an official celebratory fashion. Handshakes or hugs are given according to the custom of the land. Players have been invited to royal and presidential palaces, and offered vacations with all expenses paid .They've also appeared on countless television shows, documentaries, and news shows, and special government jobs have been offered to at least one of their close relatives. They're treated as champions who represented the nation well in the global soccer."

"Of course, they'd love to be treated as great players," noted Billie. "This means that necessary arrangements must be made to enable the country prepare a reception for the team members because they've done America proud. It'll be a way of helping the soccer system, rather than killing the soccer industry in the U.S."

"Let me make clear," asserted Nick, "what I think might be more helpful to soccer and continued social development in the U.S. Because of the global appetite for soccer events, our state governments, foundations, organizations, conglomerates, strong interest groups, and corporate America should reconsider the need to get more involved in revamping our soccer program. They might even form clubs that parallel Real Madrid, Arsenal, Barcelona, Chelsea, Manchester United, Juventus, Liverpool, AC Milan, and others, for the good of the nation's soccer industry and even for the nation's economy. I know that nervous thinkers might at this juncture begin to ask the following questions. Is there any possible logical link between soccer and a nation's economic growth? What are the costs and benefits of getting involved in or getting committed to soccer? Is it a suggestion or temptation that ought to be resisted and overcome? Or is it a proposal or recommendation that ought to be either watered down or killed off?"

"For me, it doesn't really matter," noted Henry, "even if the effort is only to help the nation improve the performance of her soccer team, since recent World Cup soccer have clearly indicated that our soccer teams need improvement. I mean, it's not a time to malign the coach or the organizers or to call the players' names. Some people think that might help. No, not at all. Maligning them wouldn't be fair, because these are all great guys who have sometimes done the impossible. Rather, this is a time to re-strategize and search for a better way forward."

"That's right." agreed Ramona. "It's a time to explore our uncharted inner selves, in relation to our interest in and appreciation for the potential of this soccer giant of a nation to rise. For our team's success, there might be a need for improved team chemistry and deep bench rotation. It's only high time soccer is taken seriously in this country and taken to a higher level."

"Americans ought to rally around the players," suggested Sinclair, "as they fight their way toward clinching the World Cup someday. The players need the support of every one of us in the U.S. The team definitely needs that support to attain the enviable height we all have in mind and so desperately long for. That's always the desire of any well-meaning national team the world over. I think that American players are ever more determined to show all Americans that the South African World Cup outing in 2010 didn't truly reflect the quality of their game or their true potential."

"Success will bring the U.S. the attention it has always received in most of the rest of the world," opined Grace. "Let's wait and see, and give all our players the full support that they've always deserved. Many public leaders and politicians have become gifted in talking about success and victory, but the problem remains in the implementation of those plans that lead to success and victory. It's no longer the time only to talk about success or victory — rather, it's time to achieve success and victory, for this giant to rise. It's time for action."

"Let's not use our past failures as an excuse for future breakdowns," cautioned Maxine. "We should always get our hopes up and work toward them. The day the U.S. men's soccer team brings home the Gold Medal in a global soccer contest will be a brand new day for everyone in this nation. People will hold up their hands and arms in gratitude and awe. It'll be like a triumph of the human spirit that had once been relegated to the background of the entire human existence."

"Surely it'll be heartening, and, to some, surprising." agreed Valerie. "To some people it'll be like meeting God, who's always a winner, victor, and who should always be identified, and associated, with in whatever we do. Let's stand smiling and move about radiating joy, because we know that it'll work. We know that our men's team will come through, and we've the utmost confidence that it'll be so. The U.S. has the potential to give its image in soccer a facelift and redeem its prestige on the international soccer stage, which has been on the decline in the past years."

"I've no doubt in mind," added Connor, "that in the near future, the U.S. men's soccer team will become a difficult one to beat. Our desire is to have our national men's soccer team, at the earliest possible time, soar to the ranks of becoming one of the three best teams in the world. Yes, we can do it. Yes, we can reach megastardom in the field of soccer. Let 'Yes we can' be our watchword and cliché once again, after it accomplished such a great miracle in the history of the U.S. It worked in the field of politics — it can also work in the field of soccer."

"Yes, I've always believed in the magic of that cliché, 'Yes we can!'" agreed Kelly. "Success, in this context, isn't like nailing Jell-O to the wall. Yes, we can make it happen by evolving Super Soccer Strategists (SSS) who can get the job done and make it happen without wasting an iota of time. Indeed, we seem to have them already."

"Make no mistake about it." affirmed Sheldon. "We can attain superstardom in soccer. Yes, we can accomplish this feat by first having a non-back-pedaling resolve to push our men's national soccer team to the highest possible level. Yes, we can do so with some consistency in thinking, uniformity of resolve, determination, and understanding a unique U.S. pattern and style of soccer that must be developed and strengthened over time."

"Yes, we can make it happen," reassured Eric, "by implementing unique soccer tactics and creations on the field. Yes, we can do it. Yes, we can do it by planning and corner-coining-up a vibrantly clear 'redemption victory' in the next global soccer tournament."

"As far as I know," noted Nora, "certain subtle techniques and tactics in the field of soccer are often developed by players, with the assistance of savvy coaches and technical advisers. We need more smart, tactical, and speedy strikers in our men's team. From time immemorial, soccer, like other sports, like football and basketball, has involved a division of labor, which has to do with the breakdown of functions among players."

"Thanks a lot, Nora." exclaimed Jermaine. "You spoke as if you knew what was on my mind. I was going to say that in the field of soccer, there are always those players whose job is to initiate a strategy, and that strategy will be carried through until it gets to the opponent's goal area. I prefer to call them 'soccer strategy creationists or initiators.'"

"Of course, I got the message." remarked Hank. "Those strategists or creationists must be specially trained to always be able to construct and deliver solid strategies. Tactics come in when a strategy is moved to the opponent's goal posts. As they manipulate and wiggle their way into the opponent's home, trained Soccer Field Confusionists (SFCs) among our great midfielders should make sure that those creations and strategies are properly combined, as they'd do well to stop at nothing in trying to confuse their opponents."

"I understand what you mean, Hank," replied Larry, "as a former soccer player and midfielder myself. Those tactics will enable players to get around opposing defenders, maintain control of the ball, and support teammates while on the offensive. The idea is also to out-hustle your opponents with constant efforts, no matter how strong and big they appear physically. If what you mean by 'confusionism' is properly coordinated and maintained, it could render the opponent's team, no matter how strong, frustrated and scoreless, at least for some time."

"You got it, Larry." agreed Hank. "This type of 'confusionism' would involve a certain use of swift body movements, quick eyeball shifts, and some master dribbling techniques. Some of these creative tactics are employed by most of our great basketball players. At the end of the day, the whole strategy would've looked like a well-organized conspiracy that was eventually properly executed on the field of soccer."

"Haahaahaaa, I often prefer to call these players, I mean the 'confusionists,' Master Tactical Soccer Stylists (MTSS)," observed Melvin. "Our guys could take those cues. The aim of causing this 'deliberate confusion' is to get the opponents to disintegrate and permit the midfielders to arrive at the next stage."

"Permit me to come in here, guys." interjected Frederick. "An important stage, indeed. These tactics will also enable the strategists to create a chance for a prolific front-liner, who'd move swiftly down the opponent's flank without being crowded out by the opponent's upsurge to perfectly curl the ball into the net. Again, I think that 'confusionism,' if properly piloted, could lead the engineering soccer team in question to a skillful victory over its opponents. It almost always pays off in the end."

"Don't forget the next stage," hinted Keith, "which I believe is to cross the ball, with lightning speed, to any free and ready forward-liner(s), who'd then finalize the creations with some accuracy and target precision. To do this job well, forward-liners need to be true and reliable Soccer Field Precisionists (SFCs). This is my invention. 'Precisionism' shouldn't be seen as a type of fine art or painting, but an art or skill in soccer that must be introduced at all costs in our men's soccer system. It has a basic influence in great soccer playing because, without it, one would find it hard to imagine a clean and clear goal."

"I've not stopped believing that 'precisionism' is crucial in soccer, as you just mentioned, Keith," opined Lucius, "because without precision in shooting, unorganized players would come back home to tell fans cock and bull stories. May I add that even though 'precisionism' should be a special requirement, it might be helpful if it's also considered one of the criteria in the selection of good players."

"In addition to your comments, guys," responded Glenn, "I've always believed, as a former coach in Seattle, that for any team to be outstanding, most of the players should be highly proficient in the use of both their right and left feet, as the opponents are often prone to attacking the right foot. Moreover, attackers should always develop their skills in passing, dribbling, and shooting with both their right and left feet. A two-legged player is always an asset and advantage to a team's forward lines. Forward liners, attackers, and strikers should always be those who have been tested and proven when it comes to taking those shots that will get their soccer team clean goal scores. Of course, it's always done by firing or rocketing a shot into the opponent's goal with some degree of accuracy."

"It's doable," agreed Ashley, "but that needs serious trainings not only on how to fire shots with accuracy, but also how to build stamina, achieve balance in front of the goal posts, amid the push and pull from hawks in the persons of the opponents. It's time to be serious, to do the job with all thoughtfulness and to do it right. It's a time for the forward liners to stand strongly on their two feet. Smart attackers should, in no way at all, allow the ball to stay too long on their feet. It's a good ball handling to pass the ball to one's teammates, or to fire a shot into the net at any slightest given opportunity, before one gets into trouble."

"Haha... I'm glad that I'm now an American citizen," boasted Pedro, "and feel strong enough to make some contributions in soccer. In addition to what you've said, I believe that long ranging should also be seriously adopted as an aspect of the U.S. soccer style, but again with some level of precision and accuracy. This has to do with how players, especially midfielders, handle soccer shooting when necessary. Shooting shouldn't be limited to those taken from only near the goal line or penalty box. Shots fired from a distance further out from the goalmouth can also be a good opportunity for scoring. It's always done by kicking the ball with the front of the foot from a long range."

"Your contribution is fine, Pedro," noted Harrison. "Long ranging is a good idea. If possible, it's always better to do so early in the match as one of the intimidating strategies against the opponent's goalie. It helps a lot before the main strategies commence. Furthermore, there are excellent soccer drills and tactical lessons for how and when to execute long range shooting. These drills enable the players to sharpen their shooting skills."

"I love and follow your arguments, Harrison," commented Drew. "What I've come to discover is that good players know how to score from long range or from the half line. Savvy coaches encourage long-range passing, accuracy, and finishing, as these improve soccer a great deal. On the other hand, we need well-trained Soccer Field Deflectionists (SFDs), when the opponent crosses a ball that was supposed to be heading to our goal posts. 'Deflectionism' doesn't usher in a chaotic situation; rather, it clears off what would've resulted in a chaotic situation, making it easier for the deflectors to gain some advantage over a ball that was otherwise dangerously making its way to an undesirable destination."

"Haha. I'm excited by your idea, Drew!" exclaimed Matt, "having been in that business myself. Smart players can always deflect a quick, smart crossing. Free kicks can also be deflected away from the goal posts, but only with some level of expertise. But I think that without proper Soccer Field Positionism (SFP), an accurate 'deflectionism' may not always be achieved by a soccer player. 'Positionism' is important for all players, and for all sports, since without proper positioning, a player will lose balance and may not gain the stamina and balance to score a clean goal. This also involves quickly pushing the ball onto one's stronger foot and shooting across the goal. This is where conditioning, skill, and tactical knowledge are highly needed."

"My suggestion," added Nicolas, "is that shooting wide or skimming the bar should always be discouraged. Expertise in a soccer player lies in his ability to shoot not only a moving ball on the ground, but also a bouncing ball. It takes a player who knows how to position himself well. It could begin with concentrating on forcing a save from the opponent's goalkeeper, and by consequently creating different opportunities for oneself, so as to score at the slightest chance."

"For my suggestion," noted Hugh, "I should think we need a mature, balanced, unemotional, and highly impenetrable defense machinery — a type that can always hold off dangerous strikers from the opponent's team and prevent hitting our goalkeeper with a score. Smart and experienced defenders always move the ball away from the opponents, away from the midfield and toward the touchlines. Great defenders immediately attack any ball that gets close to their goal posts, while their co-defenders subdue the attacking opponents. How? By marking up the opponent and positioning themselves between the ball and the opponent, to prevent the opponent from getting at the ball. Very important."

"Your suggestions are crucial," agreed Rudy, "because a poor defense will have all the defenders attacking the ball. Defenders should maintain the highest poise and composure under both good and bad conditions, while supporting their co-defenders at all times. All the ideas and styles discussed above sound good, but they will take great soccer leaders and players to implement them properly. For the U.S. to rise in the field of global soccer, our players and leaders should always think and act big."

"There's also need for the power of positive thinking and positive acting." affirmed Chauncey. "By thinking big and acting big in soccer, we can finally start addressing the challenges that we have in the sport, and start solving problems we used to think were unsolvable. That's the only way we can begin to make progress in our most intractable problems in major international soccer. What are those striking issues that our men's soccer team faces when preparing to compete globally with other countries that rank much higher in soccer performance than we do? In dealing with those issues, it would be rewarding if we could think of what those issues look like before, during, and after our participation in soccer contests. Our future is bright, though."

"Even though I'm not an astrologer," noted Gregg, "I seem to believe, now more than ever before, that the planets, the moon, and even the great stars of the soccer universe seem to have aligned themselves to support our growth in soccer. They seem to have aligned themselves so that the great results we're aspiring toward in our nation's soccer engagements can best be achieved by following and strongly adhering to our 'think big' resolution in future soccer involvements."

"The implication of this resolution," observed Wilson, "is that we ought to persist with an unswerving resolve, determined to realize and drop what were our past mistakes and all those things that didn't work in our favor. Great progress will be made in soccer engineering, if those blind alleys are discovered and nipped in the bud."

"Great progress will be made if we say a big welcome to the Age of New Strategies and Solutions in addressing our soccer problems," remarked Derek. "What would you consider the biggest of the Think Big and Act Big solutions? Some of those solutions have been previously advanced and will be further advanced. However, forging a true prosperity in soccer boils down to creating lasting policies and methods that will enable us to quickly reverse the relatively mediocre status in our men's soccer team; I mean when compared with the great soccer superpowers, and forging true soccer prosperity in the US."

"I'm not a prophet," noted Isaiah, "but I think that the soccer industry and soccer engagements should be seen as an investment that will most likely change the demographics and, possibly, the sociology and economy of this great country, with visible dividends, no doubt. This is my opinion. It might also be a smart move on the part of the U.S., with millions of children playing soccer, to raise the travel fees for soccer.

"Let's not be too anxious to begin to fight right away." Isaiah continued. "Let's go, but let's, for now, move on to the comic section to celebrate *Xtmas* for our eyes and ears. Hopefully, this will calm our nerves, put more marrow into our bones and more grease to our elbows, as we learn from our past mistakes and move on to a greater future in soccer. Meanwhile, let's go comic, with soccer and soccer alone, guys."

# Chapter 6
## Comic Dimension

Are you ready? Please get ready. Come, see and listen with attention. It might be the most dramatic thing you haven't heard or seen in a while. It might even be the most exciting time you'll ever enjoy with others.

Michael: "Hello. I'm Michael Big Ears [*while running a pinkie over his right ear*]. It's necessary to remark that even though we should aspire to the highest victory, any soccer win or defeat shouldn't be for us, or for any nation on earth, an opportunity to fight with one another, as sometimes obtains in some uncivilized and small nations. Failure to win in any sports engagement shouldn't be seen as a disposition toward anger, name-calling, or bickering over contracts unfulfilled. Thank goodness, we don't have such a crazy culture here."

Chris: Haahaaahaa. You're right, Mr. Big Ears. Yes, thank goodness, we don't have that sort of culture here, but we love to win and win big. I wish to add that failure to win in soccer should also not lead to a situation where some people nag others to death or bite someone's ears off; of course, such news would get around fast and become needlessly provoking."

Robert: "Haahaahaaa. I'm the Little Robert Peanuts (*while dropping peanuts into his mouth with head tilted backward*). I was gonna say that it may just be a time to eat peanuts, or lick peanut butter together with others while we're alive. Listen to what I'm going to say if you've got good ears. A farmer once wanted to know if there's really any peanuts or peanut butter in an afterlife. No one is sure, but we eat peanut butter while we're alive here on earth. Shared friendship should continue to exist among players, the coach, and soccer committee members, because any soccer contest, though highly competitive, is just a game. It should be a time to be united like never before."

Thomas: "Hi, I'm Thomas Funnyman Any type of mutual love that doesn't straddle the fence must be kept in place. Accusations of betrayal, breach of trust or jilted partnerships should all be discouraged. And, above all, we've got to have fun, alright?" (*While making funny faces and at times emitting farting sounds from his mouth, and backing it up with quick apologies! This behavior was often followed by outbursts of laughter from the audience).*

He continued: "I recall a few riddles and jokes about our past World Cup soccer involvements and the recently concluded soccer Tournament in South Africa. Our men did quite well, there's no doubt about it. But I think that it would sound sweet to tweet them on soccer websites (*laughter from the audience*). I've just thought of what it would look like when put into a fiction or comic display. No doubt, it'll get people laughing all the way to their targets, especially to the banks, for those who have biggies or some 'raw cash' sitting in abandoned accounts; it's your money, right? Call them lucky laughers. Let's see, but let's make use of our senses in hearing more. I think we all need Big Ears just for now. Have fun, and this time eat more candies and peanuts from strangers (*laughter from the audience*)."

Commentator Extraordinaire: "Dear friends. This play plus comedy promises to be delightful. If you're not the hosts or entertainers, maybe you're the spectators or the guests of honor. At last, there should be plenty of interesting invitation cards to accept, so you don't have to stay home and hide behind a book or computer.

Note that fictitious names are assigned to the referee and the three moderators in this show, but with their real names withheld. It's wise to point out that the comedy is unilateral; it covers only one side of two soccer competing teams. It's more of a message specifically directed to us to wake up and win big in soccer: "Wake up and win ... because to score big is to win big." It's purposely done to expose some soccer issues that need to be fixed and strike at some positively teachable moments, but, above all, create some fun.

The show will be more of a verbal soccer comedy than real action soccer display, since only one side (the U.S.) will be mostly represented in the five comic sessions. These are unspoken feelings that players entertain sometimes in the fields during contests, which the cast-mates put into words; it's like putting words into the mouth of our imaginary players. The intention is to douse the impact of people's and players' possible feelings, especially after all the 2010 men's FIFA World Cup and, above all, the final loss that brought the U.S. team back home winless (without winning big). In this comic display, what's needed is ignoring what you see but keeping what you hear (and what you're told) without raising any objections, unless when they are absolutely necessary. This idea would end up saving much time for the spectators and perhaps last for only about an hour. The comedy begins."

The first mock match between the U.S. and England: Inside a large auditorium in Philadelphia with all eyes on them, eleven kids and cast-mates kicked off their sneakers, put on soccer boots, and started playing with one another in a makeshift field that mimics a moderately-equipped but small field. It's remarkable that the opponents' teams weren't physically represented. The eleven kids, with one adult in his late 30s who played the part of the referee, and another in his late 40s who played the role of the coach, entered the stage within view of the spectators gathered for this event. With the exception of the referee, the coach, and the moderators, who'd help relay what the actors do, the players (the kids) were numbered according to their positions of play as if in a real field (starting with the goalkeeper as No. 1). In a prologue fashion, the first kid actor (No. 1), holding a ball in his hand as a goalkeeper would and playing the role of the goalkeeper, shouted to introduce the comic display.

Jersey No. 1 (Goalie): "Hey! What's wrong with you there, guys?

Cher! What are you doing? Are you still sleeping? Please know that we're right here in the field." Cher: "It's never too late to wake up and win; there's plenty of time to do just that, right here and right now."

Audience: *(laughter)*

Jersey No. 1: "You can't sleep or nap your way into the opponent's goalmouth, buddy. Nobody does that — it doesn't happen and never happens. That wouldn't lead us to victory."

Audience: *(laughter)*

Tony: "I'm shocked by this allegation against Cher in this field. I don't believe it — I don't think he's that kind of guy. I've been on this team with him for almost three years now, and he's been a terrific player and never naps on the field of soccer. In fact, he's among those who have kept our team in excellent shape."

Audience: *(laughter)*

No. 1: "Excellent shape? Well, I think we're doing better than England in this present face-off."

Audience: *(laughter)*

No. 1: "However, there are gross things you don't know about Cher . . . and our team."

Audience: *(laughter)*

Jersey No. 2 (Cher . . . lo): "Come on, stop it. Ugly rumors seem to be going round against me now, even when I have only the best of intentions."

Audience: *(laughter)*

He continued: "Goalie, you're accusing me of sleeping? Am I really sleeping? Who tells you that? How did you know that and how did you find out, gossip boy?"

Audience: *(laughter)*

Cher: "No, I'm not sleeping or napping. I'm walking, running, and playing at the same time; just making sure that we win and win big."

Jersey No. 1: "I know that you're doing all those stuffs now, but you forgot to mention jumping."

Audience: *(laughter)*

Jersey No. 1: "I know that you're walking, running, and playing, but indeed, not playing soccer."

Audience: *(laughter)*

Jersey No. 6: "Well, if you're running, Cher . . . Please don't run too far and too hard. I'm only worried about your boots that seem to be too tight around your feet, and in between your toes."

Audience: *(laughter)*

Jersey No. 3: "Sorry to interrupt you, but when you run too hard I'm sure you lose a lot of salt, sweating like a cow all through the match."

Audience: *(laughter)*

Jersey No. 3: "Better save some energy, for you'll need it later."

Audience: *(laughter)*

Jersey No. 8: "Also, there should be no waste of salt of any sort, at all, in here, no matter how small, for someone needs it out there . . . someone out there gotta cook."

Audience: *(laughter)*

Jersey No. 2: "Oh yeah. Salt is needed for cooking — I never thought of it that way, buddy. It's good to have people who not only think, but think out of the box."

Audience: *(laughter)*

Jersey No. 4: "If we take a cue from you, Cher . . ., we'll all end up having our arms, legs, and faces crusted in a shimmery white, salt crystal coating."

Audience: *(laughter)*

Jersey No. 2: "Don't ever let someone take up your precious time when it's about an issue that doesn't involve them…"

Audience: *(laughter)*

Jersey No. 1: "You're right. Runners spit and blow their noses all through a match. They simply do. Look across at our opponents to see someone doing just that. Over there."

Audience: *(laughter)*

Jersey No. 1: "Better get down to Fort Lauderdale where you'll have a better chance to play with kids. I mean, only with kids who aren't serious . . . but you're not gonna do that in here, on our field — for this is a global contest."

Audience: *(laughter)*

Jersey No. 2: "Don't worry about me. If my face is covered with spit and snot at the end of this match, kindly cheer me on, anyway."

Audience: *(laughter)*

Jersey No. 2: "It means that I stand out among the crowd and, therefore, need some thumbs up and perhaps some pay raise."

Audience: *(laughter)*

Chris (Mod. 1): "Get out of here, please, go and get a job out there. Tell me, are you looking for any good job that you'd wish to add to soccer playing or something?"

Audience: *(laughter)*

Jersey No. 2: "Yes, of course I do, I'm working on it, but I gotta hang in here for now, until I find a good one out there. I'm only figuring out how not to go broke."

Audience: *(laughter)*

Jersey No. 2: "By the way, I'm one of the players from Long Island, New York."

Jersey No. 1: "Okay, so you're from the Wrong Island."

Audience: *(laughter)*

Jersey No. 1: "There are millions of job seekers out there who aren't players, like you. It's good to look for a gainful job, but you gotta be sharp, driven, and hardworking to get a job out there for a living; the same applies on the field, including ours."

Audience: (laughter)

Jersey No. 2: "You're right; I wanna eke out a living in here, for now. That's what I'm doing right here on this field, to make sure that we win big so I can keep making a living for my family and myself. I'm gonna hang in here for now and never let go."

Audience: (laughter)

Matt (Mod 2): "Get out of here. No one hangs anyone here in the US."

Audience: (laughter)

Coach: "Wait a minute. That's what I'm also seeing happening here, now — you're hanging in there . . . again, napping or something. But I know and see that you wanna make a living for yourself. So, does it make any sense that you're in here hanging around and roaming about aimlessly like one of those inside-the-field fans watching us now?"

Audience: *(laughter)*

Coach: "Again, I mean hanging around for absolutely nothing."

Audience: *(laughter)*

Jersey No. 6: "Cher . . . ! Sometimes, what's best for you isn't best for the team and for our country. Your life's career is waiting for you out there. Someone gotta help you step into that pretty job out there but not in here, surely, not in here. You don't belong here, buddy."

Audience: (laughter)

Jersey No. 2: "Please stop it. Why are you all talking to me that way, as if I did anything wrong? I'm doing my best in here for everybody, including yourselves and the goalie. Otherwise, he'd not stand there at the goal post — believe me he'd be literally dead."

Audience: (laughter)

Jersey No. 4: "Of course, one man's garbage could be another man's skill, even without the garbage owner knowing or owning it."

Audience: *(laughter)*

Jersey No. 4: "That's exactly the lesson I'm learning from you, right now."

Audience: *(laughter)*

Jersey No. 7: "For now, we're gonna keep you in here, anyway, as we don't wanna let you go out there and begin to lead an indulgent life that can make the American *Caligula* blush."

Audience: *(prolonged laughter)*

Jersey No. 2: "Thank you. I'm gonna stay here anyway. I'm not yet old enough to retire now, and moreover, I have no other means of livelihood."

Audience: *(laughter)*

Jersey No. 5: "They say that if you find a job you like in life, you'll never consider it a job at all . . ."

Audience: *(laughter)*

Jersey No. 10: "Okay, guys, stop bothering him. Don't worry about only one player, as that's not gonna help us as a team. I'm already fighting and giving out the last drop of my life's blood to make sure that we win and win big."

Jersey No. 8: "We're not worried about only one player. It's not only a person's problem. Three others are involved in this mess, but we're gradually tracking them down one by one. I'm happy that you're not one of them."

Audience: *(laughter)*

Jersey No. 9 *(gesturing to Jersey No. 10)*: "Please buddy, don't drop any blood in here; we're not here for an unwelcome blood drive . . ."

Audience: (laughter)

Jersey No. 9: "We're on a football field. Just 'drop' the ball and not blood into the opponent's net. Use your right foot, left foot, your head or torso, whichever one you prefer, find suitable, healthy, or fit to do the job at this point — that's it."

Audience: *(laughter)*

Jersey No. 3 *(gesturing further to Jersey No. 10)*: "Don't invite vampires in here either, dude."

Audience: *(laughter)*

Jersey No. 3: "We know that Halloween is gently approaching. What do you plan to be when it's here, a vampire?"

Audience: *(laughter)*

Jersey No. 10: "Sorry, I've not been tricking or treating for over 15 years now . . ."

Audience: *(laughter)*

Jersey No. 7 (pointing a pinkie to Jersey No. 10): "My advice is that you remain as totally convincing as you've been in your non-suicidal and harmless role on this field."

Audience: *(laughter)*

Jersey No. 10: "Well, it doesn't matter if I drop or deposit any blood here, for, as the saying goes, it's better to give than to receive."

Audience: *(prolonged laughter)*

Jersey No. 10: "You're encouraged to give blood, as you might need it someday . . ."

Audience: (laughter)

Jersey No. 9: "You're right! Moreover, it's written in the Bible, thou shalt love thy neighbor as thyself. If donating blood can help others, then it should be your duty and joy to give."

Audience: *(laughter)*

Jersey No. 5: "No, no, no — not that stuff! Don't even give us that stuff; don't give us blood! Just give us scores and more goals; that's all we want, and that's the only way you can be generous to us and to our great nation."

Audience: *(laughter)*

All other player/actors suddenly broke out in a song: "All we're saying . . . is give us more goals . . ." (This was sung about three times by a group of three kids, following John Lennon's tune of "All we're saying, is give peace a chance.")

Audience: [*Laughter and applause*]

Coach: "A shot has just been fired into the hands of the English goalkeeper now by Clinnie, and we got a goal! Hip hip hurray! We've secured an equalizer . . . thank goodness!"

The audience roared in excitement upon hearing that it was a score for the U.S.

Jersey No. 11: "I overheard the English goalkeeper murmuring something . . ."

Jersey No. 6: "What was he saying?"

Jersey No. 11: "He said, 'I'm not a happy man . . . Something hasn't gone right. They've killed my hope! The ball has just wrongly slipped off my hands . . . is it possible I could have it back?'"

Audience: *(laughter)*

Jersey No. 5: "I've seen that invasion of privacy is what you do so well..."

Audience: *(laughter)*

Jersey No. 6: "And what was your reply to him?"

Jersey No. 11: "Can't get any more embarrassing, friend. Sorry, I can't help you. Good try, but too late for you to have it back!"

Audience: (laughter)

With all the players and actors breaking out again into song: "All we're saying . . . is give us more goals" (*sung in the tune of John Lennon's 'All we're saying, is give peace a chance ...*'), a voice from the audience says: "Wow! These kids are great singers ... but they're not from Singapore, though!"

Audience: [*Laughter and applause*]

This session ended with long, drawn out laughter and applause from the audience for the actors who exited the stage.

The second mock match between the U.S. and Slovenia: This section began with Tony (Mod 3) coming into the stage with a dim countenance.

The second moderator approached him and said he also intended the same message for the entire audience: "If you missed the World Cup between the U.S. and Slovenia, don't worry. Just be happy, for you'll catch up with it through our young comic brothers, right here."

Tony (Mod 3) and the rest of the audience: *(laughter)*

After this prologue, the entire team rushed onto the stage with a soccer ball. Stepping out, the player with Jersey No. 8 said: "The only thing I know that's happening now is that we're playing against a small and pinkie country, and we're definitely gonna win."

Jersey No. 7: "Are you sure that we're gonna win?"

Jersey No. 5: "What can a rat do to a giraffe?"

Audience: *(laughter)*

Wilson (*whispered in the audience*): "As a nation, they're small in population, but seem great. They might even be greater than what we appear to be in soccer; whoosh!"

Jersey No. 6: "You never know, 'never judge an old woman by the size of her shoes!'"

Audience: *(laughter)*

Jersey No. 5 (Sean): "Hi, Jerry, are you doing alright?"

Jersey No. 9: "Yes, of course! I can feel the heat coming out of me as I run. I also sleep well."

Audience: *(laughter)*

Jersey No. 1: "Hope not in here."

Audience: *(laughter)*

Jersey No. 9: "No! I mean when I go home."

Audience: *(laughter)*

Jersey No. 1: "Are you sure? Positive?"

Audience: *(laughter)*

Jersey No. 9: "Yes, of course! Sleep is my next best friend, but only after soccer!"

Audience: *(laughter)*

Jersey No. 2: "Come on guys, hey, hey, hey! The ball is rolling by, it's coming toward me now. In fact, it's a goooooooooal!"

Jersey No. 3: "Hey, hey, hey, grab it! Grab it! Grab that ball, please!"

Audience: *(laughter)*

Jersey No. 2: "Oh my gooo . . ., the ball bounced off my bald head and rolled into the net. You should've grabbed it for me! Oh noooh!"

Audience: *(laughter)*

Jersey No. 3: "It's the job of the goalie to grab the ball . . . not me . . ."

Audience: *(laughter)*

Jersey No. 4: "Too late! But your cry should've grabbed the attention of our lenient but great goalkeeper!"

Audience: *(laughter)*

Jersey No. 7: "But you gotta grab *Osama* first before yelling at the goalkeeper to grab the ball . . ."

Audience: *(prolonged laughter)*

Jersey No. 1: "They'd always tell us where he's hiding. But they still can't grab him!"

Audience: *(laughter)*

Jersey No. 1: "And you expect me to grab the ball? That's crazy!"

Audience: *(prolonged laughter)*

Jersey No. 8: "Someone puts a brick wall in our way whenever we appear to be closing in on him . . ."

Audience: *(laughter)*

Jersey No. 1: "How the heck you thought I could grab the ball . . . it *pee-weeed* away like the bare-footed runner and long-goateed Osama . . ."

Audience: *(laughter)*

Jersey No. 5: "Whhhh . . . but this time . . . into our net."

Audience: *(laughter)*

Jersey No. 6: "For now, four legs, good, two legs bad. I mean only now."

Audience: *(prolonged laughter)*

Jersey No. 1: "That's right. Four legs are supposed to give you an edge over your opponents and help you grab the ball faster."

Audience: *(laughter)*

Jersey No. 2: "Don't worry about it. I think that we're doing all right."

Audience: *(laughter)*

Jersey No. 2: "Americans like their players to be a little fallible, anyway."

Audience: *(laughter)*

Jersey No. 10: "Ouch! I'm feeling like stiff and sore right now, with a whacked knee and thigh that I can't even move or grab the ball anymore, much less run."

Jersey No. 2: "Oh, no! That's a disaster for us. Did you overextend it? Please fight to overcome whatever is your knee and thigh strain and injury before the next match. Sorry about that."

Audience: *(laughter)*

Jersey No. 5: "I've discovered that you have a high end and open-toe socks, and that could cost you an arm or a leg."

Audience: *(laughter)*

Jersey No. 4: "It's not soccer specific."

Audience: *(laughter)*

Jersey No 7: "As long as you don't have both arthritis and stomach upset right here in the field, we're fine with you."

Audience: *(laughter)*

Jersey No 7: "Keep hanging in there, and please keep doing your best."

Audience: *(laughter)*

Jersey No. 1 *(talking to Jersey No 10)*: "What are we gonna do? Please don't give up — keep trying."

Audience: *(laughter)*

Jersey No. 9: "I pray that you please lose the pains quickly, but not the ball, in the course of our arduous journey in here."

Audience: *(laughter)*

Jersey No. 7: "My advice is that you keep going and hanging in there."

Tony (Mod 1): "Oh boy! Nobody hangs anybody in the US, and not even in secret."

Audience: *(laughter)*

Jersey No. 9: "I'm sorry that one of us is feeling that way, but we gotta keep moving. Ouch! I'm also beginning to feel like I'm losing my right leg from the thigh down. Just feeling like a thief that got nothing but a shot in the leg."

Audience: (laughter)

Jersey No. 3: "Oh, c'mon. That's another disaster in a different wig."

Audience: *(laughter)*

Jersey No. 1: "Well, if the leg doesn't work at this point, the hand could equally do the same tricks. How's that, guys? A one-time Diego Maradona style?"

Audience: *(laughter)*

Jersey No. 6: "Please be smart enough to do that for us and all will be fine."

Audience: *(laughter)*

Jersey No. 9: "Sorry, I can't. I feel like a fowl unable to pee . . . just as other creatures comfortably do."

Audience: *(laughter)*

Coach: "No, this isn't a place for peeing. Remember, it's a soccer field."

Audience: *(laughter)*

Jersey No. 9: "Sorry, I'm using some figures of speech from my culture, as I wasn't originally born in the U.S. It's not that I'm feeling like or planning to do that."

Audience: *(laughter)*

Coach: "But you gotta figure out and know more about things and people from other cultures quite well before you say things, or use words and figures of speech like that."

Audience: *(laughter)*

Jersey No. 11: "That sounds like a pretty nasty culture."

Audience: *(laughter)*

Jersey No. 8: "Jokes aside. Please try and try, you never know. You could somehow make something happen now."

Audience: *(laughter)*

Jersey No. 9: "What do you mean by 'something'?"

Audience: *(laughter)*

Jersey No. 9: "Do you not think that we're playing against a mighty team or something? As a nation, they looked small to us, initially, but now seem quite ready to score at will. Please watch it and please read my lips."

Audience: *(laughter)*

Coach: "Hey, hey, hey, please arrest that guy swiftly heading toward our goal post for a score . . ."

Jersey No. 4: "That's the job of a cop (police)."

Audience: *(laughter)*

Coach: "I'm not a cop who arrests people . . . but they do so only after thorough investigations, anyway."

Audience: *(laughter)*

Coach: "Are you helping and shielding his effort to score against us? Look at him moving up swiftly . . . Please, there should be no bargain at our goal post."

Jersey No. 4: "I'm not shielding or helping any opponent on this field. Moreover, no one in here is a criminal for an arrest."

Audience: *(laughter)*

Coach: "Oh my God, it's a gooooal . . . This is ridiculous. See, they're now leading us 2-0 and they scored the first goal in 13 minutes."

Jersey No. 6: "We have a great goalkeeper. Surely he gotta do something next time . . ."

Audience: *(laughter)*

Jersey No. 1: "Hi, buddy, you don't wanna go through the hell of catching those missiles in the name of soccer ball shots . . . You know what I mean?"

Audience: *(laughter)*

Jersey No. 1: "You don't wanna endure that crowd that invade and besiege our goalpost under your watch, guys."

Audience: *(laughter)*

Jersey No. 1: "I'm here only to help you stop those missiles. Enough is enough."

Audience: *(laughter)*

Jersey No. 10: "Mr. Goalie and all of you, guys. Please don't worry, be happy. We gotta fight to win — that's what we're in here for."

Audience: *(laughter)*

Jersey No. 7: "I like people who are optimistic, but don't fight for a penalty award. Just get us a top-notch score from outside the penalty box."

Audience: *(laughter)*

Coach: "Oh no! My problem is our defense — what the heck are they doing there? It's becoming atrocious."

Audience: *(laughter)*

Jersey No. 10: "Whatever, we gotta get a fabulous finish."

Audience: *(laughter)*

Coach: "Thanks. That's what I wanna hear from all of you right now. Please get to work right away."

Audience: *(laughter)*

Chris (Mod. 2): "The Slovenian guy has slipped and now Lannie has the ball in his control. There he's, moving toward their goal area like lightening. He stops and looks for a pass but none was available. But we now have a shot from an angle into the net of the Slovenians . . . He's just secured the first goal for us . . . It's a goooooal . . . That will get the game right on, thank goodness." (*The spectators sprinting with thrills and excitement, while some shed tears of joy and yelled: "USA, USA, USA."*)

Coach: "Thank you, Lannie, and thank you for being here . . . I'm thrilled by this great performance . . . Again, thank you."

Tony (Mod. 1): "Why are you crying, folks?"

Audience: *(laughter)*

Two women from the audience responded: "We're not crying. Only tears of joy."

Audience: *(laughter and applause)*.

Jersey No. 10: "Thank you for cheering. You haven't seen anything yet. We're coming right back . . . again."

Matt (Commentator 1): "Here is Joie . . . he's coming, he's heading right into the box of their penalty area. Yes, he got the ball from halfway on the right. I don't care where the ball is coming from . . . my only joy is that Joie has it now. Here he's — Mike got a perfectly timed running as he got the ball from Joie . . . He fires a high one into the net, and folks, it's a goooooal again. It's a gooooooooal! Another great goal for the U.S. Thank you, Mike, and well done."

Jersey No. 1: "Thank you guys. We've woken up and won. We got a draw, but it's still a great fight and a great win. I can see our coach almost dancing. Can't believe how it's just ended."

Tony (Mod. 1): "Fantastic indeed! Great job, guys, you've done us proud. Thank you, Lannie, thank you, Joie and Mike, thank you, goalkeeper, Timmie, and above all thank you coach Bobbie, thank you, American fans. What a thrilling finish. Remain strong, for America loves you guys."

As soon as this goal was scored, all the actors exited the stage to prepare to come back for the next session. The following observations are coming from some spectators and members of the audience:

Glenn: "But why, why, and why did the referee cancel our third goal, as we would've won this match cleanly? How could he do that and never give a good reason? Isn't it a disgrace?"

Kevin *(from the audience)*: "He screwed us up and got away with it. Things like this make me not wanna be a soccer fan or a fan of any stupid sport. They never give reasons for anything, anyway, but this referee seems to be inexperienced. Unbelievable! Everything here now seems to me like a disgrace."

Andrew *(from the audience)*: "No! I beg to disagree! Everything here isn't a disgrace for me, even as the referee was a disgrace and one of our opponents feigning injury, a shitty disgrace! Our guys did a great job!"

Guy: "Soccer isn't a disgrace. It's not a stupid sport. It's beautiful and the best sport in the world as far as I know! Rather, some human beings in here among the fans are a disgrace. You don't wanna mention their names . . ."

Audience (*those who are listening to this brief exchange*): "Haaahaaahaaaaaa."

Robby: "Andrew should've suggested that the referee be banned from future World Cup and he'll be just fine, but he didn't do that. I'm making that suggestion now as a fine soccer fan!"

Andrew: "Fine soccer fan? I think you're rather a fired soccer fan . . . You're fired!

Audience: *(laughter)*

Robby: "Why? Because I know you've never been a soccer fan, anyway. I've been looking at you — you're one of those who become cheerleaders only when the going gets good on the field."

Audience: *(laughter)*

Kevin: "We shouldn't have let the Slovenians get into the game the way they did in the first place, but forget it. That looks like an American win stolen from her in a broad daylight while everyone looks on."

Audience: *(laughter)*

Guy: "Of course, people are people and would always look on, no matter what you do. You can't close their eyes, it doesn't happen!"

Audience: *(laughter)*

Peter: "What did the referee call for? Wow! Was that referee blind, some people ask?"

Rudolph: "He was not blind and perhaps had a good night's sleep. He had pretty good eyesight even when he made that decision. What he was doing was very clear to him ..."

Audience: *(laughter)*

Donald: "But what was his problem? Dimsy was said to be at the left corner, but people are asking to know what he was doing there."

Audience: *(laughter)*

Donald: "Pushing the opponents' defender or the opponents' defender pushing him?"

Audience: *(laughter)*

Kevin: "I think it has to do with one of the opponent's players feigning injury at the slightest contact . . . Isn't that ridiculous?"

Audience: *(laughter)*

Donald: "Well, let's move on to beat Algeria and forget the past."

Audience: *(laughter)*

Richard: "I'm glad all these exchanges are coming from all of us who are members of the watching audience. Beating other soccer teams sounds easy in your mouth, like ABC!"

Audience: *(laughter)*

Jersey No 7: "There are some ignorant people out there saying some dumb things . . . Some people expect that if you're a U.S. men's soccer player, you're supposed to just blow everybody out and win . . . ."

Audience: *(laughter)*

Jersey No 7: "It doesn't work that way in the global soccer . . ."

Alex: "Well, without the intention of rolling back to what Kevin said earlier, let me mention that if everything here seemed to him like a disgrace, it doesn't seem like a disgrace to me at all! I believe that we can still go ahead and build up more graces with future soccer encounters!"

Alfredo: *"Muchas gracias!"* Alex: *"De nada, amigo!"*

*The third mock soccer match between the U.S. and Algeria:* With the auditorium still packed with the audience, fans, and spectators, one of the kid actors, wearing jersey No. 3, rolls the ball into the stage to signify the start and the entrance of other player actors. "What an expected soccer match-up with Algeria," he said. "I'm glad every tough player that we have is on board."

Audience: *(laughter)*

Jersey No. 7: "I think we can take on this Algerian team. I don't see us fighting like crazy, as we did in the past matchers, hoping no one plays a spoiler."

Audience: *(laughter)*

Jersey No. 8: "Too soon to tell, because these guys may give you surprises."

Jersey No. 7: "That's not a problem, as long as their style of game doesn't grow concussive . . ."

Audience: *(laughter)*

Jersey No. 7: "Moreover, we don't have to dig deeper!"

Audience: *(laughter)*

Francine *(from the audience)*: "Too bad I missed the start of this match, but at least I'm going to catch up with the highlights, now. I'm sure it'll be fun to watch!"

Jersey No. 5 *(gesturing to the audience and spectators)*: "Are you watching? Our opponents seem to be going after us now that we haven't been able to score."

Jersey No. 1: "Well, nothing is too late as long as there's life."

Audience: *(laughter)*

Jersey No. 9: "You'll be forgiven, anyway, even if you didn't express the same confidence as you did when you missed a ball that was up for grabs in the previous match!"

Audience: *(laughter)*

Coach: "What's happening, guys? Our defense in this match looks suspect and porous."

Jersey No. 4: "It doesn't matter, sir, as long as we have an offense that's aggressive!"

Audience: *(laughter)*

Jersey No. 1: "Do you mean you wanna give them a leeway into our goalposts with a weak defense? That will look like telling them that the goalposts are open to everybody and wide open for everything to penetrate . . . Tell me, who on earth does that?"

Audience: *(prolonged laughter)*

Jersey 8: "Surely, you don't wanna leave the goalie in a hot soup, as if he was tied up to a corner."

Audience: *(laughter)*

Jersey No. 5: "Of course, you don't wanna leave the net wide open and undefended. That's not right and will never be right in any generation!"

Audience: *(laughter)*

Jersey No. 6: "That's not the type of promo, publicity, and generosity that we're calling for now!"

Audience: *(laughter)*

Coach: "Your generosity will be better and more appreciated only when you score."

Audience: *(laughter)*

Jersey No. 9: "You seem to be pulling our legs this whole time!"

Coach: "If I pull your legs, what are you gonna use to play? You need your legs to score goals for us to win."

Audience: *(laughter)*

Coach: "Shrinking tactics don't make it to the goalposts, because our goalposts aren't shielded from our opponent's shots."

Audience: *(laughter)*

Jersey No. 7: "No, I mean we gotta score in the nick of time. But that's not gonna help matters right now."

Audience: *(laughter)*

Jersey No. 3: "Thank goodness, the Algerians don't seem to be putting much pressure on us, as their counterattack isn't that threatening, The best chance they got with a short-range shot only struck the bar."

Jersey No. 6: "Okay! If that attempt to score isn't intimidating, it's annoying!"

Audience: *(laughter)*

Coach: "Hey, Joie (Jersey No. 9), what happened to those tons and tons of great chances you got to score? What are you waiting for?"

Audience: *(laughter)*

Coach: "We gotta get out and score early and not wait for penalty kick chances, as that's not the best way to decide a good winner."

Audience: *(laughter)*

Jersey No. 8: "How long are you gonna keep missing those chances that keep slipping away and never come back?"

Audience: *(laughter)*

Jersey No 9: "Hi, buddy, just be nice now! Don't cash in on that to feather your nest . . ."

Audience: *(laughter)*

Jersey No. 8: "Sorry, I don't have a nest because I'm not a bird . . ."

Audience: *(laughter)*

Jersey No. 9 (Joie): "Enough about me, let's talk about you, now."

Audience: *(laughter)*

Jersey No. 8: "Promise me not to go negative . . ."

Audience: *(laughter)*

Jersey No. 6: "Because it's not good to burden people with your negative feelings as they've got plenty of theirs."

Audience: *(laughter)*

Jersey No. 3: "Release your anger and frustration in a way that's positive and carefully controlled . . . ."

Audience: *(laughter)*

Jersey No. 7: "Only do good and avoid evil."

Audience: *(laughter)*

Jersey No. 8: "What did you say?"

Jersey No. 7: "Just wanna fend off some unpleasantness with a simple cliché."

Audience: *(laughter)*

Jersey No. 9 (Joie): "Expect to get something less poking than I got."

Audience: *(laughter)*

Jersey No. 8: "Well, let's see what happens, I'm only keeping my options open at this point . . ."

Audience: *(laughter)*

Jersey No.1: "But you don't wanna leave your options open when you get the chance to score . . ."

Audience: *(laughter)*

Coach: "Hey, hey, Mike, the ball is right there now for you to score. Please don't miss that opportunity!"

Jersey No. 8: "Sorry that one slipped off my bald head and went off the post. My follicles have been terribly fleeing. I apologize!"

Audience: *(prolonged laughter)*

Jersey No. 5: "You don't have any apology eyes, having looked you deep into the eyes!"

Audience: *(laughter)*

Commentator No. 2: "This looks like a good chance to score for the U.S. team, as the ball appears to be right there on the courts of Jersey Nos. 6 and 7. We hope they might do something meaningful and wonderful this time!"

Audience: *(laughter)*

Jersey No. 6: "Though I came all the way from the midfield…this is my opportunity to score, but my heart is pounding and sounding like the engine of the old British Morris Minor . . ."

Audience: *(laughter)*

Jersey No. 11: "Me too, my mind was screaming and screeching and almost body-popping as I waited for what would happen next . . . as the opponent got closer to our goalkeeper . . ."

Audience: *(laughter)*

Jersey No.10: "I think that they're doing their job and we gotta do our job too . . ."

Audience: *(laughter)*

Jersey No. 8: "We're not gonna score now; we gotta wait until the last minute into the game to break their hearts!"

Audience: *(laughter)*

Jersey No. 7: "No, dude! You gotta do it now, do it quick, and do it right. Please don't let the opponents break your hearts first."

Audience: *(laughter)*

Jersey No. 11: "I'm pretty sure that our goalie is at work and we're on the winning side and this is gonna be the worst defeat against Algeria."

Jersey No. 6: "I'm not sure what you're saying. I've always maintained that when a shark is hungry, it doesn't really matter how good you're in water . . . . She's gotta eat, anyway!"

Audience: *(laughter)*

Jersey No. 5: "Our goalie is doing great too, but I don't think we're gonna win the World Cup with a defense that's this weak. I don't think they'll go too far in the knock-out rounds."

Jersey No. 8: "We're getting knocked out already and you're still thinking of winning the World Cup? You must be kidding like crazy!"

Audience: *(laughter)*

Coach: "Here it comes, the ball is pushed down toward our opponent's goalposts to our clear advantage. He pushes it to Lannie, guys, and I think fortune is running in our favor now. How fortunate we are! It's a gooooal! A clean gooooooooal! Isn't it incredible?" Audience: *(shouts of joy and applause)*

Other responses from the audience and spectators:

Julie *(from the audience)*: "It's a great day to be an American and a soccer-supporting fan, no matter when the score finally came. I'm thrilled!"

Ryan: "What a breathtaking finish for us and a heartbreaking finish for Algeria."

Audience: *(laughter)*

Ryan: "I think the U.S. is gonna win the World Cup, as it's the best game of the World Cup so far. God bless America, God bless the U.S.!!!"

Carl: "Please, let everybody in here and out there go USA in soccer!!! It's an unbelievable finish and a terrific last minute win, buddy, but never count your chickens before they're hatched, as we're gonna take on Ghana for the second round soon."

Billie: "By the way, how long did it take us to score the winning goal?"

Audience: *(laughter)*

Jim: "Yes, it took almost 92 minutes! Whatever it took, a goal is a goal. Half bread is better than cookies or a stick of pretzels!"

Audience: *(laughter)*

Dannie: "Never trust a team that will wait until stoppage time to score only a goal . . ."

Audience: *(laughter)*

Dannie: "It's to console the fans!"

Audience: *(laughter)*

Genevieve: "Of course, we're not gonna put our hands down in clapping for them and cheering them on, until we grab the cup."

Audience: *(laughter)*

Chris (Mod. No. 1): "Thanks to Lannie for taking a big leap by scoring the lone goal. Thank you for being pretty creative in the field of soccer. You're world class!"

Will: "Wait a minute! Do you mean that the other players aren't world class?"

Chris: "No, I didn't say that. I'm the moderator and only moderating what I observed, and comments from fans."

Audience: *(laughter)*

Josh: "They're all doing great job, but what do you think of those ones roaming about and around the goalkeeper?"

Audience: *(laughter)*

Tony (Mod. No. 1): "Ha ha, stop it, don't go there. They're doing a whole lot of a good job in there, too. Those guys do a good and smart backdropping; too, otherwise the goalie will be in a pretty hot seat."

Audience: *(laughter)*

Kevin: "I think that our guys gotta wake up more, as I can now see our opponents itching to score."

Audience: *(laughter)*

Matt (Mod. No. 3): "I think you're right! But it's said there are only two cures for the opponent's scoring itch. What are those cures? — Injury or death!"

Audience: *(laughter)*

Matt (Mod. No. 3): "In our case, you either score or quit. The good news is that you gotta choose one."

Audience: *(laughter)*

Jersey No. 7: "Never mind, guys, we're exploring one more score in addition to the one we got!"

Audience: *(laughter)*

Tony (Mod. No. 1): "My hunch is that they won't like it when you tell them that you're exploring a score."

Audience: *(laughter)*

Jersey No. 8: "Of course, not!"

Audience: *(laughter)*

Tony (Mod. No. 1): "Thank you for sharing. I never thought of them that way, that's a pretty nice way to put things. Whatever it is, with the score we got, the U.S. has secured its spot in the next round with Ghana, for sure!"

The eleven kid actors, as usual, exited the sage and reappeared after a few minutes for the final session of another mock soccer encounter, this time with Ghana.

The mock match between the U.S. and Ghana: as they reappeared on stage, they got into their normal verbal soccer business right away and, of course, with a little demonstration with the soccer ball, as usual.

Coach: "I can see that our guys are playing, and almost playing their hearts out, but these Ghana guys seem to be closing in on us."

Audience: *(laughter)*

Jersey No. 1 *(acting as any goalkeeper would)*: "Those guys seem ready and willing to score at will, if given the chance."

Jersey No. 2: "Please don't leave that door open for them!"

Audience: *(laughter)*

Jersey No. 1: "They're on a constant move to score!"

Jersey No. 3: "Do you think so?"

Jersey No. 1: "I know so. But we're not gonna let our team get shackled up in this funny drama . . ."

Audience: *(laughter)*

Coach: "Please don't give them the leeway or the freedom to kill this team and bury it with its head sticking out of the sand, like that of an angry cat!"

Audience: *(laughter)*

Coach: "Please catch them before they catch us. If you see something this time, please kindly do something!"

Audience: *(laughter)*

Jersey No. 6: "Whoever scores in this match will get the highest cheers and the highest thumbs up! Good luck, guys, from one of your inside-the-field fans!"

Audience: *(laughter)*

Jersey No. 1: "A little bit of good luck on our side can do wonders for this team right now!"

Audience: *(laughter)*

Jersey No. 6: "Goalie, are you kidding me? I'm just wondering if you're tied up to a corner of the post."

Jersey No. 1: "No, not quite, but I'm gradually being pushed tightly to a corner . . . , if I don't get quick help from you guys right away; I may possibly lose a body part."

Audience: *(laughter)*

Jersey No. 1: "I seem to be forever saving what appears like missile shots in the name of soccer balls!"

Audience: *(laughter)*

Jersey No. 3: "Never mind, help is on the way."

Jersey No. 1: "Hope it comes so soon . . . without delay!"

Audience: *(laughter)*

Jersey No. 8: "Oh no, I can't even find my way to their goalmouth anymore."

Coach: "Do you need the GPS to get there?"

Audience: *(laughter)*

Jersey No. 8: "No thanks, not now, but maybe later!"

Audience: *(laughter)*

Coach: "So you need it at all? I promise to give you a perfect GPS that's in good shape and even talks to you, but it's only for those who fear their opponents. I don't really care, as long as you get the job done. I mean, regardless of what the GPS does for you, just get the job done!!"

Audience: *(laughter)*

Jersey No. 4: "I have one GPS on me to give you immediately, on the condition that you don't cut corners."

Audience: *(laughter)*

Jersey No. 4: "Please stop the joke! They made their defense so impenetrable that an attacker, like me, might need a good GPS to get around them, so as to make it right into their goalpost. I know that it's more than worth it at this point!"

Audience: *(laughter)*

Jersey No. 1: "Come on, leave me alone . . . ."

Coach: "Hey! Hey! Hey! The ball is heading toward our goalpost again. Okay, someone just stopped it."

Immediate Impression: Chris *(from the spectators)*: "Even though our guys are drenched in sweat, I'm proud of their performance and perseverance so far, but the problem I have is that these guys are keeping the ball away from our Yanks, who seem to have almost lost their legs in this encounter."

Audience: *(laughter)*

Hugh: "Lost their legs? What do you mean by that?

Audience: *(laughter)*

Hugh: "I think our guys are doing pretty well, as expected."

Coach: "What's happening, guys? What I'm seeing now is that another Ghana guy called Bo-eng is weaving his way through our defense. I'm afraid this is a dangerous move . . . . Hey, hey, hey! . . . He slots the ball into our goal post! . . . Folks, it's a goal! . . . Oh my . . . Where's Boca . . . and where's Demps.. . . ? Oh my . . . gush!"

Sandra: "Our guys now seem to be holding onto the ball again, thank goodness! Is that a serious incursion into Ghana's half? I'm not sure!"

Jersey No. 6: "I think the best way to solve our problem is to make quick friends in here while there's still time by promising them green cards and free immigration. . ."

Audience: *(prolonged laughter)*

Jersey No. 7: "I think we're all competitive friends already ...So what?"

Jersey No. 9: "I think that making friends will be an excellent idea and source of good luck at this point, so meet up with them at any chance you get. Hope it helps . . ."

Audience: *(laughter)*

Jersey No. 5: "Yes, I think so, and believe that it might yield some dividends, but from where do I begin? Promise them green cards now and take back my promise later?"

Audience: *(laughter)*

Jamie [*from the audience*]: "Here he comes . . . who's that? It's our captain, Lannie again, he just curled in the ball and is making his way down toward the right, he just got into their 18-yard box, and it's now a goal for the U.S . . . . Great job. Let's go USA."

Richard: "Really, an incredible job! He made it past the Ghanaian goalie. It's a goooooooal!"

Jill: "Hey! Hey! Watch; watch this Ghana guy called Gay . . . . an. He's pushing forward, about three minutes into extra time . . . ."

Coach: "Match up with him, guys, and track him down right away. Don't just watch because if you only watch him without matching him, he's gonna score . . . Please don't let their gain become our pain."

Audience: *(laughter)*

Coach: "What's funny about that? Please match up with him, Clinie . . . Here he comes, I told you so . . . He gives a stunning strike and it's almost a goal against us! What a shame!"

One of Ghana's supporters in the audience yelled: "It's a goooooooooal, a clean goooooooooooooal! *Mama mia.*"

Lynn: "Thank goodness this one isn't a goal, but I can see something is happening. It looks like an award of penalty kick. I saw that. It's his left foot shot that nearly passed our defender to zoom into our net . . . so sad! I saw that they've been awarded a penalty kick. Is that right? Whhhhh! Oh my God, it's a goal; they just scored by a penalty kick . . . so sad! I think this is another unfortunate goal that's going to send us home and we didn't come here to be sent home this way. I'm sure this will leave our Yanks upset."

Lena: "Did you not see their penalty goal scorer now dancing from victory? Isn't he a 'star'?"

Tipper: "Yes, I see him, but I don't wanna dance with stars this time. I wanna dance later, only with superstars and perhaps with some Bristols and Mayers."

Audience: *(laughter)*

Rudy: "As long as it's not a dance with some twitchy twists . . ."

Audience: *(laughter)*

Camille: "I'd wanna dance but don't wanna be whipped in the finale . . ."

Audience: *(laughter)*

Pillar: "Did you not see one of our players almost 'crying'?"

Gregg: "I'll say to any baby crying in here, quit crying and go shopping at Wal-Mart or take a drive thru at McDonalds for some relief — for it's more than worth it!"

Audience: *(laughter)*

Larry: "Maybe a little pat down might do some good tricks . . ."

Audience: *(laughter)*

Jersey No. 10: "Losing this game makes me feel as if I wanna curl up and die!"

Jersey No. 9: "Come on, be nice, buddy! There's a chance you may be suffering from a complicated grief syndrome."

Audience: *(laughter)*

Jersey No. 6: "If you kick the bucket, who's gonna fight for us next year?"

Audience: *(laughter)*

Jersey No.11: "I figured you're mature enough to make decisions about yourself. That means that you've got a better view of what you want and where you'll wanna go to find it."

Audience: *(laughter)*

Jersey No. 1: "I'm also feeling as if I wanna pass out."

Jersey No. 7: "Do what? Please don't pass out in this 'defeat', for that's not good for us and for all U.S. fans. Moreover, your house pets aren't gonna run away when you get home, buddy, and your family is never gonna disown you, so why worry!"

Audience: *(laughter)*

Wilson *(from the audience)*: "I wanna thank all of you for fighting hard to finish, especially to Tim, for stopping the shot from one of those bad but nice looking guys that nearly sent us home earlier than they've done."

Audience: *(laughter)*

Jersey No. 10: "I'm not sure if I'll ever recover from this."

Jersey No. 8: "Do you mean from your whacked knee?"

Audience: *(laughter)*

Jersey No. 8: "Please get over it!"

Audience: *(laughter)*

Coach: "Whhhh! I feel like I'm a hopeless mess. If I do nothing now, I'm never going to do anything, and there's nothing worse than doing nothing. I feel like it's time to make a decision about whether I wanna leave or stay."

Jersey No. 6: "It's no big deal! You need to spend some time with your thoughts. It's up to you to figure out what's best to do next, but I'd wish that you be fast about it . . . ."

Audience: *(laughter)*

Jersey No. 7: "Good bye, see you sometime . . . and somewhere else!"

Audience: *(laughter)*

Coach: "What's the best exit strategy?"

Jersey No. 8: "Exit strategy for what? I don't know. All I know is that it's not confusing at all. Thankfully there are no rubber-necking traffic delays anymore on the Throgs Neck and George Washington Bridges, and even the New Jersey Turnpike is pretty free today . . . Route 78 interstate highway would be a good route for heading back home."

Audience: *(prolonged laughter)*

Jersey No. 10 *(gesturing at the coach)*: "I never thought that it was your fault in any way at all, sir, so I'm not sure why you're worrying unnecessarily."

Jersey No. 11: "Your thought is as good as mine. That we lost this match doesn't make you the culprit, sir. You did everything well and gave your all to help us, so I'm not sure why you're feeling this devastated."

Jersey No. 5: "What type of car do you have, sir? Just, wondering if you need some help to head back home for good."

Audience: *(laughter)*

Jersey No. 6: "It doesn't matter at this point, guys. He can as well fly back to his state of origin for good . . . if he so desires. Basically, speed is only what matters at this point!"

Audience: *(laughter)*

Jersey No. 9: "Don't be afraid of any stigma against you, sir. There's no stigma in knowing more about yourself and making the right decision at the right time. It takes courage and determination to do that. Timing is the most important part of your job."

Audience: *(laughter)*

Jersey No. 4: "It only takes a soul-searching strategy, or call it tactics, if you so desire."

Audience: *(laughter)*

Jersey No. 3: "Dear Mr. Bing! . . . it's pretty important that you don't jinx it . . . We would appreciate it if you leave it better than you found it, while you head home for good."

Audience: (laughter)

With this last laugh, this comic session of verbal mock-soccer show ended, with great applause from the audience! The next session will usher in a period of questions, answers, and reflections among the players, and fans, and it's flavored all through with a comic touch. A big question requiring a good answer: the eleven kids came out again with their organizers and moderators to waiting fans and supporters, after a few who were upset with the final defeat left the auditorium.

The first kid actor speaks out: "Many times in recent months, I've met a question that troubles me. What's the question? Not so much about the question itself, but because I didn't understand what prompted the question. Listen to the question, all you who are here: 'Does anyone know the worst defeat in history?'"

The second kid actor: "Haaahaaaa. What makes me wince a bit about this question is that the art of finding ways not to answer questions of this nature seems to have become quite polished . . ."

Audience: *(laughter)*

The second kid actor: "The question has come in a couple of different forms, but has roused my defense. Let someone help us out this time."

Audience: *(laughter)*

First Moderator: "While answering this question, please don't roll back to time immemorial. I mean back to the time of Adam, as you talk about it and try to give us an answer."

Third kid actor: "Just think and talk more about now and not about then, as we're itching to get a better answer."

Audience: *(laughter)*

Third kid actor: "Talk about the ones that happened in our time. I mean the ones that are as young and old as we are…"

The second kid: *(laughter)* "The answer which I'll give, if there's any hope of making a good U-turn and changing things, is pretty easy … For now, I think it was the soccer match in which our nation's team missed the world's best scoring chances seven times."

Audience: *(laughter)*

First kid actor: "Do you mean only seven times or seventy times?"

Audience: *(prolonged laughter)*

The second kid actor: "Too hot, or too cold! Hold on for a minute, let's get someone's opinion, as the whole situation was like a mess!"

Audience: *(laughter)*

Second kid actor: "I'm hearing the voice of the yesteryear's coach, Arey at the background."

First kid actor: "What did he say?"

Second kid actor: "Miss me yet?"

Audience: *(laughter)*

First kid actor: "What did coach, Brad … say?"

Second kid: "He said, 'leave me alone. I've not committed any impeachable offence. Also, when all votes are well-counted, and no one denied the right to vote, I'm gonna be the winner again."

Audience: *(laughter)*

Third kid: "I think I've been surfing the internet, without success, to find a score that would help me answer that subtle question. But recently I stumbled upon one — the recent FIFA World Cup soccer match between Portugal and North Korea that ended in 7-0 victory against North Korea. I think that's the worst defeat in soccer history."

Audience: *(laughter)*

Second kid: "Do you think so?"

Third kid: "Yes, he's right! I think it's one of those international soccer games where North Korea lost 7-0 to Portugal in a soccer tournament."

Fourth kid: "Wow! Where did that happen and when?"

Audience: *(laughter)*

Fifth kid: "Come on, do you think it's only America that has suffered defeat before? Others pass through the same tunnel, short but good, though!"

Audience: *(laughter)*

Sixth kid actor: "You're right, America gracefully passed through a short tunnel, but this country, called North Korea, passed through a wide gulf of a tunnel! It tingles and tickles my ears to hear that: 7-0?"

Audience: *(laughter)*

Fifth kid actor: "Really, a pretty big and deep tunnel, haahaaa. But was there any light at the end of that tunnel?"

Sixth kid actor: "Oh, no!

Fifth kid actor: (laughter) "Well, defeat comes and goes. That's where consolation comes from!"

Audience: *(laughter)*

The seventh kid: "No, it doesn't go that way. This one is too much and too bad; a 7-0 defeat?"

Sixth kid actor: "Do you mean they didn't redeem even one goal? That's too bad. Portugal was so mean!"

Audience: *(laughter)*

The eighth kid: "What do you mean by saying that Portugal was so mean? Please let's not get into those emotions and specifics about how you feel for the North. They should now come to know that this is soccer contest, not saber-rattling!"

Audience: (laughter)

The fourth kid actor: "You're right! They've been met by the harsh reality of what it means to get involved in a global soccer contest in a global village."

The ninth kid: "Of course, you gotta be mean to win big. And I think Portugal did that job well! I think they already finished the job for the world."

Audience: *(laughter)*

The tenth kid: "Do we need to talk to the North more about diplomacy? Do we need to send our men there for anything more?"

The eleventh kid: "No, not anymore. The job is finished."

Audience: *(laughter)*

The eleventh kid: "A well-timed global soccer contest has done it right! I think that they're no longer a threat, at least for now, with this job well done by Portugal."

Audience: *(laughter)*

The seventh kid: "Who's next, guys?"

Audience: *(laughter)*

The first moderator: "It's you, Lannie. It's time to throw some questions at you, but I'm not gonna throw soccer boots at you!"

Audience: *(laughter)*

The first moderator: "I'm sure you're smart and agile enough like G.W. Bush to dodge all of them, at sight!"

All the kid actors and the audience: *(laughter)*

The first moderator: "By the way, hope this isn't about that notorious Iraqi journalist?"

Audience: *(laughter)*

The second moderator: "We know that you're a smart soccer player, but please don't dodge the question as you would dodge soccer boots if they were thrown at you. As if they were coming from the Iraqi journalist. You know what I mean."

Audience: *(laughter)*

The seventh kid actor: "Not the soccer boots now, but the opponent's goalie is good at dodging the balls when they're sent into their goalposts like missiles!"

Audience: *(laughter)*

The seventh kid actor: "He's pretty good at it!"

Audience: *(laughter)*

The third moderator: "Hi, Lannie, talk to me. Were you thrilled, at all, after all the soccer matches?"

Lannie: "Of course, only a corpse wouldn't be thrilled at all. The truth is that I wasn't much thrilled after all the matches, but I was thrilled when we defeated Algeria, because I thought it was a real throw-down."

Audience: *(laughter)*

First moderator: "Yes, Lannie, I think you're right to be thrilled. I was also thrilled while watching the game in a beer parlor, where I downed four bottles of beer with my boss after the great win. Booze! I heard someone slap his desk as the goal was scored. It's a win that will make you hug and even kiss strangers, with all their kids."

Second moderator: "Did you flee your workplace with your boss for the bar, buddy?"

Audience: *(laughter)*

First moderator: "No, I was already at the bar with my boss waiting for the victory to happen."

The second kid: "When the victory eventually happened, did you recall remembering your last name, and what you did last before heading to the bar?"

Audience: *(laughter)*

First kid actor: *(laughter)* "Yes, I did remember them a little bit."

The second kid: "Just a little bit?"

First kid actor: *(laughter)* "Thanks for the nice victory compliments for our beloved men's team!"

The second kid: "Go ahead, Lannie. Never mind our detour!"

Lannie: "Thanks, that's not a problem! I was also thrilled a little bit when we secured a draw game with England."

Third kid actor: "So you were thrilled at all, from what I'm hearing from you?"

Lannie: "Yes, of course. I was thrilled, even though it was a tie game. Because, England was believed to have been favored more by her supporters than we were in that match!"

The fourth kid actor: "Hmmm . . . . Then tell me now, what happened when Ghana defeated you? Were you also thrilled? Did any of you, including the coach, attempt to wiggle onto a quick flight back to the U.S. without his suitcase?"

Audience: *(laughter)*

Lannie: "Hahahaha. Not that I'm aware of. It didn't get to that point! Whoops! I'm feeling pretty spent. Can we'll talk about it another time?"

Lannie took a time out and came back about five minutes later. The questions resumed.

The fourth kid actor: "Please talk to me, Lannie. Could you please continue from where you stopped?"

Audience: *(laughter)*

Lannie: "Of course. I thought that I fought too hard all through the games. I did that to get our team to win big, but it's too bad we didn't make it, finally."

The seventh kid actor: "You just admitted that you didn't make it. Did anybody die?"

Audience: *(laughter)*

Lannie: "Nooooh! Nope! That's not a hospital situation type of thing. It's in a football game that we didn't win. Please, let's put whatever trauma that goes with that defeat behind us and move on. Thanks!"

The third kid: "How about Clinnie? Do you think he could give us a good answer to this question? And how about Mikel?"

Lannie: "Go ahead, I think that every player has to talk for himself and share his feelings. I wish you good luck on your continued search!"

Audience: *(laughter)*

The third kid actor: "Hi, Clinnie, how did you feel after all the soccer encounters?"

Clinnie: "I felt bad. When it happened, I felt as if I was gonna hide away in a close-by closet! But overall, I believe we did a great job in all the soccer encounters."

The kids and the audience: *(laughter)*

The third kid actor: "Why hide away?"

Clinnie: "Because we thought the last defeat was 'awful'! I felt so bad for our goalkeeper, who was the only final savior when those guys were hustling and bustling non-stop."

The fourth kid actor: "Why did you not stop them?"

All the kid actors and the audience: *(laughter)*

Clinnie: "I was so exhausted that I thought I was gonna pass out or collapse on the field at that point. Again, thanks to our goalkeeper."

The fourth kid actor: "So the goalkeeper did the job during your match with Ghana?"

Clinnie: "No, we all did it, but more credit to Lannie and, of course, our renowned and world class goalkeeper. I think that without them, we would've gone home much earlier than we did."

The kids and the audience: *(laughter)*

Clinnie: "I still believe that most of our players hid away after the whole encounter."

The fifth kid actor: "Where do you believe they hid themselves after the encounter?"

Clinnie: "I'm not sure. Maybe in some empty closets."

The kid actors and the audience: *(laughter)* Moderator: "I think we need to move to another player now, for lack of time."

The eighth kid actor: "Hi, Joie, please tell me — where are they all hiding after they were de-feeted? In the closet? Really?"

Joie: "After what and hiding in what? That's a crazy talk! Clinnie didn't say the 'closet'. You introduced that word. We weren't de-feeted in the first place, or in the real sense of the word, de-feet. If we're de-feeted, we'd all be in the hospital now and I'd not be standing here on my two feet, talking to you."

Audience: *(laughter)*

Joie: "Better look for another word."

Audience: (laughter)

Michelo: "No one took away our feet from us. No one cut them off. It never happens on the field of soccer!"

Audience: *(laughter)*

Peter: "I have mine, here, as I talk to you. My teammates and I all have our pairs of feet, including our socks and boots."

Audience: *(laughter)*

Christophe: "We're all well and good and walking about unperturbed on our two pairs of feet. Thank goodness!"

Audience: *(laughter)*

Christophe: "Their feet weren't stronger than our feet, even though some of them came from the tropics. What's the difference?"

Audience: *(laughter)*

Simon: "We didn't lose anything. Everything we have is intact. Thanks for your concern and for thinking about us!"

Audience: *(laughter)*

The eighth kid actor: "I mean 'defeat,' that is, being a loser in a soccer match!"

Leonard: "Is that 'defeat'? Is that what you mean?"

Audience: *(laughter)*

The eighth kid actor: "Yes, of course!"

Leonard: "Sorry, we deleted that word from our lexicon a thousand years ago."

Audience: *(prolonged laughter)*

Leonard: "It's not a small achievement."

Audience: *(prolonged laughter)*

Gilbert: "That will need some public option or opinion debate!"

Audience: *(laughter)*

The ninth kid actor: "You surely didn't lose anything except the scores, winning, and bringing the Gold Medal and trophy home!"

Audience: *(laughter)*

The tenth kid actor: "We know that you came back home safely, bringing all your pairs of feet and shoes, but we're not gonna hang them on the wall or place them on the counters to serve as trophies and Gold Medals."

Audience: *(laughter)*

The eighth kid actor: "Sorry for my English and my pronunciation. Please forgive two of them! I know that I have some accent, for which I believe I need some cure."

Audience: *(laughter)*

Clinnie: "What are you sorry about? I think that you've said all that you planned to say clearly, to the hearing of all the members of our audience here, including the players."

Stephen: "Oh yeah, I think your accent and English, now, shaped the way you thought and spoke. Maybe your mother tongue isn't limiting what you're able to think as much as say."

Audience: *(laughter)*

Kingston: "I believe that your mother tongue is now imposing on you a picture of reality that's totally different from what I have within my head."

The kids and the audience: *(laughter)*

The tenth kid actor: "No, I know that accent occasionally wanders and hovers over much of the western and southern US."

Audience: *(laughter)*

The eleventh kid actor: "Do you not think that having an accent might be a problem for a good soccer player?"

Audience: *(laughter)*

The sixth kid actor: "Order, please! Please, don't change our discussion. I'm asking where the players were hiding after they were defeated in soccer."

Clinnie: "Oh, now I see what you mean. What about that? You know that I'm one of them, so what do you mean by hiding?

Audience: *(laughter)*

Clinnie: "Even if we hide, it wouldn't be inside the closet, as that can only accommodate one person . . . eh?"

Audience: *(laughter)*

Samuel: "You're right, because even when there are many people in a good bunker, the oxygen level will definitely begin to drop . . ."

Audience: *(laughter)*

Samuel: "A closet isn't that big as we need to breathe fresh air after fighting hard in the field . . ."

Audience: *(laughter)*

Samuel: "You don't wanna have anyone run out of air." The kids and the audience: *(laughter)*

The fourth kid: "Are you serious? What type of fight did you fight? You mean soccer fight? We're trying to be considerate, to get all of you a good place to hide in and eat good food. To help you refresh, since some of you were running in the field as if you were starved forty full days before the match!"

Audience: *(prolonged laughter)*

Clinnie: "The second offer would be a nice gesture of hospitality!"

Audience: *(laughter)*

Clinnie: "Thanks for that offer, but get us a good place where we can dine and not hide, where we can rest and finally get a good sleep in good hotel rooms, and not a place to hide. Hide for what?"

Audience: *(laughter)*

The fourth kid: "Let's think of the kitchen first, as an alternative, since it's already time for diner. Do you know what I mean?"

Audience: *(laughter)*

The fifth kid: "You're right, they're 11 players, and the number 11 is too big a population to occupy a closet. I believe that's why they chose to remain in the open and take defeat graciously, so that they could breathe the fresh air of recovery, survival, and arrival back on the U.S. soil."

Audience: *(laughter)*

The sixth kid: "You're right. They need to breathe fresh air, as that's good for them, so they can get the strength after resting to wake up, to begin to fight again in future tournaments, and perhaps to learn how to win and win big!"

Audience: *(laughter)*

The sixth kid: "They need to eat too, since they're exhausted. They took that defeat graciously."

Audience: *(laughter)*

Mikel: "Took what graciously? De . . . feet? Oh, thanks for being nice and coming back again with that word, de-feet. I thought it disappeared . . . and *pieweeed* away too, long ago."

Audience: *(laughter)*

Mikel: "What's so funny about that? Again, we all have our feet, as I'm standing on mine and looking at all of our teammates now, but some have already removed their soccer socks and boots."

Audience: *(laughter)*

The sixth kid: "Do those things hurt?"

Audience: *(laughter)*

Mikel: "No! There's nothing funny about you."

The sixth kid actor: "Nothing funny about me? Well, I'm not a soccer player, neither am I the coach nor the goalkeeper, period."

Audience: *(laughter)*

Mikel: "If you're not any of those, why then are you asking? However, you don't have to be any of them to ask. You're only an American and those guys belong to us, so what's so funny about that?"

Audience: *(laughter)*

The sixth kid: "Not 'those guys,' for you're one of them. And you're one of the players who performed well on the field. I did watch you play elegantly. Thank you."

Audience: *(laughter)*

Mikel: "Oh, thanks for those nice words and compliments."

The sixth kid: "But I'm trying to find out how you're feeling after the defeat."

Mikel: "You wanna know if I'm breaking my head or dying? Of course not."

Audience: *(laughter)*

The sixth kid: "I wanna know."

Mikel: "You wanna know what?"

The seventh kid: "Please talk to us before we talk about your eating."

Audience: *(laughter)*

Mikel: "You wanna starve me? Do you mean I don't have the right to eat anymore?"

Audience: *(laughter)*

The seventh kid actor: "I didn't say that. Neither did I imply that in any way at all!"

Audience: *(laughter)*

Mikel: "I', feeling hungry and wanna either eat first, or drink. Whichever one comes first is good, anyway."

Audience: *(laughter)*

The sixth kid: "Sorry, a deep feeling down inside me makes me feel like laughing harder."

Audience: *(laughter)*

Mikel: "Me too."

Audience: *(laughter)*

The eighth kid actor: "Of course, you can laugh as hard as you can, but don't break your ribs."

Audience: *(laughter)*

The eleventh kid actor: "We have other types of meat but no ribs. I gotta offer you food and drink and you gotta pay."

Audience: *(laughter)*

Spokesman for all the players: "Of course, right away, buddy!"

Joie: "I think I'm gonna eat first, as that's more important to me than anything else right now."

Audience: *(laughter)*

Waitress: "Okay, the first thing I'm gonna offer you is an appetizer, and after that the octopus!"

Joie: "Shhh . . . h, come on, don't get me the octopus. It's not my food!!"

The rest of the players and the audience: *(laughter)*

Joie: "You have no single idea what that little guy did to us during the World Cup. As a matter of fact, it's one of the reasons we didn't win and bring the World Cup and the Gold medal home. He knew so well that if we'd found our way we would devastate Germany and the rest of the great teams at the World Cup."

Audience: *(laughter)*

Restaurant manager: "No, not the octopus that we have here in our restaurant menu. It's only the psychic octopus named *Paul* that did that to your team, if at all, he did it! We don't have him here!"

Audience: *(laughter)*

Joie: "No, I don't believe you. They're all the same as long they have eight legs, appear slimy, and look alike. Please don't put that into my plate . . . Shiit!"

Audience: "*(laughter)*

Chris: "Always think before you eat, as every bite you take is a choice."

Audience: *(laughter)*

Joie: "Of course, that's not the type of animal any player would wish to have on his plate right now."

The rest of the players and the audience: *(laughter)*

Joie: "No one, and I seriously mean that no one would like to have such a creature in front of him or her for now!"

Audience: *(laughter)*

Eleventh kid actor: "Do you mean in front of your table or house?"

Audience: *(laughter)*

Joie: "I mean both and more than both, including your aquarium or swimming pool. Shiiit! You don't wanna swim with such a despicable organism."

Audience: *(laughter)*

The second moderator: "Come on, stop it! But that innocent little creature didn't do anything wrong to you or to the U.S. team, so why refer to the innocent creature as despicable? If *Paul* the octopus did offend anyone, it was only the Germans. I mean, if he offended them at all. So please, leave him alone!"

Joie: "I thought I said de ... capable and not despicable."

Audience: *(prolonged laughter)*

Joie: "But I tell you, the man octopus isn't innocent at all. He did it! He did it and he did it!"

Audience: *(laughter)*

The seventh kid: "He did what? He did what nature intended him to do by making a simple and clear prediction that offended the German soccer team, and what about it? But what of the Staten Island groundhog that predicts annually the length of the winter season with pinpoint accuracy and Princess the Camel that makes predictions about Super Bowl winners?"

Joie: "That's okay! Those other animals do what's good!"

Audience: *(laughter)*

Joie: "Moreover, I don't like to eat a Carmel or a rodent either . . ."

Audience: *(laughter)*

Joie: "What do you call a simple and clear prediction? He offended us too, not only the Germans. Do you mean the terribly subtle predictions that got rid of many of us out of the World Cup, before he ever pounced upon the next stage of the tournament to predict the one between Germany and Spain? He devastated his country and us too."

Audience: *(laughter)*

The second moderator: "Again, he didn't do any wrong to America or to their team."

Joie: "Nope! Predicting our defeat was right there on his mind and it came to fruition eventually when he finished the job."

Audience: *(laughter)*

The eighth kid actor: "Finished the job?" "How did you get into his mind? Does he have a mind like a human being?"

Joie: "If you claim that he doesn't have a mind, then why did they name him *Paul*?"

Audience: *(laughter)*

Joie: "Are you sure he's an animal? Only the Germans, to whom he belongs, can help us figure out the man octopus and who he really is."

Audience: "*(laughter)*"

The eighth kid: "Again, if he offended anybody, it was only the Germans."

Joie: "Germans are our allies, and we're all the same."

The third moderator: "Okay, you've come to realize only now that you're allies. We have no allies in soccer either you win or you lose, that's it! Soccer is beyond political, social, and cultural relationships among nations. It's about sports contest. Come out on the field and give us your best. It's about being the first to wake up and win big in a soccer tournament."

Joie: "Back to the menu . . ."

Audience: *(laughter)*

Joie: "Could you please get me some crabs, oysters, and salmon, for those are my friends and the friends of my teammates. The other one, I mean the man octopus, belongs to the Germans."

Audience: *(laughter)*

Mike: "In support of Joie, it would be nice if we could have salmon, crabs, and oysters. What a beautiful coincidence and match, since my wife is driving down from Oyster Bay, New York to meet me here for this great get-together!"

Audience: *(laughter)*

Restaurant manager: "This is turning out to be more like a party for Real Soccer Victors!"

Audience: *(laughter)*

Robert: "Joie, it's okay, let's end that issue. We'll go with your menu this time . . . . Hahahahahahaha."

The ninth kid actor: "Joie, before we continue, let me take you back to what you just said. How could *Paul* the octopus belong at the same time to the Germans if he was against them?"

Joie: "I mean he was born and raised in Germany. He's a full-fledged German citizen by birth."

Audience: *(laughter)*

The eleventh kid actor: "But the Spaniards, at some point, wanted to adopt him as their baby."

Audience: *(laughter)*

Joie: "Oh sure, they can have'im, they can have'im. After all, they won their game against Germany as the man, octopus *Paul*, predicted the victory in their favor."

Audience: *(laughter)*

The first moderator: "You'd better like the octopus, otherwise he's gonna ban you from all future World Cup matches and thereby order you to spend the rest of your adult life watching the outdated sports in your poor state, eating only shrimp, crab, and salmon — only if you have him, that's, because by then the little you'll have saved in your account could've run dry."

Audience: *(laughter)*

Joie: "The octopus doesn't have all the power that you mentioned before this fabulous dinner organized for us!"

The ninth kid: "If he doesn't have that power, how come you believed he had the power to stop you from winning the World Cup? Isn't that stupid and superstitious? I'm sure you're a Christian and Christians don't believe that way."

Joie: "This issue has nothing to do with religion. It's all about soccer and what the octopus did! He did something! And if you're talking of religion, are you sure I'm not already a convert to '*tintuism*'?"

Audience: *(laughter)*

Moderator 2: "What religion is that?"

Joie: "I'm not gonna tell you that now. I'll do so when I come with all my teammates for dinner again tomorrow. But for now, don't put the octopus on my plate, please."

Audience: *(laughter)*

The restaurant manager: "Since we're running a befitting restaurant that strives to bring diners something special, we always want to provide more than just food on the table. We're also about providing you a delicious meal in a comfortable atmosphere, a warm and inviting place where you can share conversation with friends and family too. I don't wanna offer a meal to players that will be a contentious talk of the town . . ."

Audience: *(laughter)*

The restaurant manager: ". . . dinners such as that, from my experience, can't rest at ease inside anyone's gut who dislikes an octopus . . ."

Audience: *(laughter)*

The restaurant manager: ". . . . Our exclusive decision has always been to offer and dazzle people with the best we have to offer — a tasting menu with a rarefied dinner experience. We don't wanna have any customer throw up or throw down the contents of his plate upon inspection . . . You definitely don't wanna have that happen here."

Audience: *(laughter)*

Chef: "You're right, boss. We've seen that you don't get things right here with the octopus on the menu for the players, since they all seem to be supporting of one pretty vocal person. You don't wanna make room for a painful dinner here."

Audience: *(laughter)*

Moderator: "I agree with you, because the dinner is intended to spark a dialogue among ourselves to figure out what to do to make our men's soccer team better. We thought it would be cool if you could have all the surprises and treats of a tasty menu, and even cooler if you don't get the octopus involved in any way at all, while we keep charting a better course for the U.S. men's soccer team in a get-together fashion."

Audience: *(laughter)*

The tenth kid *(gesturing to the players and audience)*: "Do not forget that whatever we're serving you is already cooked, which means that the animal you're afraid of is literally dead. I think that it would be the height of bad manners not to eat seafood here at least three times a year, to keep healthy!"

Audience: *(laughter)*

Joie: "No, I don't believe you when it comes to serving me the octopus. Any creature that can make such correct and accurate predictions can as well pop up alive at anytime, anywhere, and from anyone's plate!"

Audience: *(laughter)*

Joie: "No, it wouldn't be from my plate, not mine!"

Audience: *(prolonged laughter)*

The tenth kid: "You're pretty funny, my friend. They say you're what you eat."

Audience: *(laughter)*

Joie: "That's right, but I don't wanna be that!"

Audience: *(laughter)*

Third moderator *(unaware that the microphone is close by his mouth, whispering into the ears of one of the servers)*: "Come on, get organized, you don't always let your guests know your plans . . ."

As this message resonated embarrassingly to the hearing of everyone, the audience broke out into a wild laughter.

Realizing that other listeners heard him, he continued: "Sorry about that. I can ask them to get you guys; I mean our players, catfish in place of the octopus."

Audience: *(laughter)*

Joie: "I caught your joke. No, no, and no! I can't eat catfish either, as that would remind me of a cat that one night used her paws to press the power-on button in a home. The heat started a blaze that eventually led to a conflagration that razed an entire duplex down to the ground. Thank goodness, no persons or animals were hurt. They all made it out with their dear lives, with the backs of their feet touching the backs of their heads as they ran!"

Audience: *(laughter)*

Joie: "They all piweeeeeed away!"

Audience: *(laughter)*

Third moderator: "Let me remind you of another story about a hell cat that leapt six feet into the air and viciously attacked a woman in the Bronx, leaving her with serious injuries. The bites were so severe that she lost the use of her four fingers and warmly had them amputated . . . I've never seen a cat behave like that in my life before . . ."

Audience: *(laughter)*

Third moderator: "That's not funny! But the point remains that a catfish didn't do that; a cat did."

Joie: "I know that, but I can't trust a catfish either."

Audience: *(laughter)*

Joie: "Please don't hang up, don't hang up!"

Audience: *(laughter)*

The ninth kid actor: "You could just as well think of a dogfish, if there are any. Of course, that would also remind you that your dogs are smart too, and that the nose of your dog knows a lot."

Audience: *(laughter)*

The seventh kid actor: "That's right! Your dog also senses when something unusual is happening or has happened. Yes, she possibly smells and senses all that you've done during the day . . . ."

Audience: *(laughter)*

The fifth kid actor: "And I wonder how many among all of you sitting here and listening to our soccer drama and comedy now, would wish that their five-year-old Chihuahuas, Beagles, or Labradors could talk?"

Audience: *(laughter)*

The second kid actor: "That's right! If you do something unusual, your dog will sense that right away, but she may not tell your mom, dad, or report you to the police. How nice of her!"

Audience: *(laughter)*

The first kid actor: "No Wikileaks this time!"

Audience: *(laughter)*

The third kid actor: "Even though they live in the same house with you, surely their senses of right and wrong aren't equivalent to yours."

Audience: *(laughter)*

Joie: "Does my dog know that we've just been decimated in soccer?"

Audience: *(laughter)*

Third kid actor: "Of course she knows but wouldn't report you to anyone, so you can have a restful and happy day . . ."

Audience: *(laughter)*

Fourth kid actor: "Congratulations, there are no Wikileaks from your pets!"

Audience: *(laughter)*

Eighth kid actor: "Do you mean that controversial whistleblower?"

Audience: *(laughter)*

During the comedy, the restaurant seemed to be running short of time for both entertainment and light refreshment, so the drama was cut short to give room for other items on the agenda.

The tenth kid actor: "Again, nice talking to you and have a good evening, all!"

Now the restaurant waiters and waitresses served food to all the mock players, as the audience looked on while having their individual snacks. At this time, there was noticeably a dramatic increase in the number of audience present at the auditorium.

The players: "Thanks all! Thanks! Thanks for the food and for the wine! That's all fun! That's what we want right now!"

Joie: "Oops! Okay, not on my plate, the bad guy isn't on my plate, thanks!"

*(The audience and the rest of the players burst into prolonged laughter following Joie's comments upon the arrival of the food).*

The restaurant chef: "Realizing that one of the players hated having the octopus on his menu and plate because he felt that *Paul* the psychic octopus had made a prediction that didn't favor him and his team, makes me feel that I've just lost a friend in a soccer player."

Audience: *(laughter)*

A short break was observed for an organized and delicious dinner, for the players, with the help of the three moderators. Everybody who came to this comic forum was in good spirits, as the organizers tried their best to keep the audience comfortable with entertainment and light refreshments.

Comments and remarks from other spectators and fans:

Julie: "I'm glad I attended the verbal soccer show by those kids, with the last dinner for the mock players. It was fun, but with pretty interesting unspoken messages about soccer encounters, not to mention thoughts and ideas that need to be deeply analyzed. For me, it was a soccer comedy explosion! It satisfied that come-and-see comic wonder statement that had been clearly spelled out in the invitation. It was a job well done by such a fabulously creative and pretty smart high school kids, their organizers, and their moderators."

Jessie: *(laughter)*. It was an explosive comic display of verbal soccer entertainment. From beginning to end, the show was absolutely ravishing! I'm glad to have been a part of it. At some point I felt challenged by the creativity of those kids. That was fun!"

Noah: "This whole piece, as I saw it, was put into a fictional comic display by a group of high school soccer-loving kids, who took their turns in a well-planned mock soccer holiday presentation, concluding with delightfully fresh refreshments. It felt like a feel-good movie of the year!"

Emily: "It's interesting that eleven kids did the melodramatic exhibition with three moderators among them. At some point, they were doubling, tripling, and quadrupling roles, but I think that's pretty permissible in a field encounter, I guess! I watched the drama from A to Z, and I thought they were realistic performances, which reveal savory and unspoken comic aspects of soccer as a form of global sport. And another thing — how does the final funny dinner drama connect to the choices we make in soccer preparations, and in soccer outings? Bravo, young guys and future hopes for the entertainment business!"

Tim: "What I saw was a team-up of ever-delicious youngsters, who love to promote soccer in the U.S. in a way that we could never have imagined. The show will make it easy to forget that you're watching actors playing an otherwise near heart-breaking but non-stinging defeat in soccer, which was inadvertently incurred by our men's soccer team. Great lessons were also learned from the dinner section of the drama, when it comes to satisfying your customers and implicitly satisfying the fans in the real soccer arena. It's not all about food and eating. The Joie part of the dinner show and *Paul* the psychic octopus were funny! I think they did a great job!"

Ari: "I think that the whole piece, though in four sections, was delivered as simple soccer jokes! But what struck me most was that there were several well-staged encounters and comic set pieces devised by a well-grounded soccer comic composer, enabling the listener who wasn't a spectator to think that their opponent's team was actually present on the field for those mock soccer encounters. I think that they did a marvelous job. While listening to the get-together for the dinner part of it, a novice in comedy would feel removed from soccer, but it was all about soccer and the choices we make, both on the field, but also in leadership and management. I'll spray more grease onto their willing elbows!"

Crystal: "There was no doubt in my mind that we had great fun. I wish to give the organizers and actors a big credit for deciding not to impersonate real people or give their real names. Perhaps that was why the names were either changed or mutilated, so that the cast mates would be free to shape their characters without inhibition. Moreover, care was taken to keep different sessions of the play and drama from overlapping, as information from a different session could've possibly brought in confusion in presentation. Bravo to all who took part in this simple show!"

Gregory: "No doubt, the entire show was breathtaking! However, what caught my first attention upon my arrival at the venue where the entertainment took place, was my vision of the vast expanse of land that the campus occupies, some 85,000 square feet. The auditorium was almost overcrowded by spectators. Cars were parked down the street, where the display took place. At some point, the auditorium almost became chaotic with noise coming from the audience, who were all laughing, given the nature of the show. In the midst of the chaos that was finally controlled, there was an indescribable energy alive in the air that left me completely stupefied! It was great — and a great job from those kids!"

Natalie: "What made the most impression on me was the message that was comically conveyed in a touching fashion by the young actors and cast mates. Astonishingly, it was more verbally than physically done, even though spectators would see the ball passed from one player to another at the show. The microphone system helped a lot too. All in all, a pretty good job!"

Reese: "My joyful excitement began with the reality that there was a giant pileup of spectators at the auditorium where the mock soccer drama took place. I discovered that the presentation and displays were built on a series of soccer scenes unevenly strung together, with the composer and directors following them closely. I think that those guys did an outstanding job!"

Camille: "It was a tough and rough crowd last night at the auditorium. It was full of fun, and no one ever forgot to laugh! Also, I thought that the display looked a bit untidy and chaotic, but it was pretty big fun. Indeed, an eccentric comic thriller filled with enough laughs that people would be most willing to overlook the fact that it makes virtually no sense as a real soccer thriller!"

Ryan: "I enjoyed what those kids did at the auditorium with their mock verbal soccer display. I know they wanted to convey some interesting but funny message, and each one of them played his role pretty well. I've been a soccer player for years and ended up in my career as a high school coach. I should think that the entire comedy, from the beginning to the end, was a welcome revelation. It was a joy for me to be there!"

Sandra: "Anyone who spends sometime around young people, or anyone who has once been a young person for that matter, knows that kids, and many adults, are prone to mixing joy and sorrow stuff when they wanna have fun. I think that was what took place during the soccer drama and comedy. I'm describing this attitude, but not necessarily endorsing it, especially when the poor creature, octopus *Paul*, was comically attacked by one of the players — who apparently didn't wanna eat it! I felt bad because I'm an animal lover. But overall, I think that was all fun!"

Tia: "Having great fun playing against one's national men's team would appear weird to the uninterested, and to the uninformed soccer fan. Nonetheless, there's a clear sense of objectivity in the whole thing. But I think those were smart kids, as the idea of defeat of the U.S. men's soccer team was at some point quickly dropped and in some places revisited. I thought they were considerate or perhaps blindly patriotic. By and by, it was unusually elaborate, but didn't look like an excruciatingly long vanity production, judging from the manner of its presentation!"

Suri: "As a soccer lover and an animal lover, I was almost pissed off following the kids' detour from soccer to discussing animals, until I discovered where they were going, and upon recalling that the whole thing was intended to create fun and convey some previously unspoken messages lurking in the minds of some players and fans. I think their display was strikingly creative."

Holly: "Aside from the verbal soccer drama, which I did enjoy, there were other extraordinary moments that took my breath away. I saw that as one of those things that measures our lives, and not necessarily the number of times we take a breath. The dinner organized for the players provided a relaxed setting for me! Tension about our losses and defeats in soccer relaxed so much at that table."

Tina: "What I enjoyed about the dinner was how easy it was to have conversation, especially on how to move our men's soccer team forward. There was a natural flow, and at no point did I ever think of walking away. Ronnie and I listened to the jokes together, and laughed together, especially to the microphone-amplified verbal soccer-display and jokes that were really, really fun! What remains was how to move our men's soccer team forward, amid a suspended struggle to find common ground."

Owen: "Fascinating! That's good to know! I believe that after all the fun that we had in abundance, we need to move on together to figure out how to make a big difference in soccer by developing a winning program. We can begin to think of our soccer as not just good, but as the best in the world, and that will help us move forward better, and perhaps end up winning big, by coming out as the best!"

Blake: "We need to begin working now until we get to a point where we can't be stopped by our soccer opponents or any soccer giant in the world. It's important to know what we want, what we need, and what we must do to get there. The important questions that we should ask ourselves are as follows: 'Do we want excellence or do we want mediocrity? What are we waiting for?' Let's do it now or not at all!"

The above comic show should also help promote good spirits in soccer, emphasize the good in soccer itself, and lift the spirits of frustrated fans with some ingredients and recipes for laughter.

Above all, we need to wake up and win big in international soccer contests!

# Chapter 7
## Soccer and Soccer Fans

Sounds good! What's good about soccer and its fans? Some people hawk the illusion that soccer is unpopular, while some soccer adversaries believe the idea that we shouldn't engage in "a game that keeps us winless." Should we then crush soccer? What do you think?

If care isn't taken, these ideas and cynical statements could undermine the huge benefits that soccer brings, and the domestic support it gains from well-meaning fans. Of course, if that were a proposal, it definitely wouldn't fly. The ancient and modern justification of soccer as a beautiful sport is that soccer will forever remain an exciting game and the number one spectator sport in our world! Why? Because it's heavily global and will continue to be.

Think of how many nations that took part in the 2010 World Cup and in previous World Cup contests — why does soccer remain an attraction for all these nations, both great and small? Isn't it interesting to note? Participants in soccer compete in an arena that's pretty real. And if you hear that it's real, think it's real and get the gist that it's real, it means that it's really real! Call it a real arena that's well organized before every global soccer fiesta kicks off, with as many nations as possible involved. It's an exciting event. It remains true that the real challenge of promoting soccer locally in the U.S. is that it's a nation of Baseball, Football, and Basketball (BFB).

Soccer is a beautiful game to watch. Organizers, fans and promoters can testify to this fact. No doubt, soccer is a fascinating and beautiful game to watch. It's such a large-scale sport indeed, fielding 11 players on each team, with the goalkeeper unavoidably present. It's a mental-application game, and involves much physical interaction. It's a nation-building sport. We should drop any possible pretense of trying to relegate this great game to the background or to trample it underfoot.

How does soccer playing begin, sprout, and blossom? People who excel in soccer most of the time begin playing when they're young. Boys and girls who get involved in soccer playing not only strengthen their muscles, they also strengthen their character. Improving basic skills in soccer involves vigorous training, which invites good tryouts with good outcomes expected.

In some developing nations, soccer normally begins with bare-footed street children running around and finally coming together at the village playgrounds and fields, with some humble and simple beginnings. Think of countries like Brazil, Argentina, South Korea, Nigeria, Ghana, and the Philippines. As they gather together from various parts of their nation for primary, elementary, and high school soccer contests, the entire nation apparently comes together. These children and youth make friends across their nation of origin and increase their mutual positive self-esteem through their involvement in soccer.

Commitment to soccer doesn't require any prior applications; neither does it need vetting any documents to determine qualifications on the part of those get-together kids. Surely, it's good for children, youth, and adults, boys and girls, men and women alike, which means that it also bridges the gender gap and doesn't in any way at all offend modern tastes. Many of our children, youth, and young adults are fighting obesity today and its attendant health risks, as a result of inactivity and sedentary life habits. Soccer has been recommended as a sport that encourages children to turn off the television and video games, and to get off the floor and couches to get some exercise.

Most Americans are serious about slimming down, and there's no doubt in the mind of any well-meaning and right-thinking person that the first question from concerned Americans would always be: how do I begin? It's not often easy to determine how best to get started, especially when someone is looking for a game of choice. It's good not to bite off more than one can chew. Aside from eating clean and drinking clean, we also need to figure out a way to do more and better professionally.

If you have a weight problem and want to lose, soccer playing is good for you. If you want to lose weight, keep in shape, get skinny and strong, go soccer! Losing weight many times seems like an impossible task, but you couldn't believe how easy it would be to get into the field once a week. Soccer isn't only about getting healthy, it's also life-changing. A lot of people, beginning with kids who came to love soccer, didn't change their minds about any other games. A simple comparison is to look at those who play football and those who play soccer, and the difference will be clear in a twinkle of an eye. Soccer has remained a high-impact form of sport. People who went into soccer witnessed how fast the fat in their body melted away, like butter left under mid-afternoon scorching sunshine. Wait a minute and listen to these testimonials to soccer, as they're important disclosures.

"In 1992," recalled Rose, "I had a friend named Louise who was deeply into high school soccer. Once in a while we would get into a debate over which form of sports was best suited for losing weight. Because I had loved to watch football and baseball, I was arguing in favor of the two games while relegating soccer playing to the background. Then it happened that I got engaged in 1996 to a man in Texas while I was in the state of Louisiana. We finally proposed to get married in church in the spring of 1998. While our wedding day was drawing near with the weeks and months rolling by, I discovered that I had gained a lot of weight, to such an extent that it became certain that I had to shed some of it before the wedding.

"As at 1996," continued Rose, "I was 5 ft. 8 inches and 155 lbs., but by November 1997 I was 180 pounds. It became necessary to go to the gym and perhaps follow some dietary programs. The urge to get started made much sense to me, as I didn't want to fight to fit into my wedding outfit. My friend advised me to join her on a private field in Lawtell, Louisiana, where she trained in soccer with other girls of her age range. Initially, I felt unwilling to do that, but finally I changed my mind to give it a trial, because I was skeptical about the result, as I wanted to shed at least 20 pounds before our wedding that was coming up in April. I made the decision to finally join them in their weekly practices

"When at last I picked up courage," revealed Rose, "and attended soccer practices with them for two weeks, I must tell you that I was astonished to discover that I shed the entire 20 pounds within two weeks. I was even a little afraid to grow too skinny before the wedding, because I grew up in a culture where being too skinny wasn't always desirable, but being skinny is okay. But I did well, blending the exercise with good food, so that by April 1998, before our wedding, I was 150 pounds, or five pounds below my 1996 weight. I loved what I looked like, and had a happy and lovely wedding, with my good friend Louise and a couple of her soccer friends present. I've ever since enjoyed a happy life, both in the family and at the workplace, because of my involvement in soccer. From that experience, I've come to discover what good playing soccer can do for a person of my type. Ever since, I've been in love with soccer, and will remain forever thankful to Louise for helping to change my life forever. After that experience, I saw firsthand that a friend in need is a friend in deed! Did I argue with her again regarding whether football and baseball could help a person lose weight faster than soccer? The answer is a big No! After my experience I now believe her message about soccer, because I've seen and believed her words to be credible and trustworthy, since I didn't need to do any other research work on that. It was for me a practical experience. Soccer is for me a reliable, weight losing sport. It's a sport for all seasons, especially during winter, since you can keep warmer during this nasty season by running and kicking all the time."

"My son Jonathan was classified obese at the age of 7," observed Cherry. "Whenever he did little things, he got tired easily as a result of his weight. People recommended many things that would help my husband and me stop Jonathan from gaining more weight, since that's not good for a boy of his age. Some people even recommended colon cleansing products, which they claimed would help eliminate toxins that built up over the years, get rid of gas and bloating, remove sludge from the walls of the colon, and help regulate metabolism. I was concerned that these types of products were good for only adults. As I was trying to research the products on the website, one of my college friends called me.

"When I was sharing my worry about my son and the product I was about to research," Cherry went on, "she told me that she and her husband has a son who's now 14 and who was obese when he was 8, like my son. She mentioned that the only way they fixed the problem was to introduce him to a village park soccer coach, who allowed him to join the other kids in soccer practices at least twice every week. As soon as the boy joined the practices, they began to see striking results, beginning from the boy's neck. As the weeks and months rolled by, the boy slimmed from 140 pounds to 105 pounds. For them it was a tough journey, but they made it.

"After listening to my friend," confessed Cherry, "we made our way, the following day, down to the village recreational park to enroll our son into a kids' soccer association through a coach we'd known in church. As soon as our son started joining them for practices and training, we saw a dramatic result. The workouts helped his body work, plus burned calories quickly and more efficiently. After about four months of regular attendance at those trainings, we had a new boy with a new face. We discovered that his energy level was high again, with no shortness of breath as before. He now sleeps more soundly, without tossing and turning like before. Thanks to God, thanks to our friends, thanks to the coach, and thanks to soccer! It's amazing what soccer can do for people!

"Whoever remains doubtful of these outcomes needs to try it for himself or herself," Cherry concluded, "as the results are real. Remember that these people who share their experiences and impressions about soccer with us had their previous doubts and concerns, until they tried it and saw for themselves and were quickly turned into believers. All it takes is to compare soccer players with those who play other sports and record the difference. There must be an excitingly sporting way of sending a strong message that America takes losing and shedding weight seriously. What other ways would be better than engaging in soccer playing and exercises?"

Children and youth participants in soccer seem to burn more calories than you could ever imagine and increase muscle mass. Of course, some people would like to know what kinds of muscles it helps to build. This type of curiosity is good for research, because soccer is oftentimes physically demanding and provides a great workout for kids and the youth.

"I've been a soccer lover all my life," remarked Sharon, "and I've also been a soccer player in high school here in the state of Vermont for over three years now. It helps you develop good stamina, strong legs, and more!"

"I've been a soccer coach for more than 12 years now," boasted Rich, "here in this great city of Los Angeles. The issue isn't whether soccer helps to develop strong stamina or keep people in good shape. People know that, I believe. Many other games and activities exist that people introduce their children to, and they help work out various parts of the human body, but what I've seen in soccer is unique. I say get involved, if you so desire, and you'll see what other kids and young people of your age who are already involved in soccer look like and are able to do. Does that interest or excite you? See if it's true and go soccer, alright? Many people tend to think that children who play sports like soccer are much more likely to think and learn about how to eat properly and be aware of the type of foods and snacks that might do them good and not harm."

"I recently learned that the First Lady, Michelle Obama, is advocating her 'Let's Move' initiative," added Laura. "That should become America's move to raise a healthier generation of kids. In essence, it'll be a fight against the challenge of obesity in children and the youth. I'm pretty excited about that initiative, and I think that we've got to move fast with her to help achieve that goal. As a soccer mom and a staunch Chicago resident, I thought of sending her a beautiful note and flowers in the mail to thank her for her pretty thoughtful and brilliant project, and to suggest including soccer for kids, knowing what soccer has done for me and for my kids. I know this might sound funny, but I was almost tempted to suggest that soccer be made compulsory for kids in primary schools up to the high school level, but later decided not to push it, as people might begin to think I'm a soccer fanatic rather than a passionate soccer fan."

"Thank you, Laura, for bringing that to light," responded Kieran. "My wife Helen and I've benefited a lot from soccer. Our kids also love soccer so much. It isn't only an exercise, it's also fun for kids and the youth, as various skills and tactics are established during any type of soccer training. Kids like soccer as a fun sport, because it encourages them to do better every time they play."

"I'm a fitness expert here in the state of Delaware," bragged Jeremy. "Even though I'm not going to give up my fitness industry, I still believe in soccer. I've seen what soccer can do for people who want to keep fit. A lot of this might be helpful to people who run fitness and health classes here in the US. However, what's unique and far more interesting about soccer is that when kids get involved in it, they learn both discipline and how to get along with others."

Discipline on the field doesn't take place only by thinking of it; it takes place by being involved in it. It doesn't take place without some lasting positive effects, such as being able to handle tensions and failures in future endeavors, learning how to take successes and failures with maturity, and how to problem-solve in general social life.

"It's amazing," chimed Kieran, "the benefits one can derive from getting involved in soccer. What's astonishing is that sometimes the players don't immediately realize the unseen benefits that come from engaging in soccer. I'm talking from my experience since high school and now in college here in Boston. From playing soccer, I've gained major benefits, including emotional maturity and stability that have helped me so much in life in general, in relationships, and in business. Emotional maturity and stability make up the essential parts of every person's life. The way we relate with other people summarizes the patterns of our lives, because no one is able to hide his self-awareness and self-control for far too long. As we interact, communicate, and listen to one another, make important decisions and follow through on those decisions, our entire life style is revealed. Emotional maturity enables us to become good, inspirational, and transformative leaders, who get along with others, keep and maintain friendships, communicate properly, and judge wisely in our relationship with others. This maturity will help us deal with conflicts, mistakes, defeats, and losses in our daily lives and solve problems promptly without depending solely on other people."

"For me, as a longtime soccer player and now a veteran," affirmed Johnson, "I believe that an enduring engagement in soccer playing will leave the soccer player with a bombshell of discoveries about this beautiful sport. The field of soccer could be the ideal place to develop and groom emotional maturity and stability. Getting along with others means acquiring that ability a player needs to interact well with other kids and adults."

"One of the rewarding discoveries that I've made as a soccer player in Rhode Island," recounted Nestor, "is that in relationship with fellow teammates, coaches, and technical advisors, these interactions should include politeness, listening to others and relating to them with respect, while maintaining your uniqueness and individuality in sharing talents and skills with others on the field and in other team-building engagements. It doesn't matter if those players decide to play other sports — they still tend to maintain the same discipline and healthy lifestyles that come from emotional maturity and stability."

"Without any single doubt in my mind," asserted Kelly, "one of the smartest moves my husband and I've made was to get our two young kids into soccer. My son Sean plays both in high school and for the youth soccer team here in Virginia, while my daughter Sallie plays girls soccer at her school in Connecticut. It's my belief that wise moms and dads who want to encourage their kids to get involved in a healthy lifestyle will be interested in soccer, because it might help them make better life choices. But it's for them to decide for themselves, with their kids, whether soccer is the best sport for them, as you can't force it on them. Parents will naturally want to know the impact a sport will have on their children before they think of committing. But they've got to make it clear to them that, among other games, soccer has been viewed as a much more sensible game with much less concussion risk than in other sports!"

"I think that we should never be afraid to tell children the truth," noted Jason, "even as you don't force them into what you'd wish them to do, as only narrow-minded people do that. Good schools that care for their kids encourage them to get involved in sports, such as soccer and other extracurricular activities. It won't only help the kids when they're still kids, it'll also help them form good habits of healthier living as they grow older."

A force for good and a boost for less immorality: doesn't it sound good?

Of course, it does. The involvement of children and youth in soccer is believed to help children and youth in general avoid criminal behaviors that contradict the life of discipline and orderliness they practice on the field of soccer, like dealing in drugs and belonging to street gangs. Some people strongly believe that soccer can help overcome certain forms of addiction. Addictions are frustrating and painful, not only for the addicts but also for their friends, family members, and loved ones. Addiction affects the addict, and those close to him both emotionally and psychologically. Soccer for Social Change has for some time now advanced a solution for these ills. Soccer for Social Change is the mission of Street Soccer USA, which seeks to bring about positive social change to reduce social marginalization, social exclusion, antisocial behaviors, immorality, and homelessness in the nation. The idea is to change lives, give people the strength to keep living, build and improve self-esteem, and convey important social and moral messages.

It's intended that this program will get about 80% of kids off the streets as soon as they join the program. It begins with building relationships, which is characteristic of soccer teammates because they train together, strive together, and, above all else, listen to each other. Even the nation's professional soccer teams should look at this program as a foundational model that deserves imitation. The program integrates healthy activities that build character, social skills, and self-esteem in participants. Those kids who were abandoned by either their parents or guardians at an early age, who are striving to survive or to find food and shelter, can avail themselves of this privilege that Street Soccer USA offers. Many kids of that nature have been saved from either robbery or other social infractions. Some of these kids realized and demonstrated their natural talents and love for the game when they got the chance to play soccer with a real club team. By participating in the Street Soccer program, many of these kids garner respect that otherwise would have been denied them. It has given them the opportunity to travel and realize what it means to play soccer.

By taking part in this program, some of the kids have taken part in the Homeless World Cup tournament in countries like Brazil. Some of these players have ended up becoming stars and superstars, and could be selected to play professionally for a national team or in any league. It helps the youth kick their drug, drinking, and even smoking habits. Continually expanding the prisons and correctional centers and sending people to for-profit prisons, isn't sustainable. Get kids into soccer and they'll do wonders for the nation! We would be wiser educating kids and teaching them to play soccer.

In the U.S., there are programs already in place in about 18 cities across the country, known as Street Soccer USA. It's a national sports league for social change. In these programs, soccer teams train and compete among themselves in local leagues. What's interesting is that players make commitments toward changing their lives and life styles by setting three, six, or 12 personal goals. Here they need the assistance of their coaches and volunteers to be held accountable to their goals or to possibly exceed them.

The U.S. is a BFB nation, whereas most of the countries across the globe are mostly known for soccer. However, soccer is a game that the U.S. can further explore and excel at permanently. In fact, we can make it on the world stage of soccer if and only if we come together, think, plan, and work together, period. It takes more than an individual's efforts to grow and promote soccer in any civilized nation. It takes collective effort. We the people need to work together to either promote or grow soccer in the U.S. It isn't about news, personal opinions, or rumor mongering. It's also not about drama. It's about reality.

Working together is what the soccer culture is all about. Even in the real soccer arena, it takes collective effort to score a goal. Sometimes it gets crazy, but it's also fun trying to get into things as much and as soon as possible. It takes togetherness and team understanding. It takes collegiality of contributions and sharing resources, time, and talents. Soccer fans can show us the way.

Just as the players play together and 'fight' together, fans also think together, work together and shout support slogans together. The U.S. Soccer team and fans are a great force to be reckoned with! In the words of a U.S. player close to tears after a soccer encounter: "These fans have been helpful to us. Their presence energized and buoyed our optimism. In fact, we wouldn't have been able to score any goals but for our dear fans, who set in motion our fighting spirit by resoundingly shouting, chanting, and yelling 'USA.' all the way."

Even though success in soccer and on the field isn't determined by the number of fans and soccer supporters, it's possible that the absence of fans might go a long way toward making success and victory either illusory or pyrrhic to the team in question. Never underestimate clichés and repetitive bits! Why?

Because the feeling of being surrounded by serious and loving soccer fans is fantastic! Those feelings can reinvigorate in players the determination to win, and eliminate possible crises of confidence that are, sometimes, bound to arise as they struggle to navigate through the often murky waters that stand in their way to success on the playing fields of soccer. If you're a hardcore soccer fan, roll with it. Americans are beginning to appreciate the World Cup soccer fiesta as so much bigger than the Super Bowl.

"I've never liked to watch soccer until now," confessed Michelle, "because my husband Tim, who has been a honest, intelligent, wonderful, and humane person, had been super excited about the World Cup 2010. He's been making me watch soccer and I've come to love all of it. Permit me to mention that Tim has been a good role model for our two young sons, and has been a great supporter in my career as an actress on Broadway all these years. He often teases me for what he describes as my iconic role on the stage, and believes that I'm a super wife and mom. As one of my fans, he believes that I live daily in the hearts of my friends and fans as a wonderful actress and a gracious lady. Thanks for all of those nice words and encouragement, Tim. I love you with all my heart. I thank God for what He's doing in our lives. Hopefully, our love for soccer will increase our love for each other and for our kids all the more. Long live soccer! And long live the United States!"

"I'm getting more and more excited," beamed Barbara, "to know that soccer is becoming one of the most competitive sports for kids in our high schools and colleges. Kids who otherwise would've dropped out of high school are becoming increasingly interested in getting into college because of soccer. It's a great lure! Kids, who are great in soccer, talented and motivated, list as their first choice academically top-notch colleges that have good soccer teams, fields, and sprawling facilities. They want to be in the company of other kids who are equally motivated by the same talents and ambitions. Those kids normally work extra hard to excel in academics and in soccer so as to be able to get into those great colleges. Bravo, great kids!"

"My son Matthew, starting from the age 7, had been hopelessly absorbed in playing video games," moaned Peter, "up to the point that he'd skip lunch and even dinner. I did everything with my wife, Susan, to take it away from him, because our intention when we bought the device for him was to help him grow smarter than the kids of his age and perhaps become an engineer in the future, but that intention turned out to be hurting us. Thank goodness we succeeded in getting him out of it before he was 10. Now that he's 18, he got into smart phones and i-pod devices that he'd be playing as he walked down the streets, stairways, and sidewalks, sometimes double fisted and sometimes when he's in the bathroom. We discovered that but had no easy way of stopping him, and thought that having the internet in his pocket must have burrowed into his brain. Because of this addiction, he was very often a face-down kid. It almost came to the point where it would've been necessary to get a rehab team to teach him eye contact. Thank God we're a religious and prayerful people. After putting him in prayers for a long time, he, out of the blue, developed an interest in soccer. For over one year now, we haven't seen him with i-pods and smart phones. I think that he sold the ones he had to his friends. But we didn't bother to ask him. His life took a crucial turn for the better. Susan and I strongly believe that he reclaimed his life by that sudden interest which he developed in soccer. Thanks to God, thanks to prayers, and thanks to soccer! I'd recommend any kid that behaves that way for soccer."

"I've discovered that young people today no longer understand how to figure out their problems without the use of technology," noted Arthorine. "Most people, especially the young, sit behind a computer, thereby losing their God-given faces. So, what you see are individuals without faces, but that's changing now, thanks to soccer! Going by my experiences with some of my cousins, who were computer and electronic gizmo addicts, I've come to believe that it's a mistake to assume that addictions will stay the same with soccer. I've come to discover that when addicts stay flexible and open to the possibilities that soccer brings, they will benefit in ways they could never have imagined."

"I think you're right!" agreed Juliet. "My son Justin, who attends public high school in the suburbs of North Carolina, once confessed before me and his dad, Michael, how soccer has helped him curtail his addiction of sitting behind the computer almost 24/7. He used to be an unbridled instant-messaging-down-the-highway guru held in a longtime bondage by computer addictions, but that has shifted due to his sudden interest in soccer; courtesy of one of his peers and classmates. This is an excerpt from what Justin said: 'I think that not knowing how to relate with others got me into an addiction with computers in the first place. I used to get angry easily when I tried to relate to people or got pissed off with people because I had unresolved issues that I didn't want to discuss with anyone. I want to say that I couldn't communicate with others in a healthy manner because I felt that I was emotionally out of control. That made me get into the computer thing, and before I knew it I got badly addicted to the use of computers. One day, one of my classmates was kidding me about joining him in soccer. I thought he was God-sent. When at last I played with them on the field, down here in North Carolina, my life changed from that day, because it's like they knew and were nice to me on the field. My mom was the first person who discovered how much I improved and informed my dad. From then on, my life radically changed for the better and we began to heal, both as individuals and as a family."

"You guys all sound convincing," admitted Lindsey, "and listening to you feels encouraging to me, too. You all know me as somebody who's not new on television channels or radio news, and who's popular with the paparazzi in the whole U.S. As we prepare to ring in another year of uncertainty, I think that it would be an exciting part of my New Year's resolutions to consider getting into women's soccer, no matter how amateur it might seem to the U.S. public who, I'm pretty sure, can't wait to see me released from the rehab center. You all know that for months now I've been haunted by my inability, or as some people say, my unwillingness to shake my drunken driving addictions, which have resulted in two stints in a rehab facility and in two recent trips to jail. I believe that getting into soccer might help me keep out of trouble and away from jail. It'll be a good change in lifestyle, and will go a long way in helping me kick my addictions."

"I think that's a pretty good and thoughtful idea, Lindsey," replied Jeffrey, "you're well loved! Doing what's right takes courage and determination. It's my belief that you can do it. Why not? Just get into a women's soccer league out in Hollywood if that's your desire, and all will go well for you ever after. It's true that recovery may not be that easy for some of us, but we have a fighting chance, and I believe that, for some reasons, you have a bigger fighting chance than most rehab habitués. Make the sacrifices you need to make and you'll be fine. Soccer is the only sport that helps to teach us how to use every fighting chance. I've been there and I know so. Also, I'm in favor of the idea that what we'll be in future so much depends on what we do in the present; even though it could take one step at a time. I must tell you that I'm excited by your promising proposal, and may even have to launch a new website to support your proposal, as I find it cool. Ride on!"

Soccer truly brings people together. Soccer events bring people together in friendship and possible networking. The time of the international soccer fiesta is a time to make myriads of friends across the globe, during and at the end of it all. No type of 'noise' whatsoever prevents people from making friends across the globe when they mean business. It's also a time to see a beautiful light at the end of the tunnel when it comes to world peace and maybe more. Having a strong bond and good relationship with other people has often been regarded as the key to happiness in various fields of human endeavor and in all walks of life. By bringing people together, soccer can unite people from different religious, cultural, and social classes. By so doing, it can help build intercultural understanding and thereby help reduce intolerance, racism, and prejudice. In summary, it helps to build a world of friendly people."

"Not too long ago," recalled Rob, "I read that even Queen Elizabeth broke with tradition by putting sports at the center of her Christmas message. I recall reading an excerpt of what she said as follows: 'In the past year of many sporting events, I've seen for myself how important sport is in bringing people together from all backgrounds, from all walks of life, and from all age groups.' I did memorize her message, because I'm a great lover of sports and soccer in particular. I sense that the Queen, while talking about sports, implied soccer, because it's the most popular of all global sports."

"You're quite right, Rob," agreed Celia. "I read that message! I found it precisely in *The New York Times* sport's section. I think that her message underscores how, in most cases, sports are played in a spirit of friendly rivalry and under standard rules across the world. There I discovered that the real sense of sports is its value. Soccer for me fits that picture more, because it crosses many more national, ethical, and religious boundaries, plus the 54 member states of the Commonwealth of Nations, of which the Queen is the titular head."

"Even though I'm not a Christian," revealed Suri, "I think that the message of the Queen at Christmas centers on the goodness, both physical and spiritual, that sports can promote. One of my friends, Nandini, believes that her message was aligned to the Christian faith, and although she doesn't think that it carries much weight as a message to the entire world, but the message still recognizes that soccer appeals to everyone, regardless of religion. She sees it as the most popular sport, which gives perfect guidelines for humanity."

"On July 12, 2010," recalled Mike, "I began my trip to South Africa for the FIFA World Cup. My experience when I arrived at the stadium in Pretoria was that the weather was perfect, warm, and breezy. You couldn't ask for a nicer climate. The teams had finished stretching and practicing, and headed for the locker rooms. In truth, the match hadn't started, but I could observe American and Algerian fans having a great time together. A good time for fun together! As I was pondering the diplomatic relationship existing between the U.S. and Algeria, I also discovered that the Algerian embassy was only a block from the stadium, where a garden party was staged. Several divisions of Uncle Sam's Army marched past, shouting friendly greetings and the chants of 'USA.'"

Fans love to see their favorite team excel on the field during an encounter. So, it's exciting to win in front of one's fans. That, of course, leaves them thrilled and excited. Fans in international soccer fiestas rejoice and cheer for an anticipated carry-through of a continuing success, victory, and triumph. They're sometimes seen mounted on city streets and corners leading to the celebrating arena, to herald the emergence and arrival of the great players who did them proud.

It might be a surprising thing for a novice sports lover to get the gist about how far fans can go to raise the morale of their teams. Fans can travel any imaginable distance to watch multi-sporting activities of their choice, be it by air, land, or, yes, by sea. Because of the way they behave and react, fans are sometimes qualified with the words swarm, mob, or gang. That qualification is fine because of the way they most often descend on cities where the contests take place. Sometimes fans descend on cities in advance; sometimes they do so on the day of the encounter, depending on distances and circumstances linked to logistics. Soccer fans have been known to brashly make themselves feel at home wherever they go. Fans give their players hope.

In various countries across the globe they gather in tens of thousands, and even in millions, at a rally or at the teams' headquarters, training facilities, large parking lots, or fields to wish them the best of luck before the teams set out for the encounter. Most of them wouldn't mind trekking or traveling a long distance to do that, sometimes braving bitterly and brutally cold weather, or scorching heat waves in hot, sweltering weather, to get at least a glimpse of their soccer heroes before they set out. They do the same thing whenever their team comes back home from the encounter in flying colors, by either winning the Gold Medal or bringing the trophy home. Sometimes, a pretty sympathetic section of them and faithful followers wouldn't mind doing the same when their team only came close to bringing the same trophy home.

A lot of factors drive fans to travel to far distant lands to cheer their beloved teams on, no matter how expensive the cost of the trip. Primarily, fans travel to distant lands because they get some feelings in the air of a possible or an assured victory, and that's often what drives attendance to any tournament. Some do it to support their favorite teams. When fans and supporters travel those long distances to cheer their players and team on, they often have it in the back of their heads not only that the encounter is theirs, but also that they didn't travel all that long way to lose. Many fans regard such events as special occasions in their lives, during which they might get the chance to travel with friends and family for some vacation or preplanned enjoyment on a foreign soil. Others see it as an opportunity to not only cheer on their favorite team, but also a rare opportunity to get to know a new culture and a new social environment.

"I promised myself during the year," boasted Jeffrey, "that if our men's soccer team qualified for the FIFA World Cup soccer, I'd make it down to South Africa with my whole family for the World Cup soccer and for some vacation. We'll definitely board a flight from Indiana to South Africa, no matter the cost of the flight or the distance. Moreover, I had it at the bottom of my heart to go to South Africa with my family. We ended up among those who made it to South Africa to cheer on our men's soccer team. It was quite a beautiful trip for Juliet, me, and our three kids. That was part of my New Year's resolutions."

Jeffrey believed he'd shell out about $35,000 for the entire trip and booked a flight in advance as soon as they got the news that the U.S. men's national soccer team qualified for the FIFA World Cup soccer for 2010. He knew it was a lot of money, but he insisted he'd be going with his entire family to witness history and that no one, according to him, could put a price on such a desire and resolve. He eventually made it to South Africa with his whole family, and couldn't imagine how in the world he could miss that 'once in a lifetime' opportunity, with the basic promise to himself that their journey wouldn't be in vain. Within the US, fans have flown from California to New York to watch basketball, football, baseball, or soccer, and vice versa. Soccer fans have traveled from Washington State to watch soccer face-offs in Pittsburgh. Internationally, fans and soccer aficionados have traveled from the U.S. to countries like Japan, South Korea, China, Australia, Mexico, and, of recent, South Africa, to watch the World Cup soccer.

"Don't drop or yank the trophy or let it get so much excited at the shouts of joyful fans and jump off the bus loaded with rejoicing winner players," advised Madrid.

The U.S. soccer fans, regardless of how small their population, have often rejoiced up to the point of being on fire whenever our men's team got closer to a possible victory, or whenever their dream nearly came true. They rejoice with other excited and captivated fans and admirers across the globe. In many cases their families are present, during which the players hug their wives and loved ones and kiss their kids (*if they have any*). There would often be the most cheery ones, who'd shout out slogans and clichés, forever and ever, while others laugh and jeer at their defeated or about-to-be-defeated opponents.

The unity, oneness, perseverance, and determination of the fans are among the qualities that impress their admirers. Nations explode in joy and jubilation to see their soccer teams come out first in the ranks of victory. If a team came out unexpectedly victorious, fans are expectedly fascinated. This emotional attitude often finds expression in a stunning silence, but that doesn't last long. Fans want to see stars and superstars in their players. We need a large body of soccer fans. The presence of large numbers of fans is good news for every soccer-loving nation.

Americans are, generally, fun-loving people who love to win and win big. They love waking up to victory. They love to win. The reactions of the U.S. fans have been exciting and attractive, in recent years, to people who otherwise have little or no interest in soccer. Not many Americans are soccer lovers, but the national men's team performance in 2010 World Cup enthralled them. In recent years, people are captivated by the show, bars and sport bars are filled to the brim with fans, an indication that soccer is gradually gaining a huge American following and perhaps will become a major spectator sport in the U.S. It's not uncommon to hear or read that most of the fields in the nation are booked by fans every summer season. The more popularity soccer gains among people, the more enjoyable it becomes. The U.S. is beginning to see soccer fans and supporters spring from many states across the nation, mostly from Illinois, Ohio, Massachusetts, Connecticut, Pennsylvania, Maryland, Florida, Texas, and California. The cheering fans can't ever be ignored.

Contest is a way of life in our culture. Listen to what soccer aficionados normally shout. Also, listen to what the fans say. Hear them chant: "We're number one! We're the best! Let's go soccer!! Let's go Brazil! Let's go Argentina. Let's go USA."

A cliché like "Let's go USA" can have a lasting and even permanent impact on the minds of U.S. sport fans, and even generate more interest from the public in soccer. Does it sound like something that will get them tuned in, only to tune away when the whole fiesta is over? Not quite! The excitement over soccer because of its global overtones will be sufficient to elicit positive responses from the masses. Soccer is affiliated with the World Cup and shines too brightly to be extinguished.

The casual sports fan that ordinarily doesn't watch soccer can be enticed to tune in and even pick up interest, to the point of showing interest whenever soccer events come up. In recent years, Americans watch soccer in growing numbers more than ever before, as they gain a better knowledge of what soccer truly is, what happens in the arena, why the players are there, and soccer's impact on the world village. It's not ramming the sport down the throats of anyone. No, we now hear many people say, "I'm going to watch soccer." It's a sign that a real test or taste of America's interest in soccer has been set in motion. It's no longer the previous sorry message to fans, when little interest was found in soccer. It's no longer, "Who cares whether the U.S. beats Germany, Brazil, or Argentina?" Yes, now we care and should begin to care! Many people have begun to consider it unbelievable how soccer has become this popular, with deep expressions of joy in seeing the U.S. take great interest in the world's most popular sport. Cheer our team on with the shouts of "USA, all the way!" Forward ever, backward never! With this attitude, we'll be able to rightly wake up and win. I hope our nation will get to love soccer in greater numbers. What, then, can fans do?

"I'm a 28-year-old U.S. military captain," announced Lawrence, "and a great lover of soccer. I seized the opportunity during my leave and vacation from Afghanistan to travel to South Africa for the World

Cup soccer contest. My first experience and feelings as soon as I arrived at the stadium and saw U.S. fans was a real cross-sample of America. I was given a ride to the stadium by a friend, in whose house I spent the night before moving to a hotel. I ate lunch next to a Microsoft graphic designer at the hotel restaurant. As I was eating, I could hear the fans singing the U.S. national anthem on the broadcast. A few minutes later, the soccer tournament was under way and the barroom cheered for an early goal. To me it looked like a great turnout of Yanks in the stadium. I also heard the beehive sounds of the vuvuzelas, from South Africans and from some visiting fans from afar. Soccer fans are ready to do anything to get the teams they're rooting for to win. This is yet another one of the powerful aspects of soccer. Fans shout these slogans on various occasions in support of their darling teams, thereby creating certain euphoria among themselves when things are working in their team's favor. In other words, a certain sense of feeling good when their team seems to be doing well! These are competitive cheers."

"Powered by their great passion for soccer," Lawrence observed, "a lot of people become fans to entertain spectators and players, to boost their morale. By boosting the morale of players, fans do a similar job that 'Burnout Bursting Committees' (BBCs) do in workplaces. The members of these committees give out candies, small bars of chocolate, free gift cards, humor cards, and stress relief toys, to make people happy in workplaces. It might sound funny, but it's true. Encouragement multiplied by thousands of cheering fans becomes the home court advantage in sport contests.

"Soccer fans of today are getting pretty good at being creative in what they do," Lawrence concluded. "Think of face paintings and little gadgets that make funny sounds, or sing encouraging songs! No doubt, high-profile contests have some deep impact on the fans, well-wishers, and promoters; an impact that could be physical, emotional, and sometimes psychological. Fans form emotional bonds at every sports contest, so that their responses are almost collective. Do we need many more fans to win future FIFA World Cup soccer? We do."

# Chapter 8
## Future FIFA World Cups

What do soccer lovers and fans think of the future FIFA World Cup soccer contests?

"Let the music play on and the soccer journey roll," suggested Lionel. "It's never too late for a beginning, as it's always a beginning, anyway! The conventional wisdom of 'measuring twice and cutting once' shouldn't be wasted in our time. We should try to learn from history and not let history repeat itself unnecessarily, unless we choose to ignore it."

"Let's not remain where we were, before the realities of past years struck us," added Diana. "We should be ready now to recognize reality and deal with the new world of soccer as we find it. The U.S. should begin now to prepare for the next FIFA global soccer contest and beyond, in addition to striking a deal to possibly secure a bid to host either the 2018 or 2022 world soccer tournament."

"You're right, Diana," agreed Whitney, "but the U.S. has recently withdrawn from the 2018 bid and rather focused exclusively on the 2022 bidding process and campaign. Saddled with many responsibilities and with several projects under her belt, we still hope that the U.S. Soccer Federation has the drive and judgment to lead our men's national soccer team to its deserved summit of greatness."

"Those leaders and members of the soccer federation have every chance, and hopefully will get the chance to save soccer through unblemished, courageous, and transformative leadership," opined Lee Ann W. "The urge to start something new should be extra strong and rife by now. That's what I think!"

"Even though most of us speaking now have somewhat been into the world of music and entertainment, I've always loved soccer," claimed Josh. "I believe that now is the time for members of the USSF to get to work. It could also be a time for them to cushion themselves from the blows of people who may in one way or another disagree with their policies."

"You're right, but they will be asking, perhaps begging, for people's cooperation and support, both from within and without," reasoned Bruce. "Even though we didn't get the Gold Medal in the past soccer World Cup, it's not a time to bury our lasting love for soccer. Rather, more than ever before, it's a time to wake up and win, and not just win but win big."

"Sing it to me! It's a time to rise up to victory, and say a beautiful good morning to a different America in global soccer contests!" exclaimed Marc Anthony. "America's untapped but profound love for soccer will never go away, so whoever has been trying to have it go that way should stop trying."

"I can't agree more with you, Marc!" replied Jennifer. "I think that it'll be laughable for the U.S. to allow herself to be boxed or to become comfortable with mediocrity in international soccer. If this persists, it might lead to soccer inferiority complex."

"As Lionel mentioned earlier," added Sharon G., "let the soccer music play on. Let the music play! Our men's soccer team has made great efforts to win in their previous soccer encounters. So please, let's not be tempted to think of our past soccer failures as evidence of our virtues. I don't want to believe that!"

"Indeed, America may have learned from her past mistakes in soccer outings," noted Gloria, "especially in previous FIFA World Cup matches. Now, we can choose to ignore those mistakes or remain thick-skinned over negative criticisms when they come. It's better to remain open to facts and positive messages that will, over time, favor progress for our national soccer system."

"I think that it's also about keeping an open mind, and taking things in stride," observed Cindy. "Of course, there would always be reasons, big and small, soccer teams lose during contests, some of them obvious, others less so. The performance of our men's national soccer team in previous matches may have exposed certain flaws that might have appeared near fatal in those days, but ours is no longer a time to dwell on mistakes forever. Rather, it's time to leave behind the past, move on with new vigor, and win big in soccer. But we've also got to have fun as we do so."

"I'd say jump in with both feet and grasp the challenge, for life is forever changing," advised Mariah. "Some people are afraid of any change from previously established ways and routines of life, because they view change as disruptive, among other reasons. Fortunately, many people don't mind change if it keeps life from sliding into boredom."

"It depends on what you mean by change, Mariah!" contested Crystal. "I'm a soccer lover, too. Whenever you want to make a positive change in any field of life, be prepared for great challenges, as the hydra-headed monster could show its ugly face to prevent something good from happening. But sometimes you've got to be ready to step on toes, without necessarily hurting those toes."

"Hahaahaa. I believe that it only takes courage, guts, and humility to get to overcome challenges," argued Celine. "The power of love for whatever you want to do will often help. Soccer isn't different! But let's never forget to wake up and win — win the bid, win the game, and above all win the world soccer contests and come back home great!"

But as we brace for the challenges of future FIFA soccer games, what do we mean about change in soccer? Is it change of people, or a change in things? Is it a change in organization, structure, ideas, strategies, habits, or ways of doing things? Is there a need to change the culture of our men's soccer administration? How soon would that change be expected to kick in? Tell us what you think.

"I've read, and believed, that in all of our life endeavors, insanity consists in doing the same thing over and over again, and expecting a different result or outcome," cautioned Justin T.

The major change that every soccer leadership would naturally talk about and target is how to get the job done by changing whatever culture is connected to any losing soccer program, policy or system that we've been previously peddling.

"It's believed and sung, that it depends on where we — meaning you and I — belong," noted Pat Ben—r. "It's about understanding what you observe, being able to explain it to yourself and your to fellow co-workers, and then applying ways to correct it. Such an approach would benefit any soccer team organizers a great deal."

"It takes trust — that's probably the biggest thing," suggested Brenda. "Chances are that you'll trust someone if you're sure that he'll be where you want him to be. For players, it means putting the ball where you know it'll be safe, and where someone can make a great catch and perhaps a great score."

"Haaahaaa. First of all, it's about getting used to one another, trying to fit everyone into the system and getting them going at once," advised Bonnie M. "It also demands an honest and sincere communication process among members of a committee, federation, and soccer team for a lively chemistry to build up."

"As a singer and entertainer in the 70s and 80s, and a soccer lover," asserted Litz, "I think from experience that it's all about breaking a habit that never worked, while, at the same time, getting into the good habit of inhabiting first place and winning victories. It's time for our men's team to be continually associated with winning, and to stay with that attitude."

"By the way, when it comes to winning," noted Marcia, "no one soccer player actually knows how to win. It takes a team to come together and figure it out. It'll be a challenging project, but the result will be superb."

"There are little things, often ignored, that could help players win big, and that might help in future FIFA soccer match preparations," observed Rocky. "Listen to this small but great suggestion. The provision of services and routines that are running short of the morning wake-up calls for players ought to be reviewed by any fresh soccer leadership and perhaps changed. This might give the team a bit of a facelift."

"That sounds funny, but still makes great sense!" exclaimed Marge. "But I think that it's about doing everything at the start to provide a true leadership of change. Understanding where the problems lie is crucial for assessing what type of innovation in leadership is needed to address the many soccer challenges that lie ahead. Think of teamwork —there's scarcely any soccer victory without teamwork."

"We're on the same track, Marge," agreed Fred, "but we have to think not only of the role of players, but also about the organizers. I agree that with good teamwork any soccer team can challenge and overcome gifted opponents on the field of soccer. With teamwork, every possession of the ball can be defended from the beginning to the end. Any goal that's carefully fired into the net is usually the result of teamwork. But I think that the same should be applied to the organizers, too."

"To keep up to date," added William, "let's think of our time as something unique and precious. It's a time to rise and shine most brightly in the soccer arena, as we would in good virtue before God and man. It may also be a perfect period to engage in a debate, if we so desire, with other people as to the best way to move soccer forward and get the Gold Medal and trophy home to the U.S. I think that both good soccer playing and good leadership can achieve that."

The discussion turned to leadership in general, soccer organization and management in particular. For some people, it may have sounded unlikely to open a lively conversation about what needs to be done to achieve meaningful results. But that process works in every field of human endeavor, soccer included. This approach is good because many times ideas appear clearer when shared with others, rather than kept to oneself. When we see things through different eyes or lenses, it can give us a refreshing outlook on new approaches and ideas. Among other things, prudence as well as wisdom is needed when dealing with people in general. This quality supports, enhances, and enriches good leadership writ large. Your genuine interest in others, and in their progress, will help foster your popularity.

"I've been in women's soccer team management in Alabama for almost two decades," cautioned Elena. "When it comes to leadership, and especially soccer management, be careful about and aware of what messages you send out to others. Make sure they're not misunderstood or misinterpreted. What I've discovered is that we don't often lack strong opinions, but we do sometimes lack tact in expressing them, and that could be an issue."

"I've done the same job in Arizona for almost fifteen years before I retired," argued Chuck. "It's not usually what we say that matters — it's how we say it. If you need the support of others, find a polite way to get your point across. It's better to find out the details without being needlessly probing. Also, be wary of projecting a single favorite idea of yours, for that might have a damaging effect on the entire system. This remains only a caveat. This doesn't imply that a leader who's been tested and proven to have good insights should hand over control to any other person, since it's sometimes best to make one's decisions, depending on what's at stake."

"I've learned from my experience in general soccer administration that you could also listen to what friends, family, and work colleagues will tell you," added Jim, "especially if they're giving you advice on how to improve the nation's soccer system. In soccer management, there's no such thing as secret leadership. Sometimes we think we know best, but making assumptions can prove costly."

"I've been a great soccer fan for almost three decades now," advised Patricia. "I'd like our men's team to do great in future FIFA World Cup soccer contests. My experience in the field of higher education has shown me that for any leadership to be effective, there must be a strong desire for, and the implementation of, shared governance. I feel that this idea shouldn't be restricted to the field of education alone. The idea of shared leadership or governance could have great influence on soccer management and organization."

"For me, there's no big deal about that." enjoined Bill. "Just make sure that the suggestion boxes are fully stuffed all the time! Don't underestimate the power of sharing, since you may not always get the best from yourself alone. Rather, it could come from someone closest to you or from an outsider, provided they have your interest, and the interest of the national soccer team, at heart. They've got to be people who want the team to emerge victorious in its soccer encounters."

"Yes, valuing the opinion of a devoted person who has your interest and the interest of the nation at heart is indispensable," agreed Henry. "If you're not sure of a situation or an opinion, wait for more clarity before making a move, as failing to do so could be costly. This shouldn't only apply to general administration, but to soccer management and governance, too. Or, as the old quote goes, when in doubt do not act."

"Other people's brilliant opinions are indispensable." added Manny. "For instance, when someone is in conflict as to what to do next, confusion is bound to arise, but as more and clearer information begins to trickle in, the dew, mist, and fog of uncertainty will clear up."

"I've been in men's soccer administration for decades here in the state of Oregon," responded Michael. "However, despite other people's opinions, be smart enough to reject anyone who has a negative, self-sabotaging attitude toward soccer, as this person might, in all innocence, pull you down. Where circumstances force you to make a decision, try to seek the opinion of someone you trust, believe, and consider wiser than yourself. Or let sound inner voices guide you to make wise decisions, especially in player selections. It takes some form of flexibility in our way of life, and in our mode of operation, in soccer management and administration."

"I think by this point it's safe to say that we all want our men's soccer team to do well in the future FIFA World Cup soccer," stated Dorothy. "I believe that openness and tolerance can, surprisingly, improve any status quo, including a nation's standing in a great sport like soccer. If something needs to be dealt with, please don't delay. Do it now, rather than be sorry you didn't put the time and energy into getting something important done. Don't delay — priorities are often key. Useful ones, though."

"Soccer administration isn't something new to me," reflected Portia. "All you need to do is figure out what's most important, put that at the top, and then go about implementing it. My only advice to every soccer administrator, whether local or national, is this: to get things up and running for a better performance in the future, you've got to be really smart. Be ready to take advantage of any situation when the opportunity knocks at your door. Sometimes we might be ready to listen to, and welcome, opinions that may inconvenience us a bit, without carrying the facts too far."

"I've always been in support of welcoming other people's opinions, and our national soccer leadership does that well," confirmed Annette. "But in addition to what they do, a fair analysis of those opinions with other soccer experts and veterans would put soccer policy and decision-making, with team selection, in good stead, provided they're guided by an ardent desire for a genuine victory. This idea will help make any exchange of opinions in soccer less challenging, I think."

"I want to go by people's opinions," admitted Paul. "I suggest that extra care be taken not to over-analyze people's opinions, since we can easily get confused and distracted when we get caught up in too much individual details. That wouldn't be good for our progress in soccer. All we need to do is reorganize and begin to learn what we're not learning."

What does learning mean, when it comes to taking our men's soccer team to a higher level of performance? How can we create something new and better from what we've learned? We can begin to take steps to implement the solutions we've learned.

"The only question that needs to be asked is this: what would it take for us to rise and shine most brightly on the fields of soccer from now on?" asked Roger. "Listen to my simple prayer: May the reality of our men's soccer team's performance this year and in past years herald a period of combined, spirited, and non-desperate attempts to develop a solid soccer structure in our nation, that will henceforth guide us in future FIFA World Cup soccer matches, and in the Olympics as well."

"For us to do well in future FIFA World cup contests," noted Frank, "there's no doubt that U.S. soccer has to come up with something radical and new. Sounds like a real change —something uncommon that suits our stature, resources, and capability as a great nation and people. But first we have to figure out the possible root causes and explanations for our past troubles in the World Cup soccer games and the Olympics."

"In preparing for the World Cup soccer," suggested Eileen, "it's essential to remember that all areas of soccer life are important, and that neglecting any single aspect of this great sport will lead us into overlooking something special. But we need to ask ourselves a number of questions. Do we have minor or major problems in soccer? What's the root cause of our lack of high achievement, or call it top-notch success, that has long prevented any national celebration for our men's soccer team? Is that problem solvable? Are we able to figure it out? Do we need to agree that there's something still missing in our men's soccer team's general performance? Or do we gloss it over, remain firmly in denial, and continue to believe that we're quite okay and fine with what we have for now? And if we determine on further reflection that there's something missing, then the next question would be: What's that?"

"We have been celebrating our good performances," replied Wilma, "but one day, as a nation, we need to celebrate a clear and absolute victory in a FIFA World Cup soccer. Should we publicly proclaim that we're pretty comfortable with the performances of our men's soccer team, in their past and previous global soccer encounters?"

"I completely agree with Sunil Gulati, head of the USSF," stated Adolph, "who once said during one of those 2010 FIFA World Cup games that 'a loss and two hard-fought ties wasn't what the U.S. was looking for.' As we keep trying to get things right with the American public about our stand in soccer, it's important to first of all get our stand in soccer right. Then, public understanding and support will automatically follow."

"Thanks, Adolph," responded Ranoly. "I think that your suggestion, if implemented, will help spare us from possible future public fury for not seriously waking up to win a big victory in our men's soccer. We shouldn't be surprised if the citizenry has apparently become nearly deranged by its anxieties and fears, almost to the point where they will begin to ask, 'What is wrong with our men's soccer team? Why can't we bring the World Cup home at least for once or get closer to getting the Gold Medal? Is it impossible for us to do that? Why or why not?'"

"I can assure you that a lot of small whys have been coming up," complained Robert, "but haven't yet boiled over or exploded into a big why, which only comes when people are fed up, upset, and no longer able to think clearly, due to prolonged disappointments and frustrations over our men's heretofore dismal global soccer performances."

"I contend that opening a whole new branch of soccer engineering might help uncover a better and more immediate answer to the most crucial question: why?" rejoined Alfred. "But of course, this engineering would begin with our nation's soccer analysts, organizers, strategists, and the players themselves, for, in the final analysis, we can't do without them. Our men's soccer team needs a strong and new foundation to get the citizens motivated to become appreciative and grateful. It's time to do the right thing and forge ahead."

"Though a medical practitioner by profession, I've been a longtime lover of soccer," noted Lorraine, "and would wish that our men's soccer team wins big in their future FIFA World Cup outings. When we get many factors working in our favor, then we'll begin to see some light at the end of the tunnel, and then things will get better. It's about moving closer to achieving whatever is our dream in soccer. Indeed, the players, organizers, strategists, and analysts will have a better explanation. Better, because it's presumed that a more reliable diagnosis would often come from insiders, because what we don't see from the outside, they can see better from the inside. They know where the problems are, what the possible causes may have been, and how to advance a proper solution to them."

As we keep working toward better future FIFA World Cup soccer performances by our men's national team, let's think of how to promote soccer as a world game, to make it appear big in the US. The need to have that mission accomplished has grown more apparent ever since the beginning of the new millennium. Soccer is usually viewed as the most popular recreational sport in the U.S. because almost everyone grew up playing it, but interest seems to fade as young people approach high school and college.

What solutions could be advanced to help promote soccer in the minds of the youth, so as to impart a long lasting impression in them? About 100 million of the nation's citizens are believed to have developed an interest in watching soccer. What can the nation do to generate a buzz about soccer, so as to increase the pool of talents in the U.S. college sports system and beyond?

A few ideas are hereby suggested for immediate consumption.

First, soccer that's socially engineered by the media and entertainment industries.

"It'll be cool and even super-cool," suggested Lena, "to use what we have to promote what we have, what we're and what we'd someday wish to be. The more soccer is promoted through global stellar soccer performances, the more the American public will support this beautiful sport *en masse*."

"Yes, of course." agreed Philomena, "but this might also need some smart strategies and searching out fresh ideas to promote soccer here in the U.S. Popular celebrities could be booked to promote soccer, serving as a bold frontier to raise awareness about the 'coolness quotient' of the sport. Famous artists can help the nation take soccer to new heights by employing popular pop culture and translating it into a more desirable and appreciable bottom line. Top notch, though."

"Although I'm not sure how much she's into soccer, a popular celebrity like Oprah Winfrey could easily convince Americans that soccer is worth our commitment because of its value as a global sport," advised Kimberly. "She's well-loved across the globe because of her exceptional gift of speech, philanthropy, and creative giving. As far I'm concerned, it'll take only one show on her network (OWN) to get the thing up and running. But I think that will happen only if we mean business. I'm prone to say this because I've been a regular viewer of her television shows for almost 15 years, and will vouch for her and what she's able to do. I think she's got a God-given talent that's unmatched."

"Your ideas are good, Philo and Kim!" exclaimed Werner. "Besides your suggestions, I also think that companies can host performances of country and pop sensations to get Americans understand and appreciate what soccer is all about — a sport that's second to none. It'll get fans and people in general, talking about soccer, and talking really loud."

"Certainly." agreed John Peter. "These types of media might help shock Americans to the point of waking up to the reality of soccer as an appealing industry, and a globally popular sport that demands their maximum interest."

"Your ideas are good, guys." observed Esther. "Because, many times, like in doing works of charity, we discover that it's not that people in general don't care or don't want to do something. Rather, it's because most of them never thought of it quite the way it's supposed to be or understood what it is, in the first place. Some people need motivation, some need challenges, some need inspiration, and some need mobilization."

"What a classic idea on how to promote soccer culture and similar industries in the U.S." exploded Chris. "I'll be quick in recommending singers and performers who can give it a good promo, at least those I remember.

In addition to other great musicians and super celebrity entertainers that America has, the following celebrities could become great assets in this arrangement: Cyndi Lauper, Celine Dion, Pat Benatar, Whitney Houston, Lee Ann Womack, Sharon Greene, Josh Groban, Marc Anthony, Bruce Springsteen, Elton John, Justin Timberlake, and the youngest but not the least, Justin Bieber."

"Thank you, Chris," remarked Lesley, "but many other artists whom you didn't remember to mention can do the same. All those you mentioned seem to specialize in certain types of inspirational music, and major crossover music hits. However, all we need to do is get them going, anyway. It could be done in a concert series, which would definitely pay off for the U.S. men's soccer team and soccer in general. It could be structured in such a way as to generate a buzz, so that people who watched or listened would then wish to become soccer fans or players. In short, it's about developing great interest in soccer and moving soccer forward in the U.S."

"That's correct." agreed Britney. "It's about advancing superstardom in soccer and creating soccer awareness, with the help of popular celebrities, and with me not counted out. The concerts will also help soccer differentiate itself from other sports in the U.S., as a global sport with distinguishing marks highlighted."

"You're right, Britney" responded Christine. "It'll be another clever strategy to elevate performers like myself, players and our beloved nation's soccer industry. These celebrities can perform in soccer stadiums or in other public theaters and auditoriums." "Those performances could also be watched not only at home," suggested Mariah, "but also live in midair flights through in-flight entertainment systems."

"Some people rarely think of soccer as a pleasurable and rewarding type of sport and experience," noted Jennifer. "The open performances will be an opportunity to interact with celebrities and engage existing fans and potential new soccer fans in places and ways they never considered previously. It's about having people come away saying: 'I've never experienced such a thing before.'"

"We'll end up having all the listeners and spectators go home saying, 'I've never seen a thing like this before in my life,'" agreed Lee Ann W. "It'll make some difference, I promise. Now is the perfect time to consider planting that seed of wonder for future success and maximum victory in soccer. It's time for us to get into best possible shape for the coming soccer games and beyond. Our men's soccer team has to win and win big internationally, and that will become good news for all Americans. Those who never had a spark of interest in soccer will develop interest in a twinkling of an eye. Seriously! Americans want and need good news, and no one should be shy or quiet about this fact. It feels good to get good news, and all of us must stay positive, forward looking, and hopeful."

"My recent experience during the special ball-dropping event for New Year's Eve in Times Square, which I covered as a major News Channel correspondent, tells me that such an event could be a pretty good forum to promote soccer," recalled Nancy. "Why? Because right there you've at least a million people ready to have a ball, as it drops. This event could be ushered in by some of our great performers here in the U.S. At least a million people from across the globe are expected to fill Times Square every New Year's Eve, for the world-famous count-down *fiesta* to midnight entertainment. The great producers could help design the ball to look like a big soccer ball. This could replace the traditional crystal ball, especially on any New Year's Eve following a U.S. victory by either the men's or women's teams in the FIFA World Cup tournament. It would be an exciting and golden moment."

"Thank you, Nancy." concurred Glenn. "That's a pretty good and smart idea. I think that such an event would be pretty cool, as it would be the celebration of a great win by our guys. You would have millions watching the event on television and the web, not just here in the US, but from around the world. It's also one of Times Square's official events, and will enjoy live coverage from great companies like Apple and Android, being available on their devices. Besides, a shower of soccer gifts or precious materials with soccer promo inscriptions could be released from Times Square rooftops onto the waiting crowd, which is often expected to top the one million mark. Again, it's a pretty good idea."

Good news in soccer development in the U.S.

"I feel excited already about how much I was able to dig up!" exclaimed Gary. "For me, it's good to hear that the well-loved and cherished man, Brad Pitt, who's an Academy Award nominated actor, a tireless advocate for charitable organizations and relief efforts around the world, recently accepted an invitation to be on the Board of Directors of the U.S. bid committee, to bring home the FIFA World Cup to the U.S. in 2018 or 2022."

"Though a charitable man myself, I respect Brad so much" conceded Chris. "Americans will continue to talk about, and write about, how deeply involved Brad has been in charitable works across the globe and how much they appreciate it. Interestingly, Brad is now a companion to more than 435,000 people who have already expressed their support for this ongoing quest."

"I'm also excited to learn that someone of his age range is on the bid committee," noted Andrew. "I read his statement in a magazine recently, which read as follows: 'Soccer is a truly global sport and the opportunity to join the effort to have the U.S. host the world's greatest sporting event again is a great honor. FIFA has set a world standard for using sport as a tool for a positive social change, and I'm proud to be associated with a U.S. World Cup Bid that has so ardently adhered to the principles formulated by FIFA.'"

"You're right, guys." observed Ruth. "I believe that Brad, who founded the Make it Right Foundation in 2006 in the aftermath of Hurricane Katrina, which organized housing professionals in New Orleans to finance and construct 150 sustainable, affordable new houses in New Orleans's Ninth Ward, can also help 'make right' our soccer system. What came to my mind is that he can do something good to help promote soccer in the U.S."

"I thought as much when I read the same on the website, Ruth." agreed Nancy. "It should also be recalled that in the same 2006, Brad and Angelina Jolie established a charitable organization, the Jolie-Pitt Foundation, to aid humanitarian causes around the world. Bravo to Brad and Angelina."

"I think that the committee made a good choice in Brad." added Mandy. "I believe he'll be a great asset to soccer development in the U.S. Brad has been exposed to global social and cultural perspectives in his career, coupled with his connection to soccer via his diverse family. This experience may have afforded him a unique understanding of the unifying aspects of the game. I think he's one of the guys to consult with when it comes to recruiting foreign players, if that ever becomes necessary. Moreover, his consistent philanthropic efforts exemplify the bid's desire to use soccer as a tool for positive change. Another great guy that I'd have loved to have on the committee is Bono. I think he's a nice guy. That's just my opinion, as I thought there might have been other qualifications."

Whether or not the bidding process will turn out in favor of the U.S. remains the most touching question of the moment. For now, it sounds good and feels right, but we're not sure how it's going to end. Thoughtful consideration should be given to how the bidding process by various soccer nations works, without skipping key factors that reveal the difficulty of winning a FIFA World Cup hosting bid. No matter how the results turn out, this nation's interest in soccer and her ardent desire to win and win big in soccer contests will never wane. We should never be discouraged by the outcome of the bid, even if it turns out not in our favor. All we need to do is keep our hopes in check, because we're not certain how the result is going to turn out.

"Like me, many soccer fans and enthusiasts don't know how the process works," revealed Brian. "This is a paraphrase of a statement attributed to Sunil Gulati, Chairman of the U.S.A. Bid Committee and President of U.S. Soccer. Here's how the bidding process works. The U.S. and other competing nations submitted their official bid books to FIFA in a formal ceremony that took place in Zurich, Switzerland on May 14, 2010. The next step was that FIFA's 24-member Executive Committee studied the bids, conducted site visits, and named the hosts for the 2018 and 2022 soccer events on December 2, 2010."

"As a follow-up to your disclosure of the bidding process," added Scott, "from all I know, this process will complete a 21-month bid and review process. Suffice it to say that among the nations that have officially expressed their interest to host the FIFA World Cup in 2018 and 2022, aside from the U.S., are Australia, England, and Russia."

"I also read in a local newspaper that Netherlands-Belgium and Portugal-Spain have each submitted joint bids for the 2018 and 2022 tournaments," noted Mitchell, "whereas Japan, Qatar, and South Korea have only applied as candidates to host the tournament in 2022. I'm not sure if any nations made attempts to withdraw their bids."

"Yes, Mexico and Indonesia were said to have withdrawn their bids in September 2009 and March 2010, respectively," reported Lazarus.

"All I know is that the U.S. has great competitors in its quest for the 2022 bid to host the soccer World Cup," responded Justin. "My only worry at this point is that the slight edge which Australia and Qatar may possibly have over the U.S. is that neither of these two bidding nations has hosted a World Cup before, unlike the U.S. FIFA leadership has been pretty keen about rotating this global event from one part of the globe to another, as they still consider the trip to South Africa to have been a huge success."

"Justin, you sound like someone who's inspired!" exclaimed Rene. "I also recall that Australia hosted the 2000 Summer Olympics. This took place in Sydney, following their winning of the FIFA award to do the hosting, in preference over Beijing, Istanbul, Berlin, and Manchester, after four rounds of voting."

"Let me mention this in addition to your comments," interrupted Jonny. "On the one hand, Australia received high scores for hosting the 2000 Summer Olympics, even though the location, dates, and time zone were inconvenient for European broadcasters. On the other hand, if Qatar happens to win the bid, she'd be the Middle Eastern pioneer in hosting the World Cup, and that seems likely to happen."

"Oh, gee!" lamented Martin. "If that ever happens, it means that she'd take the World Cup to the Middle East for the first time. That for me would be a big blow to the U.S., but shouldn't derail our journey toward future greatness in soccer. However, whether that would be possible, with Qatar's tiny population of roughly 1.7 million, remains a million dollar question."

"You seem to be making a strong point, Marty!" exclaimed Audrey. "Also, even though Qatar has an enticing and alluring proposal to build some stadiums in a compact area, there are concerns about the health and accommodation for players, spectators, and fans in summer temperatures that can sometimes reach 100°F or above. This issue will remain a big problem, notwithstanding Qatar's plan to provide cooling systems at the stadiums. Well, let's just wait and see what happens finally."

"It's on record that in 2002, South Korea and Japan co-hosted the FIFA World Cup from May 31 to June 30," observed Lynn, "after the two countries were chosen as hosts by FIFA in May 1996. It was unique because it was the first World Cup to be hosted by two nations, the first in Asia and the last in which the golden goal rule was applied. Just like the U.S., these two nations have complete and well-equipped stadiums, and the logistical and technological resources to run such a great event. As you may know, FIFA leadership has had a longstanding interest in using soccer to possibly unite the Korean peninsula, but North Korea ignored its offer to host some matches in 2002. Continued tensions between these two sister nations would undoubtedly stifle the use of soccer for such good intentions."

"I'm seriously inclined to think that with China expressing deep interest in hosting the 2026 World Cup," reasoned Sherrie, "there's the likelihood that the South Korean, Australian, and Japanese bids may be undercut. FIFA may be strongly interested in taking the event to China, which appears to be the world's biggest market so far. So, if either Qatar or Australia succeeds in winning the 2022 bid, I'm concerned about the fate of the U.S."

"Don't worry, guys." counseled Austin. "For the 2022 bid, the U.S. hopefully remains the prospective winner, according to various predictions. I think that FIFA could select the U.S. at any time for World Cup soccer, as one strong incentive is her dollar power. It would be hard to find another nation that would be able to generate as much cash for FIFA as the U.S., because no other country has the number of stadiums that we have. But the bid committee has to strengthen efforts toward achieving that feat, otherwise the process of promoting soccer among 320 million consumers, who are already intrigued and excited about this forward moving and forward looking game, will be tragically derailed should the U.S. fail to secure the bid."

"I know you're trying to be optimistic about that, Austin," teased Daniel, "but it's hard to anticipate or predict the direction of FIFA decisions now. However, I believe that whatever happens, the process of promoting soccer in the U.S. can never be derailed by anything, regardless of the bid's outcome. What all the members of the bid committee need to do now is to just play their cards well. No matter who finally celebrates victory in FIFA's selection for the 2022 FIFA World Cup hosting, the U.S. will continue to work toward making soccer the most loved and watched sport in the entire nation. Promise?"

"You're absolutely right, Dan," agreed Connie. "There's no need to predict events that could catch every one of us by surprise. I think that failure to secure victory in the bidding will only mean a derailment in our focus, but not a deletion of our long-standing focus on soccer. We're all ready to keep moving forward. We're ready to support our national men's soccer team, all the way to the finish."

What is the scope of the functions of the bid committee? It's important to mention at this point that the U.S. Bid Committee is a nonprofit organization created to prepare a successful application to host the FIFA World Cup in 2018 or 2022. Hopefully, the scope of the committee's functions could be extended to helping organize a strong men's soccer team that's both super and superb. The direction, shape, and future beauty of the country's men's soccer team will be heavily determined by the way this committee and the U.S. Soccer Federation in general, work toward a possibly assured Gold Medal soccer victory in 2014. The members of the bid committee, and myriads of fans and supporters who are looking forward to the 2014 World Cup, should FOREVER recall that interest in soccer in the U.S. grew considerably following the hosting of the 1994 World Cup by the U.S. Interest in soccer will predictably gain further momentum if the U.S. succeeds in her future bids to host the World Cup soccer.

"Our hope is that the FIFA governing body would consider granting this soccer-hosting favor once again in the future to the U.S.," stated Mortimer. "But my greatest hope is that the bid committee will extend its reach in helping to give us a team that will stand the test of global soccer contests, without quickly falling to defeats midway through the matches, as they've been prone to do from time immemorial."

"Hahaaha. Falling to defeats, in any form at all," countered Stuart, "isn't an American tradition and should never be our tradition. Neither should we hand that legacy over to future generations. How can we prove our commitment to excellence? By waking up to victory. Just by waking up to win and win big."

"Everybody will be excited to learn that the members of the U.S. Bid Committee are those we hold in high esteem," remarked Kirsten, "such as the U.S. Soccer Federation President Sunil Gulati, who's the chairman of the committee. Without doubt, Sunil has shaped his powerful office to fit the needs of the times, but he needs more enhanced powers to do a better job than in the past."

"Hopefully, this committee won't stop at the bid job, but will work to save the U.S. from future soccer embarrassments," observed Teri. "I encourage whoever has the American flag to wave it with joy from the rooftops of every building, after reading and knowing the names of all the members of this bid committee. What a beautiful thing to know that we've great people in this country who can help move soccer forward, with ease and creative strategies."

"Why do Americans need the members of this committee?" asked Arthur. "Well, I believe that we need them and people like them badly now to keep our soccer and nation's flags, flying higher and higher. Soccer is like that little thing that's at the core of every progress-loving society, a thing that can help a nation make its way, with ease, through the world."

"Surely, Americans need members of the committee to help save us from future unnecessary defeats in international soccer," added Gretchen. "We need them because they're among the smartest people in the U.S., and have the God-given talents necessary to meet the challenges we face on the global playing fields of international soccer. These are people who can make positive changes for the better, but this takes vision, common sense, instincts, and guts. What they will be able to give us as a nation are things that we don't frequently see, since each one of them is, apparently, a super strategist in the making."

"There's not a single doubt about that in my mind." agreed Rochelle. "We can see in them shining examples of human excellence, but if and only if they're driven by a united and committed purpose to put successful plans into action. May they leave no success or victory behind, nor any stone unturned, in trying to move our men's national soccer team to greater heights in whatever ways they can."

"I'm not saying this just because my guy is a member of the committee," revealed Sarah, "but I believe that they're men of timber and caliber who can use their intelligence, talents, and sheer genius to save the U.S. from further downfalls in men's soccer."

"When you talk about downfalls in our men's soccer, you get me close to becoming infuriated," fumed Rebecca. "Our guys are doing pretty well in soccer. All they need is just to win and win big in the next FIFA World Cup soccer tournament."

"I agree with the point you're making, Sarah!" exclaimed Clare. "The members of the bid committee aren't only celebrities, but are also heroes who can transform the state of the American soccer with their talents and leadership style. We need people like that, both now and in the future, who have the ability to accomplish something wonderful. It's about more than just getting the bid — the fate of our men's soccer team is at stake."

"I follow you, Clare." affirmed Doug. "They can rouse support from millions of Americans, and motivate and inspire them as the occasion demands. Let's all rally around them and support them, with Sunil Gulati, and they'll get the job done for us. Let everybody support them, and wake up to victory."

"Let them know that they're not alone, whenever they work to lift our soccer team to greater heights," exhorted Edwin. "Your brothers and sisters all over the U.S. are with you and support your commitments. It's time to use leadership capably, creatively, and successfully, as a force for the common good. It's time to throw ourselves at the problem of poor soccer performance. It's time to trust that our nation can do whatever is necessary to bring us much deserved triumphs on the global soccer scene. It's time to do certain vital and urgently needed things to improve our men's soccer team, so that it finally ranks among the highest-rated teams on earth. It's time to show that we have something great in the U.S. and that something is truly working here. Viva U.S.A. Long live the US!"

You may be surprised to know the power of good rhetoric and speech in creating a great master plan to get our men's soccer team to win future FIFA World Cup soccer contests. A passionate, powerful, and fiery speech can awaken a sleeping giant in soccer. All it takes is a speech that can rattle the ears of the players with strong but uplifting messages. This can help us immeasurably in promoting soccer and in putting together a good team that can claim its rightful glory on the international stage.

"The US, among all the nations of the world," argued Dick, "has been gifted with great people, presidents, and leaders who can raise the morale of people and players with their powerful styles of speech and gifts of oratory. Just think of the presidents as examples, and we don't have to roll back to the time of President Franklin Roosevelt (FDR). Just think from president JFK all the way down to the current President Obama."

"A rousing speech by a president and commander-in-chief with an imposing stature," suggested Roy, "can send the players out to the soccer arena on fire, prepared to come back as great winners. The same is applicable to fiery pre-game speeches from savvy coaches or wily managers. The well-known clichés "wake up and win big, "rise and shine," "wake up to victory," and the ever-popular "Yes we can" can do a whole lot of magic as regards our men's soccer outings. From a psychological perspective, any well-prepared and well-crafted pre-game or post-training speech could have a transformative effect on players; just as such speeches often do in other sports. They can be an incredible game changer."

Various soccer managers and coaches have, in the past, delivered fiery and stirring pre-tournament speeches, with marvelous impacts on the players. Some players believe that such speeches will keep your blood pumping, especially when it's loaded with inspirational and encouraging clichés.

Do you know the proper way to speak to players? To start, be positive and optimistic, even when the going isn't all that good. Consider using the following inspirational phrases:

"I love you because you go to the field of soccer to win."

"The opposing team won't be a problem for you at all."

"We've played big and we're going to win big."

"I'm proud of you, so go out and win."

"As always, come back a winner."

"Be a winner."

In contrast, a public message like "I don't know what's going to happen" might be 'honest' but totally sounds like a self-defeating statement.

"I was recently impressed by the message from the New York Jets coach in their training camp," observed Olga. "A correspondent from a popular radio channel in New York asked the coach what he thought would happen the following day when the Jets encountered their opponent on the playing field. Without any hesitation the coach stated, 'It's a done deal, we're going to win . . . I haven't a single doubt that we'll win.' What a powerful, inspirational, and reassuring statement from a coach. I thought that was a great speech."

"Knowing how to treat your players," advised Felix, "can make you one of the most memorable managers in soccer history. Let there never be a dull moment in your willingness and readiness to lift the spirits of the players. It takes a smart guy who understands people, public relations, and who knows how to treat people with class. A coach who's even-keeled, always in a good mood, and upbeat is a blessing to soccer, and will be greatly missed when he's gone. What a tribute!"

Now, can you guess who the members of the American World Cup bid committee are? Perhaps, and hopefully, the ones you have in mind are among those appointed as bid committee members. Go google to see who they are!

"I think that by merely looking at the names and faces of these great American sons and daughters," remarked Ernest, people's noses will wrinkle no longer and the situation of the U.S. men's soccer team will appear pretty exciting to many. It's like being stricken by an epiphany and a sense of gratitude that runs like this:

"At last, all powerful Master, you're now coming to the rescue of our men's national soccer team, though indirectly, with the choice of these great American guys and gals. It's a time to sing the *Sun Is Shining, We Are the Champions, I'm Still Standing* or *Life's Been Good*. The future of our men's soccer team is bright. Thank you, Lord, and now let's keep our fingers crossed."

"With this caliber of people," enthused Frank, "the hopeful project of getting our men's national soccer team to greatness won't drag on endlessly, but this will only happen if committee members do their jobs quickly, promptly, and efficiently. It'll be a great pleasure to see them bring their gifts and talents to soccer."

"As far as I'm concerned," noted Trish, "the two major projects they have are winning the bid and getting our men's national soccer team bring home the Cup and Gold Medal in the upcoming World Cup soccer tournament. This achievement will push interest in soccer to heights never before witnessed in the entire history of the U.S."

"I pretty much think that the committee members will be able to put their heads together and chart the best way forward for our nation's men's soccer team," averred Ron. "It's no longer a time to be ashamed of past undeserved defeats, but rather be proud of our men and what they will be able to achieve from now on."

"No matter what, we're not going to do this by bullying," cautioned Dave. "I mean the bidding thing, as that wouldn't be a good approach for an aspiring world power in soccer like the U.S. No one does well by bullying anyone; such tricks don't always work. We're going to achieve our goals by employing our masterly strategic prowess to quickly reorganize our men's soccer team for the 2014 soccer encounters and beyond. That's it, and that's what I think."

"Guys, it's time for implementation," chimed Kelly. "It's time to put our brain power and genius into action. These strategies will be honored and will continue to be honored by Americans, if they finally pay off as hoped. The Soccer Federation should kick start a love affair between soccer in the U.S. and its many fans in the nation."

"I think you're right, Kelly." admitted Victor. "Sunil Gulati promises to fix the problem of soccer in the U.S. and has remained unmoved by setbacks, whether minor or major. Gulati, an Indian-American and charismatic economics lecturer at Columbia University, is one of the influential and brilliant men in American soccer, and will be a great asset in moving the U.S. soccer forward. He beams with confidence. Forward ever, backward never."

"That's correct." agreed Joel. "Going by his experience in soccer over the course of three decades, and his help in securing and organizing the 1994 tournament and running Major League soccer in 1996, he may be considered equal to the task and has proven himself to be just that. Still, he needs to do more. He also brings his unbeatable optimism to the job. Bravo and more grease to your elbows, Mr. Gulati. The nation wants you to add to your accomplishments so far."

From what we've just read, we can affirm that progress in the U.S. soccer began with her winning the World Cup hosting bid in 1988. The U.S. returned to the soccer tournament after a 40-year absence, qualifying for the tournament with a team of college players who came out from nowhere and did us proud in 1989, even without any professional experience, so to speak. Hope for more progress grew even stronger when our women's team won the inaugural Women's World Cup in 1991.

Moreover, the 1994 World Cup hosted by the U.S. still remains a landmark event. Our women won again in 1999, with our men reaching the quarterfinals for the first time in 2002. The U.S. has shown that it can be competitive in the World Cup soccer. After reaching the quarterfinals in 2002, the men's team earned a draw against the ultimate champion Italy in group play in 2006. "I think the perception of the American team has been good in recent years, because they've performed exceptionally well in the past soccer World Cups," observed former English soccer star Steve McManaman.

"I've never had any doubt in my mind," added Rex, "that the further the U.S. advances in soccer, the more Americans will be likely to tune in. Soccer has grown substantially in the last 20 years in America, going from a niche sport to one that now features a viable and professional league in Major League Soccer (MLS), with robust coverage of international matches on television and the Internet."

"From the records I've kept so far, more than 17 million people in North America tuned in to the World Cup final between Italy and France in 2006," noted Tony, "and more that 120 million people watched at least one minute of the World Cup tournament. In the four years since the last World Cup, soccer coverage has increased both on television and online. Such networks as the Fox Soccer Channel and ESPN have expanded the availability of games from the English Premier League and the tournament involving the top Europeans."

"Hi, Tony," greeted Rob. "I think that the record you kept seems pretty accurate. As a follow up to your report, I read recently that top European clubs, including Real Madrid, AC Milan, and others, have attracted sellout crowds during tours of major U.S. cities. Television coverage of MLS games is said to have been flat, with only a handful of games airing nationally each week. While the league is growing in size, I think that it'll expand from 16 to 19 teams by 2012. I believe that it has struggled to overcome the perception that it isn't as competitive as the European leagues."

"I recently discovered that soccer's television ratings and attendance fall well short of the established major sports in America," remarked Chris, "but sports marketing experts reassure us that winning a single soccer game, or the biggest match in the world, will fix that. To cite one example, IBIS World, a research firm, reported this week that the average attendance at MLS games is up nearly 11% from the same period last year. The company expects attendance to rise more than 15% overall for the 2010 season."

"Whatever is the case," cautioned Howard, "I don't think our approach should be one of make it or break it. From all I know, one of the biggest obstacles that soccer faces is a lack of exposure. You have to find a way to capitalize on increased exposure, one way or another."

Is there hope for more progress in future FIFA World Cup contests? Yes, there's plenty of hope for more progress, as U.S. qualifies again for the 2014 World cup tournament. Great job indeed, but what remains is clinching the cup at the finals at least once, before we secure the bid to host the tournament coming up in 2022. I mean, if we're fortunate enough to win the bid eventually.

"Yes, we can." affirmed George. "We can find our way to the finals and win if we create a Super Ball (Bowl) attitude in soccer. It's high time we remember that we've come of age in soccer in recent years, and should not hide behind cozy excuses that the U.S. has no soccer roots or foundation. We have to emerge from the group soccer contest stage, survive the elimination stage, and win the finals."

"We have all it takes to get there." bragged Ralph. "Tell me, what do we lack to achieve that? Let's not forget that for more than 95 years the U.S. Soccer Federation, as the governing body of the sport, has helped, in no less remarkable fashion, to chart the course for soccer in the U.S.A. Yes, Americans can help the Soccer Federation in its mission to make soccer a pre-eminent sport in the US, and to continue growing the game at all entertaining and competitive levels."

"The time is ripe," agreed Eli. "It's no longer a time to be a soccer fan and a believer in the sport, but rather a time to push that interest forward and propel it to greater heights. The U.S. men's national team represents the U.S. in international soccer contests, and has been officially controlled by the U.S. Soccer Federation. It's the Federation's job to elect and appoint people to various functions and recruit players for our national soccer team. If not, it should be highly recommended."

"What we're not supposed to overlook," advised Hank, "is that many of the staffs and players they appointed have performed exceptionally well, and have positively influenced soccer over the past decades, even though they may have seldom made news headlines. The USSF is now blessed with strong and effective leaders, unlike anything this nation has seen in decades. This is about their body of work — both the remarkable works they've already accomplished, and the work they should continue to do, individually and collectively to strengthen soccer in the federation."

"I'm not sure if I completely agree with you, Hank." protested Willie. "All I know is that the success and future of soccer reform in the U.S. don't depend on any one individual. Everyone's hand must be on deck in the effort to advance and push soccer forward in the current and coming decades. There's no doubt that with everyone's cooperation, the leadership will leave a legacy that persists, even after they leave the top soccer federation offices. Ours should be seen as an era for men's soccer expansion."

"We can't wait to have our men's soccer team and its leadership walk through victory doors to receive great honors," enthused Simone, "which the nation has been longing to give them. It'll be like making it to the great Hall of Fame. It would be most desirable if the effort would begin and continue with the present leadership of the U.S. Soccer Federation, a leadership that has been truly great and strong for so long now. The USSF, meanwhile, has impending challenges to overcome in the interests of our men's soccer team — to prove cynics and pundits wrong, to defend itself against being labelled impotent, and to work harder to propel our soccer team to lofty heights, as the contests come up in a few years' time."

"This challenge may have to entail doing more with less, to push progress in soccer," noted Candy. "People are desperate to have the U.S. compete aggressively in the global soccer market. At the same time, this type of progress might need a rethinking of the century-old model of soccer, where some teams prefer to look good on the field without coming home victorious. Scoring is the key to victory, not just looking good on the field of play, especially for our men's national soccer team. We need this progress in an era when Americans want and deserve their global soccer representatives to meaningfully evaluate and produce highly skilled professional players."

"This isn't an era to massage any decline in our soccer commitments," observed Rachel. "It's about fighting to get the victory and keeping it. Let's

look at it another way. The Soccer Federation has to think deeply about many things and ask itself questions like: what have other great teams across the globe done that the U.S. men's team hasn't done? What can we do to promote and sustain the development of our men's soccer? Some people think we should wake up to the reality of soccer rise and examine the effects that tenure has on our soccer managers."

"A point of correction, Rachel." urged Arthur. "If by tenure you mean job security, as we have it in our nation's education system, I'll tell you now that soccer managers don't have that, unless you're talking about the duration of their appointments to leadership positions in our nation's soccer administration. Do our soccer managers actually have tenure? If they do, what does that mean and how long does that last? Does it affect their performances negatively, or does it actually help them do better? If there's tenure in our soccer system management, doesn't it need some review? Would that do the trick and take care of the shocks of instability that hit soccer programs at the arrival of every new soccer manager? Would that negatively affect making pools of decisions without much knowledge of soccer? Does it matter whether you've any knowledge of soccer at all, or do we need people who'll get the job done?"

"A long and involved, but ultimately compelling, train of thought, Arthur." replied Jenkins. "I think that section needs a more and better enlightenment. I only know that there's a school of thought that has been advocating some application of checks and balances when it comes to our nation's soccer management, since it has a strong global touch. Which department will be the overseer and do it well? All these remain big questions. It's a clear presumption that since a majority of people are interested in the progress of sporting entertainment of whatsoever description in our nation, we should all endeavor to sacrifice our personal interests for sports, especially the type of sport that has global impact on our beloved nation."

"I'm not quite sure what you're saying," confessed Mitch. "What I know is that we need to bring the U.S. soccer into a modern world that's pretty crazy with contests. How we would like to do that is a different cup of coffee. However, it's important to think of, look at, where our players were before the present administration and give a fair analysis of the leadership. Again, and again, it's an analysis you should make regardless of whether or not you agree with the leadership on certain issues. It's an analysis you should do whether you love or hate the leadership. Meanwhile, the leadership represents a true innovation, but that innovation must be supported with more action. It's an analysis that you should do without prejudice and only with fairness, while expressing your strong position, opinion, and wish for the entire nation when it comes to soccer."

As we keep preparing for future FIFA World Cup contests, the questions that ordinary soccer lovers and fans would naturally ask are as follows: How do we select players that best represent us in international soccer contests? Are they the best players that a nation of almost 300 million can produce? The latter should remain the overarching question.

"Without a good selection of players for any match," cautioned Brookes, "there would always be lots of cock and bull stories to be told afterwards. Without the proper training and drills needed for players to move up, the direction will always be pointed downward. The bottom line remains that there are challenges involved. The challenge of one day lifting the trophy by lifting our men's soccer team higher won't be a cakewalk, unless there's an adequate preparation and performances that are impressive."

"Apart from making efforts to give the players top-notch training in soccer," suggested Felicia, "I think that empowering soccer managers and coaches is of crucial importance. We ought to be ready to give soccer managers and coaches just about anything they might need to succeed. We should support every smart step they take to achieve success, so that we'll have no reason to accept excuses for failure or defeat. Failure shouldn't be part of any consideration that we make, and we want to leave it at that. Without doubt, leadership is the summit of the entire process, with different approaches to attaining that pinnacle. Moreover, we know that there are some criteria and qualities that are more or less important than others in this arrangement."

"Inasmuch as managerial experience is important in making the choice of soccer managers, organizers, and coaches," noted Jackson, "we should not forget that they need empowerment from the powers that be and from the general public. In every sporting management, fans are able to distinguish between true patience and indifference, between keeping busy and looking busy. Getting down to specifics, let me point out that while bold gestures, unguarded and directionless actions shouldn't be mistaken as competence, no-nonsense types, and disciplinarians, motivators, and people who operate in the same fashion, are often considered favorites for soccer managing jobs. That has been my impression."

"Of course, that truth is as naked as it can be." concurred Lisa. "It's a good place to begin, when thinking of people to hire for that type of job. People with such qualities, plus smart, should be good for every team, and not only soccer because they have fiery, tough, and good disciplinarian qualities that enable them to sometimes kick the players in the butts to forestall an unnecessarily early relaxations and laissez-faire attitudes in the players. Indeed, coaches should be master motivators, born with an untouchable gift of perspectives, not to mention an uncanny way of pushing the right buttons with their players."

"I understand what you mean, Lisa." beamed Kate. "It's fine that they have those qualities, which you've mentioned. They should, at the same time, not be 'the rolling stones that gather no moss.' For me, remaining tight-lipped at all times doesn't feel right. The long and short of this is that a coach's attitude could be a great inspiration for his or her players. Good communication skills could have a significantly positive impact on the performance of the players on the field. It could be a significant factor in leading players to victories in matches, but again, it wholly depends on how strong and powerful the message sounds to its listeners."

"I think that you're right, ladies." enthused Doug. "Let me add that being a good communicator with a great power of persuasion will always be a plus, as such a quality is often inspirational and motivational for all players. I'm talking from my experience as a soccer player in the state of Mississippi. Such qualities get the attention of players and lift their spirits. Could a soccer manager or coach not have these exceptional qualities, remain a quiet soccer tactician, and still get the job done? Yes, indeed. But he could ask for a volunteer from among the players, someone who has the earlier mentioned qualities and can serve as a liaison or messenger between the coach and the team. In this setup, the coach would once in a while delegate to the volunteer player all that he wants done with and for the entire team."

"That sounds good, Doug." noted Roseanne. "I know a coach who has done that. But, in any case, the messenger and volunteer must be popular, aggressive, a star player, well-loved and trusted by his fellow teammates, and a player who'll be able to carry out undiluted instructions from the coach."

"It's crucial to mention here," added Jack, "that in trying to streamline a team's discipline in soccer, the managers and coaches should never be afraid to assert authority over the players in a friendly but strong manner. They should be people who are able to build loyalty beyond reason, and able to get people to totally believe that winning big is possible and poised toward accomplishing it. They should be able to make clear to every player what he should be doing, while trying to convince the rest of the players that what they're doing is important and why it's so. Also, there must be some consistency in their willingness and readiness to set up an environment in which the players will completely trust them. This will make the players go away as individuals, only to return with a commitment to contributing to the greater success of the team."

"The point you're making now reminds me of the case of my brother," stated Dolores, "who's been a great soccer player in Idaho. From our casual discussions about the sport, I've gathered that the type of commitment you mentioned might make every player determined to become a man of the year, decade, or century, depending on what they plan to achieve and how they plan to end up achieving it, as an individual and as a team member."

"I can't wait to add to your idea," urged Clemens, "that while the coaches and managers strive to get along with the players, at the same time they've got to question the team's discipline at all times. Otherwise, it would become uncontrollably frustrating and thereby not auguring well for the team's general performances. In essence, desired passion for proper protocol, when it comes to a soccer team's discipline, should neither be lacking nor overlooked."

"What I've discovered from my years as a soccer player," added Edwin, "is that with their sense of detail, disciplinarians and no-nonsense quality soccer managers and coaches get the players well-prepared to focus and play up to their potential. We've got to deal with the soccer world as we find it, and work through the finer points of forming a formidable men's soccer team that's beyond reproach."

"I had a coach in college soccer who was a staunch disciplinarian and a creative leader," announced Rick. "There's something unique about him. One of the things I loved about him is that he always wanted to see his soccer team improve every New Year, or show plausible plans for becoming better every new soccer season. He'd promise to never leave the team hanging. I believe that without his astute coaching and personality that commanded respect, leadership would've become an oddity for him, thereby resulting in little good getting done. His philosophy of life was: if promises were made, then the people who made them should make good on those promises."

"Rick, he sounds pretty much like my coach and soccer manager in high school, about fifteen years ago," interrupted Randy. "The slight difference between the two is that my coach, who we referred to as "The Big Do," had a philosophy of life that guided him. For the key isn't to make hasty decisions. Take time to see how things play out in the field, to help you separate fantasy from reality. He often joked about cleaning up and disinfecting the environment and culture of losing and defeat, if there was any. Defeat was the only word lacking in his helpful lexicon. For him, any culture that celebrated defeat didn't reflect well on the coaches."

"I'm looking at the issue of leadership from a different angle," opined Sid. "I've been thinking that our men's soccer leaders and managers haven't figured out a way to get the players to exude confidence. They haven't found a way to motivate our smart players. Sometimes it takes fellow players to motivate a teammate. For me, I think that nothing has changed, and maybe the leaders, coaches, and managers have to change their ways."

As we keep preparing our men's soccer team for future FIFA World Cup events, it's crucial that we allow the era of modern soccer to begin in the US, since the world is quickly changing, with millions of Americans developing interest in soccer. The majority of observers attribute this trend of growing interest to the outstanding performances of our women's soccer team, to whom some refer as "the great giants and heroines who did us proud."

Think of it for a moment. And while you keep thinking of it, please tune in and listen to more of what we have to say.

# Chapter 9
## U.S. Soccer: *What They Say*

Just listen to simple and honest evaluations: there's no doubt that U.S. players have the grit and determination that define their manner of playing and their careers in soccer. But what makes U.S. soccer fans wince seems to have been the team's inherently weak attackers and feeble forward liners and defenders.

"I've been a soccer player since high school here in Massachusetts," remarked David, "and have been watching past U.S. men's soccer encounters. My observation is that in previous U.S. men's team soccer encounters, about four decades earlier, people from great soccer nations had always looked at the U.S. fans as cheering on low-skilled players who were blessed with great coaches."

"Dave, you're absolutely right," agreed Stephanie. "I've been a witness to what some of them had often said in those days — they often tended to mumble this peculiar question as they watched our men play: 'Is your coach right for you?' Sometimes you hear them make derogatory remarks like: 'When did soccer playing become this funny?'"

"I disagree a little bit with you, David and Stephanie," objected Lisa. "Many of them saw our men as terrific players, whereas a negligible minority among them sensed naivety in the attitudes of American fans, who they believed were celebrating weakness in the name of cheering on great soccer playing."

"I don't know so much and just can't tell," mused Cindy. "All I know is that they often considered it a joke, as they looked at our men's soccer team as an easy prey, a weak and darling team that every other team would readily and willingly desire to take on anytime. They seemed to have sized us up."

Those were part of the tales told of an inexperienced soccer team's struggles in those days. However, as the years rolled by, the U.S. men's team began to match up relatively well in face-offs with some European soccer nations (with Germany, France, and Italy excluded). It was hard to observe any remarkable difference between the U.S. men's team and other low-level European teams. Nonetheless, that was a giant stride in progress, knowing what our team had been like decades ago. It's quite a remarkable progress in their long soccer journey. Things haven't gone too badly, as the team's performances remain encouraging.

Today, fans can bear witness to the rapidity with which the team has been progressing. Fans are proud that they've got a team that never quits, no matter the circumstances. They're grateful to the organizers, because the players are getting more and more physical and even proving a tough team to beat. What a great leap in progress, a type that many great nations would envy! That showed their readiness to play and participate actively in soccer. But progress seems to have been relatively slow ever since. How can the U.S. men's national soccer team improve from here?

"I've been a professional soccer player for over five years," hinted Bruce, "and have lived in Chicago all my life. I think that we have everything to become great in soccer, but we seem to have made history by having great midfielders but only low-skilled defenders and mediocre forward liners. No team ever wins major global contests with only mediocre defense and attackers."

Some disgruntled and discontented fans seem to blame the slow progress on the soccer organizers, whom they accuse of incompetence and cluelessness about the science of soccer and its engineering. Others oppose them, claiming that it's only a problem of selection and field placement.

"I'm a student of classics at Montclair, New Jersey, and an ardent soccer fan," declared Karen. "I think that our men's soccer managers haven't taken it upon themselves as a duty to make a big difference for the American people. Are they able to do so? Of course, yes. But I feel that the majority of those organizers are clueless about soccer, because they never played soccer, let alone became professional players. How could the blind lead the blind? No one gives what he has not."

"I beg to disagree with you, Karen," protested Mark. "You don't have to be a soccer genius to lead any soccer team to great heights. I think that the managers do a great job in training and drilling our men's team. I'd rather argue that our problem lies in the selection of players, as well as placing them in their proper positions. A good soccer fan and tactician will be able to place players where they belong in the field, to enable them to do a good job during any soccer tournament. It's pretty easy to spot wonderful players, and to tell when and where they do well in a soccer arena."

Some people believe that we've recently got into the swamp of pouring all resources and support into our women's soccer team, thereby neglecting our men's team.

"Our men's team seems to have been somewhat neglected," complained Tim. "When it comes to resources and management personnel. Let me cite an example with our women's team, which seems to have taken up every resource — socially, financially, and management-wise — that might be needed in the men's team. Experts were hired from abroad to drill the women's team to greater heights, which they've attained."

"I've no idea what you mean by that." objected Garry. "I live in New York and can tell you that our men's team has always received all they needed, as far as I know. They've not been lacking in anything. They have a good manager and coach, too. But I think that they need to look for more great and wonderful players across the country, and begin early to get them to know one another, and then give them excellent training for future contests. That's it. I believe that nothing is lacking in the U.S., including wonderful managers and coaches. Let me mention that the soccer managers need our cooperation as well."

Some believe that the managers are too old, although not 'ancient,' to run soccer as a sport in our great nation. However, how much we agree or disagree on these points is a different issue and ball game.

"Those guys running our men's national soccer team are too old to do that," grumbled Brian. "They seem to be too conservative and archaic in managing our national team. We need to look for young people who are charismatic enough to inspire and motivate the players. We desperately need some new blood that's innovative and will be able to run around and get the job done, anytime"

"Brian, I don't think that it really matters." objected Lauren. "None of our men's soccer managers are as old as you think. I even consider them relatively young, because none of them is 60 yet. What happens if you get a youthful person, if that's what you mean, into the system that literally doesn't know the difference between his left and his right in soccer? How would you explain that? Wouldn't that be more disastrous for our men's national soccer team?"

One of the major questions many soccer-loving fans keep asking is: why is our women's national soccer team doing exceptionally well globally, whereas our men's soccer team seems to be forever lagging behind?

"I think that Brian has made a good point." affirmed Will. "Even though managing the soccer industry needs some level of experience, we should, however, not be bothered by possible contest from young super soccer engineers. There must be a way, and some clear resolve, to inject more new blood into the system."

"Again, running a successful soccer team in any nation doesn't necessarily take the brain of a genius to accomplish," argued Mark, "but it takes some foresight, insight, and hindsight at a time and in a given situation. This may not be only about soccer, but might be applied to other fields of human endeavor. The above-mentioned attributes don't belong to the young or the old alone. We need people who'll get things done and make our men's soccer team bright and shining, regardless of whether the organizers are young or old."

"I agree with what Mark said," Sandra jumped in. "We need people who have the ability to know what's important and who can focus on the areas where they think they can make some difference in our soccer system. There's often the passion to fire those at the head of a team when things go bad. However, this doesn't always result in a helpful outcome but in potential disaster because many times the people put in a box could be faultless." Bust the bosses? Here are some responses.

"Tossing soccer managers and organizers out like old and worn-out shoes," cautioned Michael, "is never the best alternative in solving soccer problems. Indeed, firing soccer managers is like garden pruning. Sometimes you really don't know what to prune until the garden is overgrown. It's also not the most sensible way to end tenure or an era — not the best idea."

"Why not?" asked Craig.

"From my experience in sports administration," replied Michael, "layoffs are often costly and time-consuming, especially when the bigger battles are far from over. If they're absolutely necessary to push a project forward, and achieve a desired victory, then you could forge ahead with layoffs. But, as far as I know, layoffs could become administratively suicidal."

"I've been a coach in Livingston, New Jersey," declared Chris, "and a high school administrator for over six years. From my experience, if you fire a national coach or the U.S. sports and soccer manager, who has done extraordinary work to push soccer forward, whom will you put in as his replacement? How are we certain that the person we put in his place will do better or produce the intended result in the quickest possible time?"

"You're right, Chris," agreed Andrew. "They need time to study the system in the first place, to get used to it and familiarize themselves with the players and their styles of play, to enable them to make a good judgment in the selection and organization of a vibrant and solid soccer team. All these take some time. When a coach isn't doing well, he needs to be called to order on the grounds that he corrects his previous mistakes and makes some personnel, and personal, changes in his style and attitude to soccer in general. When he makes those changes and reforms, there are chances that great things will begin to happen. Every intelligent soccer coach knows what he needs to win and win big."

"Do you mean, Andy," asked Tom, "that a coach who's not performing well should be left in office as a national coach, to the detriment of a team and the entire nation? Remember that, here, we have a team that represents us internationally. How and why should one or two persons who can't perform efficiently and effectively hold the entire nation hostage? I often see it as a disgrace to any nation when her national men's soccer team is defeated in an international encounter for no strong reasons. What happens when the head coach is implicated, and indicted, as responsible for the defeat?"

"I don't mean that a coach should be kept in office at all costs or forever," countered Andrew. "A former coach is important, especially when he's done exceptionally well. But the team could promote that coach to a technical adviser status and still get a new coach, a superman who'll be able to carry the team forward to great heights."

"Andrew, I don't want us to get political in this pretty important matter," warned Laura, "but it's too early to do so now. Our men's soccer team matters to us, as much as our women's soccer team. Sometimes it takes only a simple question to move on without prejudice. Can't previous mistakes, no matter how grave, be corrected at any time? How do we correct them?"

"We'll get to the answer in few seconds," promised Andrew. "Of course, my answer is yes — nothing is too late. Correction could be made, beginning with a few courageous decisions."

"It takes some resolve, as it could be done at someone's say-so." advised Laura. "This is because politics may be driving some people's essential public functions. I've been a resident of Washington D.C. for over 15 years now, so I'm familiar with how politics works in all its ramifications."

"Laura, I appreciate your concern." replied Stacy. "I've been a policy maker for almost five years now in North Carolina. Politics can be good, sometimes, but at the same time, somewhat harmful to a people's common good and interests."

"Let's get out of politics in soccer matters, ladies," pleaded Doug. "I don't think any politics is involved in soccer management. People may not always be alerted by others to their mistakes, and given the opportunity to correct them, for some reasons. However, mistakes and losses, soccer notwithstanding, are occasions, that we need to take some time to analyze and dissect."

"I think you're right, Doug." agreed Tom. "We should see them as life-changing circumstances, both in soccer and in general daily living that we can use to think deeply of how to make things better. They also present opportunities for reflection, but with renewed energy, hope, and optimism."

"Correcting mistakes and making a few structural changes so that some embarrassments can end," noted Susan, "could be two different things altogether. Some other tactics could be smartly adopted to spare the soccer organizers and managers possible pressures of future public angst and ire. This is my humble opinion."

"All that the leaders of our soccer teams need to do as quickly as possible," added Bill, "is to re-strategize, listen to useful comments, and possibly employ a foreign coach that will technically support the team's head coach. It's also the way it is that the man who's at the helm of the ship, whether it's the *Titanic, Lusitania*, or our men's national team, always takes the blame for its failure."

"We've got team managers and coaches for our men's soccer team before," observed Lawrence, "who have been giving us great and beautiful surprises. Some have done that by shouting, yelling, pushing, and shoving, not to mention pouncing on something to make things happen and get things done. Here in Alabama, we have a manager and coach who does that and is making good things happen for our team."

"I understand what you mean, Lawrence," replied Kevin. "Our national soccer manager and head coach are both quiet looking but vigorous soccer promoters and strategists, if not super-strategists. They've been appointed to turn the U.S. soccer around, and together they can become an amazing force to influence our soccer system for the best. Their goal is to get things done right."

"I'm strongly in support of Kevin's opinion," asserted Kate. "They have done so much to help promote our soccer system to greater heights. Their commitment, like that of their predecessors, is obvious and unflinching. But these great men might need our help and support this time. Let's do it now. Together, we can achieve great success as a nation."

"Thanks, Kate!" echoed Jim. "You're a great lady. I've been a great soccer geek, even though I hold a master's degree in Classics from the University of Florida and teach courses there. I'm still into soccer and will always be. There's great harmony in togetherness, because victory also grows from harmony, *Victoria Concordia crescit*"

"It's time to win and win big with our men's soccer team," enthused Lori, "to bring home the FIFA World Cup trophy. Wake up, guys. They need our encouragement and strong support and not just negative criticisms, which don't help much but only destroy. Rather, we need to build and rebuild, as that will eventually pay off."

"I've strongly believed," remarked Adam, "that no matter what might have taken place in the past, since they entered into this business the difference has been clear and will continue to be clearer. They built on the great foundation that their predecessors laid, but now we need to do better. It's time to ask them: 'what do we need to do to help you bring home the Gold Medal, and trophy in the near 2014 global soccer contest, and beyond?'"

"You're right, Adam," concurred Meredith, "but we need to ask other questions, like: 'Do you think that you'll be able to achieve that feat? If not, how can we help you achieve a complete victory?'"

"Progress, guys!" exclaimed Michelle. "It'll only take courage to make drastic changes, after taking an in-depth look at what may have been our problems in the men's soccer."

"As an insider at the national soccer management," hinted Chris, "we know that more work needs to be done. We've never won big in any past soccer contests, but we'll continue to work to overturn that inclination, for future generations in this country."

"Thanks, Chris," chimed Debra. "Maximum victory in soccer often seems like an impossible task or challenge, but it's not. It's achievable. Achieving victory would be a great game-changer. Neither would it break into anyone's bank account, no matter how bulky."

"Haaaahaaaaa." laughed Brent. "What the leaders of this enviable sport should do now is to figure out the best ways to fix what might have appeared to the weak-minded as unfixable. Without passing judgment on the coaches' and leaders' performances, I believe that their efforts suffered from a lack of urgency. That's one of the reasons for their defeats, and those defeats shouldn't have occurred in the first place. They're undeserved brutal losses. But let's make sure that we're on the same page this time, as that will make me feel good."

"Since childhood," announced Joan, "I've believed that any problem can be fixed to save us from future global soccer embarrassments. Let them keep and maintain a positive attitude of being able to conquer all in soccer contests. The great power players in Washington, our hitherto dissatisfied fans, and the rest of the citizenry will then see them as indispensable."

"You're right, Joan." agreed Venus. "My advice to them would be that they begin to put visible machineries in place to prove that they can achieve ultimate victory, or, at worst, second place, come the year 2014 and beyond."

"You got it, Joan and Venus!" cried Frank. "It's not impossible. It's about making the right decision when it's high time the decision is made, and staying on track with few adjustments along the way."

"It's my contention," intoned Jonathan, "that the U.S. Soccer Federation has to make its broad transformational agenda crystal clear, regarding how they propose to make it to victory in 2014 and beyond."

"That's right," agreed Erin, "and if that agenda appears promising to soccer lovers, experts, and analysts, let it be advanced, and let it be so."

"The evaluation of soccer engineering among powerful soccer nations over the years and decades," noted Raymond, "would reveal that listening to what soccer fans say would help the managers, coaches, and technical advisers make better and technically helpful decisions in soccer."

"I was a coach for the women's soccer in Minneapolis for over seven years," revealed Colleen. "One of the things that helped me in making decisions was listening to my fans. Their comments were helpful and of immense benefit, especially when it came to placing the girls in their proper positions on the field of play. Listening to what they say could be a big asset in the evaluation of players to be selected for the World Cup, because they represent all of us internationally."

"I'd also think," added Patty, "that listening to the fans' suggestions could also be a value-added boost and support for the coaches' and soccer managers' efforts to enlist and recruit players for the U.S. men's World Cup soccer."

"I'm a great soccer fan," bragged Billy Joe. "All I know is that sometimes you can talk until you're blue in the face and nobody listens. But I must tell you that every soccer organizer is no fool. I've come to learn that they listen to ever growing whispers, and to ever growing talks, and will pick the ones they need and that will be helpful and convenient to them."

"One crucial thing that I'd like to suggest to soccer leaders in the U.S.," urged Rufus, "is that it's not a good idea to associate with insular people who seem to be insensitive to soccer sensibilities, people who are apparently lazy, complacent, and perhaps not perplexed as to why the U.S. men's soccer team has been losing its place in the world to people who appear to be more 'agile and dynamic' than us and more 'disciplined,' if we wish to buy that idea."

"The internet bloggers and tweeters could, in fact, be the perfect place to start if you honestly wish to listen to what they say." suggested Byron. "Could some of the remarks be incendiary or provocative? Yes. Could some of them be totally flawed? Yes. But there could be some bits of truth in them."

"Our soccer managers can do wonders," advised Melissa, "with great support from every one of us, since they can't do without you. They need your suggestions in the evaluation and assessment of the players who represent us globally. After all, they represent us."

"Well-meaning citizens and soccer fans of any nation," observed Glenn, "have the right to suggest the best ways forward in their nation's soccer team and its management, since the organizers and players represent the entire nation globally."

"Because players want to win," noted Scott, "and fans desire to have their favorite soccer teams win, there had been public outcries in various giant soccer nations in the past that the players and fans chose the coach of the national soccer team by polls."

"Your message is enlightening," Lukas replied. "I never thought of it that way because we never took soccer that seriously in this country. If we're able to do that, we'll be surprised to see who'll emerge as the winner or as an offshoot of the choices to be made by the players and fans. Such a democratic and widely acknowledged choice will be pretty interesting."

"In the sports that go international," urged Aimee, "I think that it would be a good idea to have the populace choose the person they trusted to become the head coach of their national men's soccer team. That will become a great innovation, as long as the process isn't spoiled with junk politics. It could be one of the best ways to resolve the challenges surrounding the appointment of a national coach. That's why any coach who intends to be selected in the future should never sleep until he's transformed the national men's soccer team. Just get us the Gold Medal or a trophy."

"I think that it would be hard if not impossible," observed Sarah, "to think of improvement in our men's soccer system without focusing on the effectiveness and quality of the players who make up the U.S. men's national soccer team. The quality of players is the most important factor inside the organization of a soccer team and in driving a soccer team's performance."

"The criteria for the evaluation matter so much," argued Timothy. "How you determine a good soccer player and who determines it remain big questions that need to be answered with clarity. How can you convince the fans that the players you're sending to global soccer games will represent them well?"

"Research has shown that good and outstanding players aren't necessarily determined by the managers, as some people often think," revealed Marcus. "Send out survey questionnaires to players, and then extend the survey to fans and wait for the feedback."

"You're right Marcus." agreed Sergio. "I was a professional soccer player for my country before coming over to the U.S. We knew ourselves pretty well in the field and who's best in each wing. I believe that the players themselves determine great players among them, and their best positions of play. I mean, when they do so with sincerity and without prejudice."

"Sometimes the recommendations of players could coincide with the thinking and decisions of the coach and the managers," pointed out Arthur, "and sometimes not. But it's safer to consider the recommendations of the players, since they do the playing, know themselves and one another better than anyone else does know them. They know how best to cooperate, and partner among themselves in the field of play."

"With the exception of tactical decisions," added Robert, "which are normally made by the coach and managers in the midst of every soccer tournament, broad consultations are recommended prior to any global soccer outing. These tactical decisions also include the evaluation, selection, and placement of players. People seldom get blamed or indicted for making decisions that are popular and well-vetted."

"If the current system of player evaluation uses that approach," noted Thomas, "then bravo and more grease to your elbows. It sounds worthwhile, because it seems pretty thoughtful and elaborate. It sounds like an approach that could permit soccer organizers to give sufficient attention to details."

"This approach might also be the best way to zero in on the impact of individual players on a team's achievement gains," remarked Allan. "Using this type of value-added investigation and analysis might be the best tool to help determine who's to be deployed and who's to be retrained. The method may not be perfect, but it works."

"In addition to other varied evaluation systems in place," advised Joe, "this approach may help expose the potential of players, their great performances, and even errors that otherwise would've been hidden from over-loaded coaches and soccer managers. It could help coaches make accurate as well as reliable assessments and evaluations of individual players."

"Investigating many countless stories reported by such popular soccer nations across the globe," reasoned Jamie, "as Scott previously suggested, would end up becoming a big task, as you would spend months and years listening to and reading up on available facts and details."

"However, the above suggestions from fans and soccer lovers might need a closer examination and consideration," advised Aaron. "Among the many advanced reasons most sports fail, in many people's opinion, is that sports managers, more often than not, parry suggestions from practically-minded and well-meaning sport fans. That type of attitude often ends up yielding disappointing results, both for the individuals involved and the entire team."

"Let's go with something that works in soccer," urged Terri, "as long as it's good, legal, and leads a team to an ultimate victory."

"I'd like to say that every player and organizer has to think through what his purpose is for their soccer team, and what his purpose is for our nation's soccer," observed Sarah. "Moreover, let every player bear in mind that he's representing his state on the men's national soccer team, and this type of competitive spirit will help make us rise high and shine, bright and beautiful. We've got to fight like dogs, go out there re-loading, hunting, and fighting. It has to do with knowing that it's an important win to get, and then going about getting it."

"I believe you employed a little bit of hunting language," quipped Martha, "since you're good at that. Hopefully, it's a wake-up call that can get us up and running in our efforts to win big in international soccer contests. Surely, we can be bent but not broken in soccer."

Though the U.S. men's soccer playing styles have improved a great deal over the years, some pessimistic or skeptical fans contend that their soccer styles hardly thrill, thereby exercising a weakening effect on the fans' hope for victory in global soccer contests in the near future. If you're still skeptical you're not alone, because some people are that way. Again, listen to what they say.

"If our men's soccer team were to leave behind a legacy," pictured Myra, "soccer lovers will see only something that's nearly exciting, but not necessarily exciting."

"Even when their general performance isn't that exciting," replied Theresa, "because they lagged behind too many times, their run's been pretty exciting and laudable, contrary to the previous suggestion by Myra."

"The same could be said of their clearly astonishing doggedness and resilience," added Harry. "They fought hard when the going gets tough. However, ignoring a gulf of gaping problems that has set the team up for untimely failure in World Cup soccer would be silly and absurd."

"It'll almost look like giving directions to a guest and welcoming him to a dysfunctional family gathering," contended Mitch. "By so doing, this would put him in complete confusion."

"Their past matches could be better described as merely or relatively successful," replied Dick, "never to be described as bad performances for a team that had challenges, about two decades ago, to even qualify for the tournament."

"Their performance needs to be more enticing to keep fans from not turning their backs on the game," reasoned Anthony. "It needs a serious makeover and a thorough brush-up."

"In some of the past global soccer encounters," opined Sally, "they appeared as if they went out with a whimper."

"Even in the award of penalty kicks," added Tim, "one would imagine seeing the whole nation on their knees praying, pleading, and perhaps begging whoever will take the penalty kick to get us a goal, because it takes only one kick to secure that."

"I admire our national women's soccer team," chimed Julie. "I'd suggest that our men's soccer team takes a cue from them, because our women have always finished no worse than third in the five previous tournaments that they engaged in, while also winning three Olympic Gold Medals. Of course, for them not to qualify would've been tragic. They prevail in their soccer matches with resilience and a refusal to sulk or surrender, even after their startling losses to stronger teams."

"You're right, Julie," concurred Pia. "Thanks. At the professional level, our women's soccer has encountered problems and triumphed, thereby gaining popular acceptance. However, in the sophisticated world of men's soccer as we have it today, I don't think that the U.S. will prevail by what's known as the American spirit, resilience, or by any cultural advantage over other great soccer nations that totally embraced soccer and not dismissing it as only for women. Our men's national soccer team has to get a lot more sophisticated in their soccer styles."

"Be it as it may," urged Kyle, "the performances of our men's soccer team remain encouraging and a sign of good things in store for our nation."

"Many times, fans tend to keep calling for one and only one overstretched, overworked, and overextended player to do the job of a penalty kick," drifted Cathy, "hoping that he's probably the only one to do it and do it right."

"Fans desire to see something that they could write home about," noted Yoav. "Our men's soccer team has been tested in several soccer encounters. They've also played big professional games, but they need to be tested further to ensure that they're beyond reproof."

The discussion then turned to forward liners and attackers.

"The U.S. players, in my honest opinion, are beautiful, fanciful, and elegant players," observed Emily, "but they seem to lack the needed materials in the forward lines. They also lag behind in the type of attacking system that could be styled 'reliable.' More work needs to be done."

"A lot of people believe that the forward lining, which involves attackers and strikers, is the trickiest and the riskiest," added Don. "Why? Because, defenders are looking to stop them from scoring and knock them off their feet. They need lightning-quick reflexes and vision to survive and succeed in the field."

"Yes," agreed Don. "They should be selecting players who are able to play back-to-back with the opponent's defense, but also able to make things happen in few seconds."

"All-speed-but-no-finish type of attacking," advised Jack, "or one-instant-impact types of performance should be discouraged among the forward liners and strikers. Most of the time they blow great chances, either by kicking the ball into the hands of the waiting goalkeeper or by blasting it over the bar."

"Records indicate that the U.S. men's team forward liners haven't scored a goal since the 2002 World Cup," noted Jamie, "and that those who score in other matches score few goals. Many believe that no American forward liner is considered a serious striker in European Major League Soccer."

"Some believe that even Landon Donovan, who did much to save the U.S. in the 2010 World Cup, and Clint Dempsey are sometimes brought to the forward lining," added Perry. "Otherwise, they're naturally midfielders."

"What does that tell you?" asked Todd. "We don't have forward liners, strikers, and attackers. Most of what we have are 'opportunistic attackers,' with the exception of Landon Donovan, Clint Dempsey, and Brian McBride, who are actually midfielders."

"Opportunistic attackers are also good players," responded Jennifer, "because they can score reliably when a star is besieged or held captive on the field by a group of defenders."

"You're right, Jennifer!" exclaimed Geoff. "Some smart players sometimes fake superstardom to create an avenue for opportunistic players to score in favor of their team. That's good, too, and could be considered tactical if it leads to a clean score."

"Many coaches encourage smart players to do that," remarked Carl, "for the benefit of creating confusion among the opponents, while creating scoring opportunities for themselves."

"Confusing the opponents is a pretty smart idea," argued Leonard. "It's a tactic that players, especially forward liners, should adopt, provided they don't create a situation that mimics a riotous jungle of competing vegetation. But who among our players could be said to be a solid attacker, one that should be watched or who'd be described by the opponents as 'dangerous?'"

"Hahaahaaa. A big question indeed, Leo." agreed Andrea. "I'd say that Landon Donovan, from his performance at the 2010 FIFA World

Cup soccer, seemed to have been the only one who, in my assessment, came close to that status, though not exactly, in the real sense of it. But he was definitely a star, in my view."

"Landon was obviously America's best player in the 2010 World Cup tournament," asserted Rachael. "That was obvious whenever he picked up possession of the ball. People would at least wake up, knowing that the U.S. team wasn't going to be an easy meat for everyone or a cakewalk, as some people used to think."

"We have stars among our players," concurred Stephanie, "but let's produce more stars and even superstars, if we can."

"Oh yeah!" exclaimed Eddie. "The sight of stars and superstars will be a sight that warms the hearts of the long-suffering fans of our men's soccer team."

"Everybody looks for both stars and at least one superstar in soccer," declared Ben, "so we should produce more stars and, possibly, superstars. Even if we don't succeed in getting a superstar or superstars for now, let's bring as many stars as we can to the field of play."

"It makes so much sense," replied Sean, "because if out of eleven players in the field, we're able to get at least five stars, then we should be fine with winning or something closer to it. Yes, we can challenge any strong team in the world."

"No team will be okay with only two or three stars," opined Chuck, "with the majority admired as wonderful professional players, elegant players, and the rest of them. In retrospect, let's think of a few soccer players, both past and present, that we could consider superstars: Pele, Socrates, Rossi, Careca, Maradona, Ronaldo, Beckham, Kanu and many more others."

"It's not beyond us to get people like that on our men's soccer team," suggested Danielle. "When a superstar is on the field, he's the attention of all eyes."

"Certainly," responded Kyle. "The presence of a soccer superstar is power. People know right away that he's there. His presence changes things."

"You're right." agreed Valentine. "We know superstars by the way they go for the ball. And watch when they get the ball — they carry it with persistent vigor and virility into the box 18 yards from the goal post, unless someone succeeds in stopping them."

"I think that you're right, Val!" exclaimed Clement. "But if he's the type that makes it to the 18 yards box without being stopped it's a plus, because he'd retain the stamina and tenacity to score a clean goal by out-muscling and out-hustling defenders plus intimidating the goalkeeper with his tactical skills."

"I've seen such megastar players," enthused Kate, "who have the ability to push forward and to carry their fellow players forward, until victory is gained."

"Their performance in the field," noted Charlie, "often leaves spectators star-struck. Such players have the ability to energize their fellow players and teammates with super-methodical skills. At this point, let's think of master dribblers like Pele, Zico (White Pele), Tigana, Austin Okocha, Cristiano Ronaldo, Luis Figo, Steve McManaman, Ryan Giggs, and so forth."

"I can't agree more!" cried Elliot. "Such wonderful players help in a unique way to make their teams more competitive internationally with their scoring power and ability to mobilize their teammates. A superstar strongly coordinates the ball whenever it gets to him or whenever he gets at it himself with distributive precision."

"Everyone on the field," added Miki, "sees his movement, whenever he makes it, as dangerous for the opponent. He's like a savior for a team when the going gets tough."

"One amazing thing I've observed about outstanding players," added Paula, "is that whenever they fire a goal into the net, it's a hard shot. Fans and spectators would always love to have them take the penalty kick, if that chance happens to emerge."

"Their presence motivates, energizes and lifts the spirits of other players," replied Courtney. "Such are soccer superstars. Let's get many of them, to boost our soccer image internationally and globally."

"It's more than willpower," noted Justin, "that makes them desire and work toward winning every one of their soccer encounters. They feel adrenaline running through them, to make that happen."

"I believe that they're not regularly gifted with scoring goals with precision," contested Arnold, "but they can mesmerize opponents, thereby creating opportunities for stars to score good goals. They could also be high-level and top-notch defenders during any soccer tournament and prove themselves highly impenetrable."

"Yes, they're smart players in the field," added Miller, "as they strive to do things in the right way by following the rules of the game. Depending on their temperament, they could appear serious looking on the field, unemotional, calm, resilient, but poised to get the job done."

"That's right." agreed Jennifer. "They add quality to soccer play in the field. For me, superstars aren't hidden, we see them and we know them right away. They belong to the first-class rank."

"They may not necessarily be only those wonderful players that only the coach sees and praises," reasoned Jennifer. "They're not only those praised and promoted by their friends and well-wishers. But superstars are seen and admired by almost every spectator watching the game in a stadium. These spectators might include little children who know little or nothing about soccer."

"One thing I've discovered during my career in soccer," observed Martin, "is that the teammates of a superstar are his first honest evaluators, but if and only if they do so without any imaginable fear or favor. They will give an honest evaluation of him, because they have great confidence in him. To them he's like a little god and, of course, an icon."

"It's true that there aren't too many superstars among us." noted Jill. "Some people believe that they're specially made and rare. Yes, we believe that they're made, but they can also be trained, too, since practice often makes 'perfect.'"

"Not only that practice makes perfect," agreed Barbara, "but nature can, as well, be nurtured and groomed to make it (nature) perfect too. I believe that such great gifts in nature are, most of the time, discovered at young age. We spot those wonderful talents starting from elementary schools."

"You're absolutely right!" echoed Emma. "They say: 'catch them young and begin to train them further.' If we're looking for another Pele, Diego Maradona, Cobi Jones, David Beckham, Christiano Ronaldo, and others out there, of course, we have them. All we need to do is scout them out. But the most important thing is for us to ask ourselves this real question: do we have the structure in place to be able to produce another Pele, Maradona, Jones, Bechkam, Ronaldo, and the rest of other soccer megastars? We should be able to answer this question and then go ahead to restructure American soccer, to be able to find those gifted talents and skillful players who are surely out there, but only waiting for us to discover them."

"There's no question about that!" exulted Lou. "But the only thing I know is that when we have a superstar as an attacker on the field and two stars supporting him, then we should be fine. Because a superstar not only does the job of scoring — he also motivates other players, whether he's on the field or reserved to come in later, during half time."

"The U.S. needs at least one soccer superstar," demanded Carla, "and many stars, and I firmly believe that they're not hard to find in the 50 states across our nation."

What the men's team needs to watch is that the first half is an important period for any team in soccer matches. There's an acute need for gamesmanship; to score first in the first half.

"The U.S. men's team," advised Leigh, "should always seize the chance to produce an organized and solid performance in the first half. That's absolutely necessary. Let it be an amazing start that won't only produce early scores, but will also delight supporters and fans who expect great things to happen early."

"If the U.S. men's soccer team could form the habit of scoring early goals," remarked Edgar, "it would be a great achievement. They should be encouraged to keep at it through major tournaments, without exception."

"Flick it on," agreed Denise. "It's a perfect time to show determination in playing as an outfit."

"The idea of applying the strategy of a 'strong and good start,'" noted Swen, "is to bury any thought that the U.S. men's team is an easy nut to crack or a simple cakewalk. The earlier they score during every encounter, the more scoring opportunities they will have."

"The first half is a time when our creative players are expected to surge into the opponent's goal post," advised Gregory, "not only to intimidate the opponent, but also to make the goalkeeper feel crowded out."

"From my past experience in women's soccer," recalled Florence, "and the same might be applicable to men's soccer, the first half is a time when the sides size each other up."

"Absolutely, Florence." affirmed Quinton. "Spectators have complained about the poor first halves of the U.S. men's team during most of their encounters. What are the players waiting for in the first half?"

"The first forty five minutes," replied Mattie, "are crucial for every good soccer team, be it men's or women's soccer. It's a 'never-waste-any-bit-of-time' moment in any soccer tournament."

"As a follow-up to what you observed, Mattie," commented Everett, "Some people have blamed over-confidence among our guys as responsible for those unnecessary delays. Some call it unwarranted sluggishness, while others view it as poor preparation."

"There are several creations that U.S. men's team needs to deploy in the field of play, without which their game will be meaningless and perhaps uninteresting," added Theo. "They have the first half to do that and without delay, unless they have other plans with the coach or technical manager."

"But why wait until the second half to begin to do something meaningful?" asked Pedro. "That's frustrating to fans, who are there to promote and boost morale when it begins to fade in the second half."

"Moreover, the idea of attacking at the dying minute might be too late, but again, that depends on the strength of the opponent's team," warned Ryan.

Bart added, "An attacker needs to achieve creative balance, composure, and the power to finally score when he gets to the box of 18 yards from the opponent's goalmouth."

The conversation then turned to the notoriety of draw games.

"The desire, or habit, to squeeze a draw game should be avoided by any serious team and players, if possible" advised Joel. "Sometimes match-ups might be so tight that the game remains scoreless. But it's a time to build up stamina, create opportunities for a go-ahead goal, and not a time to desire, pray, or wish for an eventual draw game, for such will be pointless."

"Sure." agreed Mark. "It's also not a time to encourage over-the-bar shots or shots that could be described as narrowly missed. And, of course, 'nearly' doesn't kill the bird at all."

We then turned to the topic of defense vulnerability. Leaving the defense susceptible to the invasion of attacking opponents can be fatal for any soccer team.

"Fast-paced players, can take advantage of a poor defense to slot the ball coolly into the net or under the legs of a defender," noted George.

"The defense isn't a place to exercise naivety," warned Derek. "On defense, no one can afford to take his finger off the pulse."

"It isn't a place to be distracted," added Ronny, "and leave your doors and windows open for your staunch opponent."

"Be careful never to expect others to fill the gaps," urged Carmelo, "or sit back and wait for them to do all the work. Be sure to block all known passage for dangerous strikers."

"It's another important area to let the opponents know that you're in control," added Sean.

"Strong defense can make a big difference in the amount of work and responsibilities that come your way as a player on the field," noted Randy.

"For defenders to be reliable in a soccer tournament," enjoined Richie, "they need to be balanced, mature, calculative, and extremely tactical. They need to have been previously tested and proven during training and other friendly match encounters."

"The two major defenders must be real 'partners,'" suggested Joaquin, "along with the three other supporting defenders for the defense, to be deemed highly impenetrable."

What about making unnecessary changes? Our discussants agreed that changes should be made only when it's absolutely necessary, at the discretion of the coach and the technical advisers.

"If possible, it's good to stick to a game plan until the end," chimed Bart. "This means staying with what the team has until the game is finally won."

"When a team is in control of the ball," advised Brian, "it's not necessary to make changes, unless for strategic and tactical reasons that are absolutely crucial."

"Without the consolidation and capitalization of the middle field and defense areas," argued Fred, "it would be hard for the soccer managers to know when and where to make changes and necessary adjustments, in a soccer tournament."

"Those who understand soccer," added Pierce, "know too well that it's wise to stick to any arrangement that works, without making unnecessary changes in players or desperate wing switches."

Jesse agreed: "Changes can come only when it's absolutely necessary. It's better to send out the best lineup at the onset."

"Coaches and soccer managers often actualize unilateral and arbitrary decisions by making unnecessary changes on the field of play out of fear, misguided frustration, and a sense of insecurity in the face of perceived imminent defeat," observed Bruce. "Again, for solid psychological reasons, changes can be made only when it's absolutely necessary, and when those changes are made, they must be tactical."

"It takes the mind of a genius to do so. Otherwise, it would only become counterproductive," agreed Bob. "What happens is that under this type of mental state and disposition, the coach or team manager might use the right player at the wrong place or the wrong player at the wrong time, thereby creating an unintended disaster for the entire team. As a result, the team may wind up losing to a weaker team that, otherwise, they might have been favored to defeat: Human shortcomings."

"It's never advisable to remove inspirational player figures from the field, unless as a result of injury," warned Dick. "They should be specially trained and brought onto the field when the morale of their fellow teammates grows low, during half time or when their team is being defeated."

We then turned to player selection and positioning.

"Let everything about the training and selection of our players, especially those who'd represent us internationally, be super and superb," boomed Maxine, "because when it comes to international soccer outings and performances involving the US, the superlatives should be allowed to fly."

"Let's aspire to have superstars among our players, or at least stars," added Cheryl. "Anything short of stars shouldn't be acceptable to our men's team, as the U.S. deserves the best."

"Superstars are superstars to everybody," noted Rogers, "at least the majority of fans and spectators acknowledge them as such. But if it happens that a negligible minority don't accept them as such; then, let them be accepted as stars, and that will be fine with anybody and all of us."

"Our men's team can't keep peddling and recycling mediocre, low-skilled or semi-star players," protested Sidney, "simply because they happened to be professionals on foreign soccer teams and clubs of low stature, or to please someone."

Britney jumped in: "Players could be pacified in many other ways that are not harmful to the common good."

"A secret that not too many people know," revealed Merton, "is that players themselves, whether local or professional, are, most of the times, the best people to choose the wing where they have the most expertise and feel comfortable covering. Why? Because, players know themselves better than any coach would, no matter his level of genius."

"Smart coaches would enlist the help of players before they make their final team selection for a tournament," observed Shorey.

"Coaches and technical advisers may ask the players to fill out a survey questionnaire," noted Jordan, "that will indicate who fits in a certain position."

"Ask them to fill in the name of any player who's best suited for a given wing," advised Dannie, "after which the coach compares notes with every respondent to see if they coincide with his thoughts, feelings, and observations. He finally looks at the statistics to make his decision."

"Why do you need the players to make those recommendations for you first?" asked Adolph. "Because they know themselves and one another too well, and will work together in the best possible way on the field."

"As a coach, once you succeed in getting great soccer partners, side by side, into their proper positions," remarked Arthur, "then rejoice, rest assured, and count your team a great success. The rest of the success will be supplied with proper training and skills, which players will cultivate as they constantly train together."

"The U.S. men's national soccer team has to get back to real solid preparations," maintained Dean. "Many fans doubt the team has seen real preparation for some time now. No need for complacency. The players may once in a while need private interviews to verify these facts, if there's any doubt."

Orvil concluded: "The experience of a head coach is golden and almost that of a 'savior' with every good training and preparation, because he can easily pick up on things that players overlook. These types of experiences can be a feel-good and confidence booster for the coach."

# Chapter 10
## Soccer and Revenue

On revenue generation, soccer is variously seen as a feel-good booster. Any statement that goes this way — "Let's go soccer, because it's a great financial booster" — shouldn't in any way at all be considered a scary proposal. It shouldn't take some nocturnal tiptoe visits to convince people and potential investors of this fact, either. Global soccer advocates should be taken seriously for myriads of reasons, one of which remains revenue generation.

"Financial sophisticates uphold the idea that even if soccer industries fail to boost the economy right away," noted Harris, "it would at least generate huge revenue that may be invested for a long-term economic development and other critical services that might help keep an economy strong and vibrant in many ways that include the health sector, among others."

Many nations and people consider involvement and success in soccer as the defining focus of their various states and federally elected governments, to such an extent, that sometimes their interest in soccer programs seems to eclipse other national projects. Soccer forms a part of their electioneering campaigns, too. It's like saying: "If you want to win and election, do it or get involved in soccer."

To those nations, soccer is many things, both to the state and to the citizenry. In some rare exceptions, governments would operate in part as a soccer-industry stakeholder by contractually yielding ownership to organizations, corporations, institutions, and clubs, thus freeing itself from certain constraints on soccer involvement. Soccer isn't only an entertainment and fundraiser, it's also a key source of income and national development. The mention of economy means the revenue aspect of the economy. Talk has just turned into specifics, thereby making this claim more believable and sensible indeed.

Attention. In an effort to explore and bring some greater economic integrity through soccer involvement, a 70-year soccer veteran once asked if full involvement in soccer contests would help promote or diminish the economy of participating nations. This issue was brought up among a group of soccer lovers, analysts, veterans, and some economic experts. Initially, there were conflicting opinions in their discussions, to the extent that figuring out which side to belong to could be an uphill task and even confusing to those experts whose job is to track such events.

Sometimes, a nearby listener would think that the discussions sounded like swanky cars stuttering in fits and starts. It would also appear like sitting at the opposite side of the negotiation table in a dialogue with people of opposing viewpoints. A lot of the debates and issues raised seemed to have been fueled by implied individual interests. To understand and unravel the implications of the debates and what they're about, discussants had to unlock and analyze those underlying interests one by one.

"The only way to get your opponents in a debate," argued Bill, "so as to reveal their true thoughts, feelings, understanding of the issues, and conflicting items of discussion is to manage the discussion by open dialogue. It's all about 'waking up and winning' your opponents in a dialogue without treating those issues as a win or lose or as a do-or-die affair. Rather, the idea would be to hammer out the differences in opinions by working through the problems and then proposing solutions."

Participants in this debate loosened up rigid but real thinking into more open perspectives, by changing conflicts into an opportunity to get a good answer. It involved the use of examples to search out and explain the practical nature of the issue. However, after a long debate with his co-veterans in a town hall but casual get-together, more points were scored in favor of strong soccer revenue. Discussants arrived at the conclusion that soccer nourishes the economic health of every nation in the long term. They came to the agreement that the major impact doesn't always take effect immediately. It's rather a forward-looking, and powerful economic indicator.

This outcome applies more to nations that are often on the winning side and attract many fans. The septuagenarian believes that any bid by any government or corporate sponsors to involve themselves in local and global soccer programs is justified for various reasons, especially on fitness and financial grounds. The soccer industry, he added, also has an additional benefit of advancing a nation's economy by reducing deflation and creating jobs. It has nothing to do with diminishing the economy of any nation. Rather, it rests on practical commitment to top promotion of public interest and economic growth.

Are vibrant soccer programs among the economic indicators that point either to success or failure of a nation's economy as a whole, or do they only reproduce some form of innovation that drive a given national economy?

Here's the thing. Soccer has great ability to spark economic growth in many countries that are soccer inclined. Why invest in soccer industries? The debaters and discussants: Anthony, Michael, Donald, Harold, Vincent, Myles, Ronnie, Paul, Justin, Andrew, Bret, Jerry, Jordan, Edward, Austin, and Innocent are fans who have developed great interests in finding out how the soccer industry could help build up a nation's economy. They get together once every week over cups of coffee, and use those opportunities to discuss soccer and how it could help boost a nation's economy, despite a few previously inaccurate descriptions of soccer programs as presumably non-revenue generating ventures.

Each of the discussants would be deeply absorbed in his or her position, so that they found it hard to come to an agreement at the beginning, but eventually they were able to reach a consensus. When they finally met, there was hope that they'd make progress on concepts. They engaged in point-counterpoints on the specifics of soccer as a good revenue-generation venture. In the course of their discussions, key issues of interest were identified that would need future closer study. Glad it wasn't a discussion of trivial things; it was only about soccer investment.

Let's join the session as they begin to discuss the issue.

First topic of conversation: what are the economic benefits of hosting the World Cup?

"How would you tell me," asked Anthony, "that any nation hosting World Cup soccer would have a successful run? I don't mean inside the arena, but outside the field, a booming economy as a result of that?"

"I agree that it's a great source of economic boom." replied Michael. "However, it may not come immediately. In brief, hosting the World Cup soccer successfully doesn't mean a quick fix for a dead economy, but it can help nurture a growing economy and even go further to take it to greater heights. Again, not right away. But there may be a foreseen economic boom a few years down the road, as the after-effect of the successful hosting of the World Cup."

"You're right Mike." Donald approved. "Even after the Olympics of 1996, during the time of President Clinton, we saw how great and wonderful our economy was in the U.S. prior to hosting the soccer Olympics. And even after the Olympics, I think that the successful hosting of that event helped our economy a lot, especially from revenue angle. I believe so."

"I agree with you, guys!" echoed Harold. "But I've read recently that in some previous cases, host nations weren't doing well economically in the year that the soccer events took place, even though the research wasn't conclusive. Moreover, some research shows that economies did better in the years before the World Cup and in the years after."

"C'mon, don't ever read that garbage!" protested Vincent. "I've read that stuff. Any research can tell you any nonsense, not only about soccer. It's also about football, baseball, basketball, and the rest of the sports. They try to create the impression that they don't generate revenue. How do you know that the research was reliable? How do you know whether they were objectively or unfairly carried out? How do you know that it met the norms of a sound research in the first place?"

"Don't even waste your saliva, Vincent." cautioned Myles. "I also read that junk but carefully. Some of those researchers sounded like people who naturally hated soccer as a sport and were, perhaps, looking for cheap ways to relegate soccer to the background. Some of their suggestions don't hold water at all. I challenge them to tell me how much the BFBs have contributed to the growth of our economy, despite not having so much to offer when it comes to global connections. How much good have they done for the U.S. economy? Understandably, they owe their roots as social entertainment to the American life and culture. As far as I'm concerned, soccer has been known to generate more cash than any other sport on earth."

"Guys! Insofar as no sport on earth is an economic engine as such, soccer remains a big and indeed the biggest revenue generating sporting program, because of the population of spectators and viewers it carries worldwide." beamed Ronnie. "Of course, no one would expect any economy to grow right away in the year of the World Cup hosting, because there are often several capital intensive projects that the host nation engages in. Those projects, I tell you, are normally undertaken to prepare a country for the influx of visitors, tourists, spectators, and fans, in the form of security details, roads, railroads, and bridges. They are expected to drain some money from the economy, but only in the short run. The final outlook of the economy, going by the amount of money generated, is what matters most."

"Soccer is such a great social entertainment," observed Paul, "that it can distract people from their jobs in the short run. That could understandably slow the economy a little bit, but it'll come back later in full force. We should never ever forget that soccer tourists, among others, mean potentially millions if not billions of dollars, let alone the sales in local businesses, such as souvenir shops, hotels, restaurants, and the rest."

"You're a thousand percent right, Paul." agreed Justin. "Let me mention that I also read the article that Harold mentioned. The researcher made it clear that there's the potential for a comeback economic boom. But those things you read were probably motivated by gloomy talks from hungry economists, naïve businessmen, and half-baked academics. Don't forget that some research works are often biased. If those research works are true to the core, why do nations keep lobbying and bidding like crazy to host the World Cup? Do those lobbyists and bidding experts want to bring some form of economic 'killer' into their nations? No, don't laugh! Nobody wants to do that, right? There's no doubt in my mind that soccer will generate a great amount of economic boom for any nation."

"I understand what Harry probably read and where he found it," declared Andrew. "Many factors can derail the growth rate of any economy. I've been a member of a national soccer management committee in a South American nation, and I discovered that investment in soccer is a healthy and lucrative business. I'm not going to give you the figures now. Soccer has the potential of boosting the economy of any nation, as far as I know; whether or not you're the host or the big winner in the field. When the revenue generated from soccer is properly managed by host nations, the economy would often giggle. One more thing that people don't usually think of deeply is that apart from investments, industries, and the rest of the things that help an economy, the nature of a nation's currency can help in pushing their economy up or down. Simple currency denominations can be the Achilles heel of some nations. However, we're fortunate here in the U.S. because our currency is well structured and well denominated. That means that its legal tender nature flows within, despite occasional bumps in the economy."

"I think that a country's economic policy remains the key, playing a great role when it comes to any nation's economic progress," agreed Bret.

"In any country where soccer contests are properly organized and hosted, the economy never remains stagnant, as long as there's a solid basis already laid down for its growth. You can't expect soccer to jumpstart an already dead economy in a poor country or in a country where revenue generation is never well-managed."

"You're right, Bret." approved Jerry. "The economic policy of a hosting nation should be working for them in the first place. Moreover, I think that the economy will be super if the host nation also happens to be the ultimate winner in the tournament. That would mean a blessing to any economy, a double win, right?"

"I thank God that we're doing pretty well here in the U.S., compared to some other countries across the globe. Also, we have the population." bragged Jordan. "Of course, countries that gamble their resources into economic decay can't expect soccer revenues to jumpstart their entire economies. That would be a clear show of naivety."

"Haaahaaaa," laughed Edward. "I know that soccer remains a great economic and financial feel good booster because it's a global sport. Its viewers and fans are measured in billions and they generate billions too. But I'm not worried whether it's a great money booster or not. I love soccer more because of its non-monetary benefits. But why should we only think of its monetary benefits this time? Why should soccer be measured in dollars and pounds, let alone in Euros and Yens? There should be no yearning on our part to do that, in any way at all. Permit me to mention that it's a global sport, as well as a great piece of entertainment that brings people and nations together. It fosters cross-cultural interactions and understanding. There's nothing sissy about holding tight to this claim."

"Like you, Ed," noted Austin, "it's not a question of being cautiously optimistic. I believe that the soccer industry, in whatever form, is a great economy booster. You forgot to mention that it's a global sport that's largely inclusive and can bring people together through peaceful contests and respect for one another. It can bring warring nations and factions to the negotiation table. With that alone, every nation should go for it and not count the cost."

"Let's think more of what possible great things and social benefits this 'most watched' sport can bring to or inspire in cities and nations," added Innocent, "and not concentrate only on the economic impacts."

Aside from the preceding town hall meeting, discussions and debates, people in general seldom think of, let alone discuss, the economy and finance in terms of soccer contests, its organizations, and hosting. But economists, lawyers, and businessmen seem to be measuring everything, even soccer-event outcomes, in monetary terms, which sometimes carry other interesting messages, enough to have us take notice. But this issue should be looked into, too, when it comes to any nation's development in soccer as an industry. It's now beginning to look like the right time to cast a fresh look over this neglected subject. Soccer events and their outcomes can help dictate the economy of any team, company, state, federal government, and nation to which the participating teams belong. It'll remain a feel-good boost, holding true for any nation. How does this happen?

To get some answers to this important question, group members discussed growth in market economies as they relate to soccer.

"A little contribution that I'll make from my research as an economist and a soccer lover," declared Marvin, "is that winning soccer nations have been known to see about 0.8% increase in their market economies after any major successful soccer encounter. Surely, most of us would be left with no alternative other than to desire ultimate soccer victories in the nearest and not-too-distant future. In the long run, the major issue well-meaning Americans, and soccer fans should support is: winning big in future global soccer events."

"This suggestion sounds good," agreed Jeff, "because to win big in the future might leave us with great prospects and put us in good stead monetarily and revenue-wise. Doesn't it?"

"I believe it would, Jeff!" cried Sylvester. "Our mantra should be not only to gain traction, but also to snowball into winning big in the future, and nothing less. Yes, we can accomplish this and proceed to beat great soccer nations in the global soccer marketplace. Yes, we can, and our men's soccer players and team managers will lead the way."

"How uplifting is this message that's well framed into a positive cliché," exulted Abigail. "Optimism is among the psychological tools that should act as our strength. Psychologically, a positive energy is believed to be among the major contributory factors to the growth of a participating soccer nation's market economy. The results of this positive energy are feelings of happiness and pride in the whole nation after victory."

"Reflecting over my past studies in Economic Psychology," enjoined Irene, "I now recall that market psychologists believe that happy people, when their pride and joy are at their highest peak, tend to engage in buying and shopping frenzies. They shop until they drop. Imagine the near-wild rush of people when the doors of the shopping malls are thrown open. Think of the multitudes of shoppers who'll be stalking the aisles hunting down possibly few supplies of products and soccer stuffs."

"I'm not a regular newspaper reader," declared Erin, "but my recent grab of a local newspaper hit me with the banner headline, showing that families and friends of players, coaches, and their organizers and fans around the country, in appreciation of victory, make trips to the malls, super centers, and grocery stores. With a great sense of patriotism, they see their country as highly blessed for winning globally in soccer."

"That's no big news to me at all," confessed Antoinette, "I've been a witness to that myself. Fans, supporters and people in general, are believed to shop until they drop in victory times. As soon as victory is announced, the whole nation often gets into the mood of organizing parties and entertainments for friends, families, fans, well-wishers and foreign guests too. This energy is created whenever a nation wins big in a World Cup contest."

"Shopping and buying in large numbers doubtless boost the economy of any nation, with special reference to revenue generation," observed Philip. "Why? Because stores, super centers, malls, and grocery stores are renovated and furnished to make shopping fun. They're also expanded and extended to make buying and selling convenient and stress free and to contain a huge influx of shoppers. Given the shopping traffic, one could easily imagine what the financial benefits might be."

"That sounds promising." agreed Melanie. "Please God, if the U.S. ever wins the global Gold Medal in the men's soccer contest, people in the U.S. will unapologetically express their pride, joy, and patriotism in many ways. I don't care, even if the celebration becomes excessive. Think of shopping — it's ingrained in the American culture and heritage to go shopping. Shopping on holidays and great events, like the World Cup, is pretty encouraging for any economy. Award galas, dinner and cocktail parties, are organized for the players. Also, tickets are sold for such events to generate amazingly huge amounts of money for the teams. Popular and celebrity philanthropists, veteran soccer players, stars and super stars in soccer are usually invited and recognized in a special way."

People, generally, love the idea of philanthropy or creative giving so much that they often go out of their way to practice, encourage, or support it. It's a gesture that's universally accepted, and that maximizes the impact of charities and creative giving. It's all about doing good.

Over the last three decades, American Philanthropists haven't only done great things within the U.S., but have also extended their tentacles of creative and charitable giving to other parts of our developing world. To encourage philanthropy, the U.S. government passed a piece of legislation in the early 1920s, offering tax-relief for personal and other donations made in charity. This came in response to concerted pressures on a growing generous population. Billions of dollars in charitable giving around the world and within the U.S. have been variously traced to the U.S. citizens.

Past events that called for charitable giving include natural disasters like the 2004 tsunami, the 2005 Hurricane Katrina, the 2010 earthquakes in Haiti and Chile and the 2011 major earthquake and tsunami in Japan. People like Andrew Carnegie, John D. Rockefeller, Howard R. Hughes Jr., Nelson Rockefeller, Margaret Olivia Slocum Sage, and many others have laid the foundation of philanthropy in the US. They were pacesetters in the charitable business, which found future expression in people like: Bill & Melinda Gates, Warren Buffett, Michael Bloomberg, Jeff & MacKenzie Bezos, Pierre & Pam Omidyar, George Soros, Mark Zuckerberg & Priscilla Chan, Craig Newmark, Stanley & Fionna Druckenmiller, John Templeton, Gordon & Betty Moore, the Walton family, James & Marilyn Simons, Dustin Moskowitz & Cari Tuna, Paul Allen, Michael & Susan Dell, Oprah Winfrey, Ted Turner, Charles & Helen Schwab, David Geffen, and most recently, John & Laura Arnold and tens of thousands of others not listed here.

What's clear is that philanthropy in America incorporates a wide range of private and public donors, both documented and undocumented. These great men and women have given millions of dollars annually to causes related to health, community welfare, education, and the arts.

"What would philanthropy mean if also applied to any nation's soccer programs?" asked Samuel. "This is a good question. Acts of philanthropy are related to soccer in many developed and developing nations. From a few soccer documentaries, I've discovered that in some soccer loving nations fans have made bold commitments to philanthropy and creative giving, even to the point of dedicating about 1% of their business profit."

"No matter how someone spins it, soccer wins in many nations attract philanthropists and creative givers, both from within and without the country," noted Mark. "Such donations are often reported to have been channeled to the welfare of the players, their team, and management, to the relief of certain budgetary burdens and projects for both their federal and state governments."

"Soccer-loving donors in developing and developed nations do wonders, whenever their national soccer teams win," added Jennifer. "It's usually amazing to see such things happen when they win big. People make huge donations to the teams, and sometimes to the governments, to help them promote soccer. Well-meaning and soccer-loving philanthropists also sponsor players and fans to attend international soccer events, thereby saving the government, clubs, organizations, and communities' major expenses."

"In cultures that have the practice of giving back, former soccer players and athletes have initiated and sustained the cycle of giving back to their communities," observed Michael. "Some of them have either sponsored or given scholarships to pupils in their communities. They've also helped numerous students go to college. They give back because those communities were great sources of support to them during their careers as professional players and athletes. This practice often winds up leaving more money in the hands of parents, who otherwise would've made a lot of expenses to send their children to school or college."

"As a teacher of economics in college," noted Frederick, "I've realized that leaving more money in the hands of parents and families not only increases their purchasing power, but saves them from the ordeal of having empty bank accounts. The impact of philanthropy is healthy for any economy."

"It has never left my mind," added David, "that when soccer is growing rapidly in the U.S., it's possible that many men and women might avail themselves of the opportunity to use their largesse to promote soccer in the U.S. Let's come together and give them that opportunity, as it'll put a smiling face on our economy. The power of creative giving or philanthropy, as regards soccer, can never be overstressed."

Sustaining any sport, including soccer, takes more than someone's time and effort. It takes some fundraising campaign that will help promote and increase the awareness of soccer and its impact on people's lives.

"Successful and well-committed soccer teams," advised Olympia, "can profitably organize fundraisers to improve the quality of life for people who suffer from devastating and incurable diseases, thereby saving the government heavy budgetary commitments and expenses."

In various countries and states, national soccer programs are organized, annually or biannually, to maintain and sustain youth participation. What happens to the funds generated from fundraisers?

"Depending on a team, club, or organization's practice," responded Hendricks, "the cash from fundraisers is used to pay for uniforms and equipment. Such funds could go a long way in helping save the government both state and federal expenses on equipment and other stuffs; to support soccer as an instrument for social change and youth empowerment."

"Apart from the cash realized from fundraisers, funds have also been raised from other sources, saving the government a lot of financial overstretch," revealed Blake "For instance, since 1995, the U.S. Soccer Foundation has awarded over $23 million in cash, equipment, and services through its annual grants program to more than 430 grantees in all 50 states. This generosity has touched the entire spectrum of soccer communities, from small clubs to the U.S. Soccer Federation, the national governing body for the sport in the U.S."

"In an exceptionally simple tradition, it could also become a major way of supporting programs and field building projects nationwide that may serve multiple purposes," noted Evan. "The U.S. Soccer Foundation is said to have invested more than $54 million in support of such projects in each of the 50 states. This includes projects that provide low income and at-risk youth in urban communities with soccer activities that promote education, healthy lifestyles, leadership, and positive options to drugs, crime, and other destructive behaviors. The cost of those projects and services could be settled with the cash derived from fundraisers as well."

In the U.S. and other nations, one of the most common ways of fundraising is to send out mailers to businesses and individuals, asking for donations to soccer program via checks, credit cards, or debit cards. Some groups hold fundraisers in restaurants. These events, which display great caring and community pride, could also be held to create jobs. They're most often huge successes, especially when organized after major soccer victories. This is one of the forums where generous people discover fine ways to serve their communities and nation.

Global recognition and renown: It's never been a secret that every nation seeks recognition in global soccer contests. Recognition from various nations for great triumphs in soccer, seems to increase the number of foreigners and travelers that visit those victorious soccer nations for trade and tourism. Think of the number of tourists and vacationers who long to visit the U.S. No one could ever imagine a better opportunity for a nation to generate revenue. This recognition from nations across the globe and the renown achieved by victory may open up a wide range of international business and investment opportunities for soccer-winner nations. It might also help promote better diplomatic relationships. Any successful bid to host world soccer events in select cities here in the U.S. could improve tourism for those cities.

Public interest: The amount of publicity given to soccer helps to raise revenue for any economy. Winning public interest can help oil the progress of soccer as an exciting national and global sport deserving our attention and strong commitment. The idea is to bring together, strengthen people's expected resolve, make a commitment and procure generous support for major soccer programs. To accomplish this feat, public interest projects could be developed using websites and social media like Facebook, Twitter, and Instagram. The idea is to give people's common interest a structure as well as provide a forum for fans. Primarily, employing social media networks would be to win the hearts and minds of fans, keeping them on message. They will help connect people with colleagues, friends, and families who work, study, and live across the globe.

The theory that economic growth and soccer victories go hand in hand holds much water. It's the spectators, promoters, media, viewers, fans, and entertainment industries that actually generate money for every world soccer tournament. So, there is a great need to appeal to public interest in soccer. We need to generate public interest, so as to guarantee popular benefits in the soccer industries. About 300 million people were believed to have watched the World Cup Final in Japan in 2002, with the number said to be much higher in Germany.

Let's look beyond this thick but bright display of hope while soaring and spiraling toward the brighter side of the same coin. It's hoped that good feasibility studies on the correlation of soccer and the economy have been completed years, if not decades ago. The U.S. can thrive in soccer, regardless of any circumstances. It's remarkable that even developing countries and countries with poor economic conditions thrive in soccer and even win big in soccer contests. They make huge progress in the revenue whenever their stadiums are not just filled but filled to the brim. Thinking of what a well-packed downtown soccer-based stadium can yield financially is a good idea. And what happens when it's close to an international airport or a busy metro-station? Doubtless, such a finance-generating project makes a great sense, even in bad economic times. Research confirms that soccer stadiums located in states like New York, California, Texas, Washington, and the rest can lure and draw more fans than those situated in smaller states.

"If you can't make money on pro soccer in Seattle," argued Church, "you must be doing something wrong." "Seattle is looking good when it comes to using soccer to generate income for a nation like the U.S. Some people feel disappointed about mismatches, especially in new soccer stadiums. Overall, glitzy soccer stadiums are good revenue generators."

An anticipated success of the U.S. in its bid to secure the 2018 or 2022 Soccer Tournament will be a sweet deal. It has been projected that the U.S. will make about 5 million in ticket sales alone, worth up to $1 billion or more in revenue, with a total economic impact of at least $5 billion. Because of her profound richness in diversity, there are clear expectations that the U.S. will guarantee full stadiums at all events, come 2022 and beyond.

This is how the calculations were broken down. The U.S. bid involves at least 21 existing stadiums, 18 of which have been built or renovated in the last 20 years, and all of which are in compliance with FIFA requirements. FIFA World Cup soccer events usually take place in one month. A month-long tournament would normally take place at 8 to 10 stadiums across the US, choosing from the existing pool of 18 cities and 21 stadiums.

Those cities that were unveiled in 2010 include the following with their seating capacities noted: Atlanta-Georgia Dome (70,868), Baltimore-M &T Bank Stadium (71,008), Boston-Gillette Stadium (73,393), Dallas Cowboys Stadium (91,600), the Cotton Bowl (89,000), Denver-Invesco Field (75,165), Houston-Reliant Stadium (76,000), Indianapolis-Lucas Oil Stadium (66,500),Kansas City-Arrowhead Stadium (75,364), Los Angeles-Rose Bowl (89,109), Los Angeles Memorial Coliseum (93,607), Miami-Dolphin Stadium (80,240), Nashville-LP Field (75,000), New Jersey-New Meadowlands Stadium (84,046), Philadelphia-Lincoln Financial Field (69,111), Phoenix-University of Phoenix Stadium (71,362), San Diego-Qualcomm Stadium (67,700), Seattle-Qwest Field (68,056), Husky Stadium (72,500), Tampa-Raymond James Stadium (75,000), and Washington-FedEx Field (86,690). Chicago, Detroit, Orlando, and San Francisco have been left out.

These select cities are considered soccer-specific and soccer-friendly. They're vibrant and beautiful cosmopolitan places with excellent public transportation networks. With an average capacity of more than 76,000 spectators, the stadiums in the U.S. bid offer a World Cup-record of five million tickets, generating $1 billion in tickets sales alone. Taking a look at the statistics of revenue generation, one would wonder if there's any sport more profitable than soccer when it comes to revenue generation. There wouldn't be any concern about overextending budgets or spending billions on the construction of stadiums and other facilities, since the U.S. has world standard soccer stadiums and multi-soccer facilities already in place. Soccer World Cups can help us reach that enviable fiscal place we want in the sporting industry, putting us on track for gradual but a steady growth. Any soccer win by the U.S. will benefit the economic, social and psychological mood of the nation and its citizenry.

Creation of jobs: A large soccer industry and programs involving the federal government as the overseer can improve the lives of many Americans by creating more jobs for the citizenry. Jobs can get an economy back on its feet. How much new employment can soccer programs create? Let's take a high-speed soccer stadium that can sit thousands of people to illustrate the point here. Of course, soccer management and fans would cherish the idea of having many such good stadiums. For instance, a soccer stadium in the U.S. is known to generate about $67 million per year, according to The Washington Post. Does one think that soccer is going to generate a lot of revenue and help create plenty of jobs?

The possibility isn't far-fetched. It's not way up there in the remotest skies. Investment in the soccer industry will become a good financial run, lending support and expanding any nation's economic base. The soccer industry across the U.S. can create at least 500,000 jobs. Aside from soccer analysts and soccer-player recruiting staff and personnel, corporate convention centers, Holiday Inns, and hotels would need administrators, staff, and management personnel. Someone's got to look for players in every nook and cranny of the U.S. 'to catch them young'. Someone's got to pick those star players in clubs, short list them, evaluate their hidden but great talents, and assess them for possible global soccer contests. The good news is that most of those who'd do these jobs won't demand $1 million a month for their salaries and stipends.

Direct revenue generation: Vast revenue is generated in a country where an approved soccer tournament is hosted, with a proportional rise in its Gross Domestic Product (GDP). The GDP may not spring up right away like the military missile, rather, it will ascend like a booster rocket, which means that the effect will come later. Sometimes, it happens right away, though. As a host nation for a world soccer tournament, a country could generate significant amount of revenue, both internally and externally. There might be a boost in the economy of its air, land, rail, and sea-based transportation industries. With the world economy not doing too well in the early part of the 21$^{st}$ Century, and with towering deficits in strategic nations, hosting the FIFA World Cup soccer in the U.S., which is undoubtedly huge in profitability, may not necessarily take so much investment of public funds. It's good news for any struggling economy.

Transportation: The main purpose of transportation is mobility. Without the mobility of people and goods, there will hardly be any progress in economic development in any civilized nation. The mobility of fans, spectators, goods, and services during major league and international soccer match-ups will, doubtless, boost the transportation industry and economy of any host nation. Mobility, in this regard, constitutes one of the major sources of economic development in any society. The promotion of private sector participation in the sponsorship of soccer leagues and ownership of soccer teams should be encouraged and promoted in the U.S., as it applies in other countries.

Ticket sales: There's no doubt that the U.S. soccer team has continued to improve on the international sporting scene. Ticket sales for both home and international games generate a huge amount of money for a team or club, which means that the sizes of the stadiums matter a lot. With the Men's League Soccer growing in popularity, and with reasons to be hopeful about the future of the League, ticket sales have also increased dramatically, partly because new stadiums are built and old ones expanded or renovated.

"Think of what soccer might be able to with ticket sales, if it gains traction across the US," reasoned Roderick. "Even for super prices people could attend the Super Bowls, and tickets are widely available on the internet and on resale websites. Could you ever believe that tickets sometimes start at $2,000 and go up as high as $100,000? That's what I recently discovered."

"That doesn't surprise me at all, Roddie!" echoed Alex. "I discovered that the average price of a Super Bowl ticket is $4,500, with the website giving the impression that's almost double the average price from the previous year. I'm from Wisconsin and can only tell you that Wisconsin residents alone have purchased three times more Super Bowl tickets on

FanSnap.com than residents of Pennsylvania. It might be of interest to think of what soccer will be able to do in ticket sales when it finally becomes popular."

"Let's now get back to soccer," suggested Cobi. "I read in *The Daily Telegraph* reports recently that Manchester United, which seats about 76,000, the same as in some standard stadiums in the US, sold about 52,000 season tickets. Its Old Trafford ground was disclosed as the richest of the English clubs, whereas Liverpool Anfield stadium holds only 45,000 by comparison. Let's look at its applicability in the U.S. in terms of potential ticket sales, which is why it would be a great win if the U.S. is able to secure the World Cup hosting bid."

"With ticket prices averaging $80, Manchester United is believed to generate as much as $50 million more than Liverpool in annual ticket sales," noted David. "High rollers like Real Madrid and A.C. Milan, not surprisingly, play in stadiums that hold about 80,000 fans and could generate up to $80 million in ticket sales."

"I'd like to apply that case to the U.S. soccer clubs' ticket sales," mused Frederick. "A club like the Los Angeles Galaxy could sell tickets for multipurpose stadiums, such as the Washington-FedEx Field, Los Angeles Memorial Coliseum (93,607), Dallas Cowboys Stadium (91,600), the Cotton Bowl (89,000), Los Angeles-Rose Bowl (89,109), or the Meadowlands Stadium (84,046), that will be used primarily for major soccer events and could generate up to $80 million, on average, for just one soccer tournament."

Soccer is seen as a big business in many ways. Soccer industry experts seem to have advanced a bold new plan to attract fans and soccer talents, from around the world. One of the ways they do this is by encouraging sponsorship and worldwide sales of soccer materials, such as replica shirts and other stuffs.

"As far as I've read and known," noted Tim, "commercial sales make up a great source of income for any team or nation. A couple of years back, Real Madrid was said to have surpassed the earnings of Manchester United, in part because the Spanish club earned 42% of its revenues from commercial income, compared with Manchester United's 27% from the same source."

"Soccer clubs and teams develop top-notch contacts with the common media and television commercial initiatives to generate revenues," claimed Steven. "For them, it's a market where they sell their team's prospects and increase their potential, through the mainstream media. They establish business relationships and contracts with major soccer kit and boot manufacturers, with whom they negotiate deals. These moves are preceded by inviting potential media and commercial partners to discuss business opportunities, which in many cases involves promos."

The skills of star players are featured both nationally and internationally in commercial advertisements. Companies like Adidas, Armani, Reebok, Nike, Coca-Cola, Pepsi, and Xerox, among others, are known for their commercial soccer promos. The commercial deals in question are normally launched in series of ads featuring star players posed in various fashions. The drive to raise commercial revenues has prompted Real Madrid to seek celebrity stars, knowing that their presence on the team can help them sell hundreds of millions of dollars in replica shirts and jerseys. The costs of soccer materials grow exponentially when linked with big-name celebrity soccer stars.

"I've watched deals that launched a series of ads featuring superstar players like David Beckham, Cristiano Ronaldo, and Landon Donovan posing in various exciting, and, in some cases, slinky fashion," remarked Harold, "either sprinting over a bridge while heading a soccer ball, or challenging the fastest accelerating cars on the planet. These business deals generate income for the company, the team, and the player."

Television rights and contracts: This is all about television, media coverage, and the broadcast of soccer events in the U.S., which is done primarily through cable sports channels. However, viewing limitations can be legally overcome by purchasing out-of-the-market packages.

"I've been an avid reader of FIFA financial reports, which revealed that FIFA's revenue in the broadcasts of the World Cup in 2002 and 2006 was worth about $2.4 million," declared Adam. "FIFA closed the year with revenue of $957 million and expenses of $773 million. Her net profit was therefore $184 million. This is only on the side of FIFA."

"Oh yeah." agreed William. "The World Cup has continued to be the principle source of revenue generation for FIFA as the most widely viewed sporting event in the world. In 2002, the U.S. was said to have generated an estimated $41 million from broadcasting rights, and the European markets generated about $152 million, with the rest of the world contributing $147 million. The total revenue for television broadcasting rights in 2003 was in the neighborhood of $340 million."

"As regards sharing the television contract and rights, let's get down to specifics," urged Francis. "In the English Premiership, this guarantees even the bottom clubs about $50 million a year, and a lot more for those in the top tier. The clubs that finish the highest in all of Europe's domestic leagues also get to play midweek games in the European Champion's League, qualification for which is worth at least an extra $20 million."

"In the US, the prospect of significantly enhanced television rights and fees appears enticing and promising indeed," argued Chris. "This is one of the major reasons why any soccer hosting bid committee would most likely secure and possibly win the FIFA World Cup soccer tournament without many tears — that is, if the committee plays its card well and, above all, has luck on its side. As an illustration, ABC, ESPN, and Univision paid $425 million to broadcast the 2010 and 2014 World Cups, not counting the 2007 and 2011 women's World Cups. Compared to the $894 million that NBC paid for rights to broadcast the 2008 Beijing Olympics, that number seems low. Moreover, one thing that appears striking to note is that fees for television rights appear to be almost doubling, which might become bigger with every World Cup event."

It bears stressing that the soccer World Cup is the most widely watched sporting event, with an estimated 715.1 million views for the final match of the 2006 FIFA World Cup that was held in Germany. The same number was estimated to have watched the FIFA World Cup in South Africa in 2010. ESPN is making a huge investment in World Cup coverage, paying $100 million for the rights to the 2010 and 2014 events, based on the conviction that Americans know and watch the beautiful game as well.

The 2006 tournament on ESPN and ABC drew the largest viewers for a World Cup outside the US. However, later research suggests that the network can do more to show the fans that it's taking the sport seriously. The long and short of the message is that soccer is becoming a U.S.A. sport. You can see it with the level of play on the fields and the amount of interest from the public. Gradually but steadily, the U.S. will come to embrace this sport more and more. Economic benefits and financial booms aren't the only things that make better nations and a better world.

It's about waking up and winning, not only in soccer, but also in all walks of life.

# Author's Postscript

I finally settled for soccer, because I didn't make up my mind on swimming, haahaa! Some people think swimming is the best form of sport too. Whatever! Both sports, to some degree, involve the use of arms and legs. But anyway, not tails and fins this time. Not like meat swimming in the gravy or an 'exercise' that might make someone feel dizzy after spinning round and round. Soccer is a real sport.

I must tell you that about two decades of arranging people's comments, opinions, thoughts, exchanges and debates about soccer in the U.S. hasn't been an easy one. This commitment involves the ability of a writer to put down and retain what you hear friends say, what you hear students say at the school lounges, what regular soccer lovers and fans discuss at restaurants, coffee shops, recreational parks, what soccer analysts say both real, over the radio and on television documentaries. You've seen for yourself that most of the characters in the book were (are) everyday people. What does it take to informally interview other sports and soccer veterans regarding their opinions about soccer in the US? What does it cost to engage in casual phone conversations (both long and short distance), e-mail exchanges and the rest of them? What does it take to get people allow you join in their discussions about soccer especially when they don't know you? I've strongly believed that it takes an investigator and author who has great interest in and love for soccer, the players and fans. It also takes discipline and dedication.

What would one think about compiling the whole stuff in an essay and composition format, to make it look fictional, lightly 'dramatic' and at the same time endeavor to retain its unique nature? Quite a huge task! I've come to know what it means to be an 'author,' especially when you have to combine such a complex project with myriads of commitments amid 'distractions' coming from colleagues, friends and family. Good distractions, though. The long and short of the game is that it ended up fun especially when you finally succeed in making it happen. Bingo!

In writing *Wake Up and Win, America,* it was my endeavor to integrate, in the simplest fashion possible, the accumulated wisdom, comments, stories, and suggestions of soccer veterans, fans, players, coaches, celebrities, trip makers, students and even previously non soccer lovers who, at least, have objectively followed the progress of soccer, with interest for quite some time here in the US. I think that this effort has turned out to become a big dream come true.

# Special Invitation and Encouragement:

Whether you are a soccer fan or not, the author invites and encourages you to continue your sporting journey and general life experiences with *Wake Up and Win, America!*

- Get involved in the 'hear the other person' exchange. Share how you feel about this book with others and read what others are saying too.

- Do well to share your insights and opinions about this book with other readers at any comment section.

- Purchase copies of *Wake Up and Win, America.*

- Readers and fans are encouraged to pass this book along to their friends and families.

- Offer people any link that will help them find *Wake Up and Win, America.*

Here are a few other ideas on how to let others know about this book:

Give to your friends, family members, co-workers, colleagues and acquaintances as gifts. This book not only contain exciting, appealing and compelling pages, It also gives you a glimpse into people's feelings, thoughts and opinions about soccer in the United States and to some extent the world over. It also contains life-touching and life-changing information and experiences that you might consider giving copies as gifts not only to high school and college students, but also to those in fitness houses, gyms, health care centers, rehabilitation homes, prisons, correctional centers and similar places where people might be really encouraged, motivated and inspired by its rich contents besides soccer.

Create and spread awareness of the book on your websites, social network sites, blogs, and by phone calls. Mention title on the e-mail lists and groups that you belong, associations, forums, sessions and meetings you attend and other places you engage people on the internet. Simply share how *Wake Up and Win, America* has impacted your thinking and feelings about soccer as a sporting activity. You could go out of your way to write an unbiased book review or even press releases that promote this title for your local, state or national media; this includes your favorite magazines or Web sites that you visit on a regular basis.

# Notes and Acknowledgements

**Chapter One**
- Greek Mythology: Theft of fire by Prometheus from the Greek god Zeus, cf. Wikipedia Free Encyclopedia for further readings.
- Carl Diem and the controversial Berlin Olympics, 1936, cf. Wikipedia Free Encyclopedia for further readings.
- *Cabernet Sauvignon*: for details confer Stevenson, T, " The Sotheby's Wine Encyclopedia" pp. 578-581 Dorling Kindersley , 2005 ISBN 0-7566-13324(Wikipedia, the Free Encyclopedia)
- *Adidas Jabulani:* The Official World Cup Ball unveiled in Cape Town for the 2010 FIFA World Cup, cf. www.soccer.com/adidas-Jabulani

**Chapter Two**
- *WASP*: 'White Anglo-Saxon Protestant' is an informal term often used humorously and sometimes with 'derogatory' connotation, cf. Wikipedia Free Encyclopedia for further readings.
- Major cities in South Africa for FIFA World Cup 2010: Rustenburg, Polokwane, Nelspruit, Manguang /Bloemfontein, Nelson Mandela, Bay/Port Elizabeth, Durban, Cape Town, Tshwane/ Pretoria, and Johannesburg. Retrieved from http://www. sa-venues.com/2010/2010-stadium.htmon October 18, 2010.
- International Wildlife Service Corporation, Nairobi: cf. Kenya Wildlife Service Website, for further reading.
- *Invictus*, Springbok: for expanded knowledge visit the internet movie database at http://www.imdb.com/tiltle/tt1055700/and Wikipedia for more illustrations.
- Vuvuzelas: known in *'lepatata Mambu'* colloquially translated as the 'plastic horn' is traditionally used during soccer in South Africa. Cf. Wikipedia.org for more information.

**Chapter Three**
- Kentucky Derby: Horse races held annually in Louisville, Kentucky on the first Sunday in May. cf. Racing Daily Form Website for more information, at http://www.drf.com/news/ Kentucky-derby or Wikipedia, the Free Encyclopedia.

- George Steinbrenner Quotes available at http://www.thinkexist. com/quotes/george_steinbrenner/3.html

## Chapter Four
- Illustration of world soccer history, cf. Wikipedia Free Encyclopedia

## Chapter Five
- PAL Red Storm Boys Soccer Team; cf. Daily News Long Island, August 26, 2010 for elaborate illustrations.
- Soccer Recap in the Tri-State Area of New York (Long Island), New Jersey & Connecticut. TV Channel 14, Long Island, Sports Documentary, March 12, 2011.
- Soccer Recap, Texas, Georgia, Florida, North Carolina and Oklahoma, cf http://www.rise.espn.go.com/boys-soccer/ article/2010/06/23-RegionIII champs.aspx.for further details retrieved March 3, 2011.
- The best soccer players in the world, partly adopted fromsoccernet. espn.go.comandfromhttp://bleacher report.com
- *Xtmas, Short form of 'Christmas'*

## Chapter Six
- Comic Reviews: Adaptation of styles from New York Times Art Sections (Cf. http://www.nytimes.com/pages/arts/index.html

## Chapter Seven
- Burnout Bursting Committees (BBC), special adaptation.

## Chapter Eight
- *Soccer Hosting Bids cf. George Vecsey,* New York Times Accounts Articles*:* 'U.S. Should Know There's No Sulking in Soccer', December 2, 2010.
- Members of the soccer bidding committee, cf. http://www. Nationalsoccerwire.com/news/460/11888 for details.
- IBIS World: Regarded by some as the largest provider of industry information in the US. Cf. http://www.ibisworld.com/about/ default.aspx

## Chapter Nine
- *Nemo dat quod non habet,* Latin, 'No one gives what he (she) hasn't.'
- *Titanic:* Constructed in Belfast, Ireland, Titanic was regarded

as the largest vessel that sailed from Southampton with 2,200 passengers and crew which later collided with an iceberg and sank on April 15, 1912.Cf. http://www.encyclopedia-titanica.org/

- *Lusitania:* Designed by Leonard Paskett and built by John Brown and Company of Clydebank, Scotland, Lusitania was deployed in a submarine warfare against Germany during WWI. Identified and torpedoed by the German U-boat U-20 on May 7, 1915 it sank in eighteen minutes. Cf. http://en.Wikipedia.org/wiki/RMS_Lusitania
- *Victoria Concordia Crescit,* Latin, 'victory grows from concord' or 'union enhances victory' adapted from the motto of Arsenal football club. Cf. http://arsenal-mania.com/forum/viewtopic.php?f=25&t=39788

**Chapter Ten**
- Names of stadiums in the U.S. and their capacity, adapted from, *Goal,* the New York Times Soccer Blog by Jack Bell, *'U.S. U-20 Team Wins Opener…and More',* March 30, 2011.

# Further Notes and Acknowledgements

To ensure accuracy of accounts and message, the author intended to convey as well as give substance and verity to the authenticity of the contents of character exchanges and discussions in some sections of this book, the following sources have provided excitingly useful ideas, supporting excerpts and insights deserving acknowledgments.

**Books, Newspapers, Journals and Magazines**
- Akron, Tony. "Soccer's Billion-Dollar Players," *Time Magazine*, August 3, 2008.
- Bell, Jack. "U.S. Selects 18 Cities and 21 Stadiums as Potential World Cup Hosts" *New York Times*, January 12, 2010
- Clarke, Liz. "U.S. Soccer Gets Upended against Ghana at World Cup, Washington Post, Sunday, June 27, 2010.
- Farley, L.K., and Curry, S.M, *Get Motivated, Daily Psych-Ups*, (New York, NY: Simon & Schuster, 1994).
- Kerr, A.K., "You'll Never Walk Alone" An Unpublished Doctoral Dissertation, University of Technology, Sydney, June, 2009.
- Matuszewski, Erik. "Super Bowl Tickets Averaging Almost $5,000'" *Bloomberg*, February 2, 2011
- Miller, Toby. "Soccer Conquers the World, The Chronicle of Higher Education, *The Chronicle Review*, May 30, 2010.
- New York Post (www.nypost.com); Daily News, New York's Hometown Newspaper (www.dailynews.com) & Newsday: The Long Island Newspaper (www.newday.com).

**Other Helpful Websites**
- http://www.foxnews.com/sports/2010/06/10/soccer-fans-hope-england-world-cup-match-boost-sports-popularity-america/.
- http://soccer.fanhouse.com/2010/06/08/espn-betting-us-soccer-fans-want-more-world-cup/
- http://www.epltalk.com/2010-world-cup-final-the-most-watched-soccer-game-in-u-s-histroy/22078).
- http://www.audleytravel.com/resources/brochures/audley-south-africa-brochure.pdf

- http://www.washingtonpost.com/wpdyn/content/article/2010/06/26/AR2010062604394.html
- http://soccernet.espn.go.com/worldcup/story/_/page/worldcup10103012010/ce/us/top-50-players2010-world-cup?cc=5901&ver=us
- www.streetsoccerusa.org.
- www.ussoccer.com
- www.US soccerfoundation.org

www.ingramcontent.com/pod-product-compliance
Lightning Source LLC
Chambersburg PA
CBHW020849090426
42736CB00008B/304